C000161299

bobby baneyjee
2/21/02
melbourne

Multinational Corporations in Political Environments

Ethics, Values and Strategies

Multinational Corporations in Political Environments

Ethics, Values and Strategies

Usha C. V. Haley

The University of Tennessee, Knoxville, USA

World Scientific
New Jersey • London • Singapore • Hong Kong

Published by

World Scientific Publishing Co. Pte. Ltd.

P O Box 128, Farrer Road, Singapore 912805

USA office: Suite 1B, 1060 Main Street, River Edge, NJ 07661

UK office: 57 Shelton Street, Covent Garden, London WC2H 9HE

British Library Cataloguing-in-Publication Data
A catalogue record for this book is available from the British Library.

MULTINATIONAL CORPORATIONS IN POLITICAL ENVIRONMENTS
Ethics, Values and Strategies

Copyright © 2001 by World Scientific Publishing Co. Pte. Ltd.

All rights reserved. This book, or parts thereof, may not be reproduced in any form or by any means, electronic or mechanical, including photocopying, recording or any information storage and retrieval system now known or to be invented, without written permission from the Publisher.

For photocopying of material in this volume, please pay a copying fee through the Copyright Clearance Center, Inc., 222 Rosewood Drive, Danvers, MA 01923, USA. In this case permission to photocopy is not required from the publisher.

ISBN 981-02-4427-4

Printed in Singapore by Mainland Press

For George T. Haley

About the Author

Usha C. V. Haley (PhD, Stern School of Business, New York University) is Associate Professor of Management, focusing on Strategic Management and International Business, in the College of Business Administration at the University of Tennessee, Knoxville. She has more than 70 books, journal articles, book chapters and research presentations on international strategic management. Her latest books include *New Asian Emperors: The Overseas Chinese, their Strategies and Competitive Advantages* (Butterworth-Heinemann); *Strategic Management in the Asia Pacific: Harnessing Regional and Organizational Change for Competitive Advantage* (Butterworth-Heinemann); and, *Asian Post-Crisis Management: Corporate and Governmental Strategies for Sustainable Competitive Advantage* (Macmillan/Palgrave). She also has a forthcoming book on *Asia's Tao of Business: The Logic of Chinese Business Strategy* (Wiley). She has taught International Business and Strategic Management at major universities in the United States (including Harvard University), Singapore (at the National University of Singapore), Australia (at the Australian National University), and Mexico (at ITESM, Monterrey Campus). Additionally, she has taught in major corporate, governmental and universities' executive-development programs, for top and middle managers and policy makers, in the United States, Australia, Mexico, Vietnam, Italy, India and Singapore. She also serves as a consultant on issues concerning strategic management and foreign direct investment for several multinational corporations in North America, Australia, Europe and Asia and as Regional Editor (Asia Pacific) for two academic journals. Please contact her at uhaley@asia-pacific.com.

CONTENTS

Foreword

By Ingo Walter:

This volume represents a valuable addition to the literature on the multinational firm, which dates back to the 1960s and continues to evolve in depth and richness. It brings out many of the subtleties associated with the interlinkage of the multinational and host countries. These include, at the very outset of the volume, the role of the multinational firm as a change agent affecting an array of interests at various levels of aggregation. This is followed by a first-rate review of the conceptual foundations of the multinational enterprise. Both discussions are then brought to bear on the involvement of multinationals in South Africa under apartheid — one of the most complex and politically-charged stories in recent memory. In retrospect, did multinationals prolong or accelerate the demise of apartheid? And conversely, what was the impact of the political pressures exerted on them, in the US and elsewhere, to withdraw or modify their South African operations in the waning years of the old regime? There is, of course, no way to run the world twice, but the analysis provided by Professor Haley provides a solid foundation for thinking about such issues. The final part of the book focuses specifically on the issues of adaptation and withdrawal, which are critical to an assessment of this question. For all of these reasons the book is likely to remain a valuable reference work on multinationals for years to come.

Ingo Walter
Charles Simon Professor of Applied Financial Economics
and Director, New York University Salomon Center
Stern School of Business
New York University

By William D. Guth:

There is considerable business and governmental interest in sanctions today, more than there was in the 1980s when multinational corporations in South Africa were the focus of organized stakeholder opposition. Stakeholder opposition continues against companies such as Nike, Shell and Disney and governments such as Myanmar's. Until the study reported in this book, however, all of the systematic research on sanctions had been done at the level of the nation state; at the level of the company, we had only anecdotal evidence. This is the first book that systematically studies why multinationals leave host states and the circumstances that prompt their leaving at the level of the company. Professor Haley has shed considerable new light on our understanding of the impact of stakeholder sanctions by including the values of top managers compared to those of other stakeholders as critical elements shaping companies' decisions. This important book identifies which sanctions by both governments and private pressure groups "work" and which do not, and explains why. It identifies the responses of corporate managements to these pressures, and demonstrates how frequently, and explains how and why, management turns situations that appear to be victories for the sanctioning parties into business-as-usual under a different format.

William D. Guth
Professor of Management and Strategy
Stern School of Business
New York University

Acknowledgements

This book stems from my doctoral dissertation completed a decade ago at the Stern School of Business, New York University. Fascinated by newspaper reports and stakeholders' activism surrounding multinational corporations in South Africa, I was surprised to find that our existing theories did not explain adequately why multinationals left a country, how they left and in what form they left. I undertook the brave (or foolhardy) task of devising such an explanation. The dissertation took three years and extracted its toll in other respects too. Two years into its writing, the end appeared nowhere in sight. At that time, Professor Donald Lessard, visiting from MIT, was delivering an invited lecture on international business at Stern. Seeing this dejected, struggling and penurious doctoral student, Don stopped to provide some insights and encouragement. He said, "These years will soon be a memory and when you leave, you will be bombarded by opportunities. You will not have the time again, to think about one idea for three years as you are doing now. Take advantage of the moment."

Don's words have rung true. After leaving Stern, I was sucked into a whirlwind of opportunities to understand and to influence multinationals and governments in Italy, Mexico, Singapore, Malaysia, Australia, Vietnam, India, China and South Korea. I wrote over 70 books and journal articles, yet, never had the time to think about one idea, by itself, for six months — let alone for three years. Recently, while discussing at Harvard efforts to sanction Myanmar, and while correspondingly exploring with friend and activist Professor David Boje, efforts to pressure Nike, I was struck again by the applicability and freshness of the ideas I had explored earlier. This book is the result. I believe the ideas hold greater validity than they did a decade ago, as the benefits of hindsight have now come to bear as well as the opportunity to influence new developments.

The ideas in this book owe a great deal to the people who supported my efforts and provided guidance over the period of my dissertation as well as later through my professional career — Professors Ingo Walter and William Guth, who co-chaired my dissertation committee. Both Ingo and Bill generously provided the opportunity to explore concepts with them as well as commented copiously on rewrite after rewrite. Both provided their unique and stellar wisdom, knowledge and experience to the understanding and completion of this monumental book project. Both showed by example as well as deed that knowledge in business schools should aim to understand as well as to influence. Professors Thomas Pugel and Janice Beyer also provided many helpful comments on my dissertation over a decade ago, especially on the methodology, which I have incorporated in part into this book. To Ingo, Bill, Tom and Jan, I express my gratitude and thanks.

Others helped on this book project. Editor Karen Quek at World Scientific, read chapters and granted more time for the completion of this project when needed, supporting its goals from the outset. In the Management Department at the University of Tennessee, Knoxville, Professors Oscar Fowler and Michael Stahl contributed greatly to an intellectually stimulating environment that encourages scholarship and research on international and strategic issues. Ms. Jackie Cook and Ms. Jane Moser in the Management Department helped me with diagrams and tables in a timely and efficient fashion. Thank you, Karen, Oscar, Mike, Jackie and Jane.

On the home front, I owe thanks to my kittens, Comet Baby and Marmalade for making life more enjoyable and less stressful. Finally, I owe a debt of undying gratitude to my husband, George Haley, who put up with me during my dissertation and later, provided comments on the manuscript and moral and emotional support throughout. To George, I dedicate this book.

Usha C. V. Haley
Associate Professor
Department of Management
College of Business Administration
University of Tennessee, Knoxville

PART I

INTRODUCTION

1. Overview and Outline

"May you live in interesting times."
Ancient Chinese curse

This book advances and tests a theory of why foreign corporations leave host states. Theories of international business have often ignored the complexity of corporate decisions about leaving foreign countries, generally assuming that the economic and competitive reasons that prompt multinational corporations (hereafter referred to as "multinationals") to enter host states (such as the desire for new markets) also explain their subsequent reasons for leaving (for example, when the markets dry up, multinationals leave). Alternatively, this book proposes a theory of how different stakeholders' values and ethics shape multinationals' strategic leaving behaviors. Tested in South Africa when US multinationals were facing diverse pressures from stockholders, governments and consumers to leave, the research provides a prism to isolate how different stakeholders' actions influenced multinationals' behaviors. Detailed analyses of subsidiary-level archival data over a period of four crucial years revealed that the multinationals engaged in diverse forms of leaving reflecting their involvements, strategies and stakeholders' influences. The research, the first to test which stakeholders' strategies, including boycotts and sanctions, influenced multinationals and which did not, and to identify their effects on multinationals' behaviors, has enormous implications for policy makers, managers and social activists. The book also applies the findings and explores implications for recent stakeholders' attempts at influencing multinationals and governments, such as Nike in Asia and Myanmar's government, through sanctions, resolutions and boycotts.

Part 2 sketches how theorists have generally portrayed multinationals as catalysts. Like catalysts, multinationals have been depicted as changing host states without substantially changing themselves. Theorists have argued that multinationals grow or decline to use intangible assets efficiently and to coordinate operations. Essentially, the multinationals' reasons for entering host states are assumed to constitute reasons for their subsequent behaviors including growth, decline or leaving. Chapter 2 reviews theories that explain the entry, growth and decline of multinationals. To decipher multinationals' behaviors, researchers have generally assumed that the multinationals employ static (as opposed to dynamic) analytical schemes, control and coordinate operations efficiently, and maintain stable relations with stakeholders. Consequently, researchers have generally argued that the reasons that prompt multinationals to enter host states also guide their subsequent growth and decline, including leaving. Chapter 3 contends that reasons for entry may not provide an adequate understanding of multinationals' subsequent behaviors. First, multinationals' analytical schemes, or how they process, codify and evaluate information, often change with experience. Second, stakeholders within multinationals may stave off managerial control and pursue their own interests; therefore, managerial control and coordination may prove illusory in reality. Finally, and partially because of the prior two reasons, multinationals' relations with key stakeholders may change over time, affecting their goals and rationales. Chapter 4 illustrates some of the issues that the theories of international business generally address and ignore. Using seven multinationals in apartheid-practicing South Africa as examples, this chapter summarizes how existing theories failed to predict or even to explain why the multinationals maintained, decreased or increased investments in South Africa.

Part 3 proposes that rather than catalysts, multinationals appear as chameleons. Like chameleons, multinationals change in response to environmental conditions. The changes help to maintain homeostatic equilibrium or stability in a system that includes headquarters and subsidiaries.

Stakeholders form major parts of multinationals' environments and their actions, ethics and values in home and host states affect managerial strategies at both headquarters and subsidiaries. These actions, ethics, values and strategies act and react in a system incorporating minor changes and frictions to display overall identifiable continuity, especially in values. For example, headquarters' managers may use competitive and noncompetitive strategies that articulate established goals, change the multinational, and yet maintain the participation and support of key stakeholders. Also, subsidiaries' managers may use symbolic strategies to placate key stakeholders with divergent ethics or values, and again maintain their participation and support. However, under some circumstances, stakeholders' ethics and values may differ so significantly from those of managers that the latter groups' strategies and symbolic efforts may prove insufficient to maintain support. These stakeholders would then induce disequilibria in the system and its disintegration. In South Africa, and elsewhere, decisions on leaving and in what form the leaving would be carried out, reflect managerial efforts to reinstate equilibrium or stability in the system; they also reflect stakeholders' power or lack of it. Chapter 5 indicates how the growth, consolidation, and decline of multinationals constitute phases in organizational development emphasizing diverse stakeholders' values and goals. The chapter also reviews contributing technical-efficiency, ideological and political forces that induce changes in relations with major stakeholders over time. Chapter 6 develops the metaphor of multinationals as chameleons. Like chameleons, multinationals fluctuate and respond to their environments; like chameleons, multinationals change from both purposive and reflex actions; and like chameleons, multinationals have limited abilities to change and simultaneously to maintain their integrity in different environments. A political-action framework captures the growth, consolidation, and decline of multinationals in host states. Several sets of hypotheses propose to test the theory on US multinationals in South Africa including the conditions and forms of their leaving.

Part 4 covers the sample and analysis of the data as well as the results. Case studies and interviews yielded seven forms of growth and decline (including leaving) of multinationals from South Africa. The theory is tested on the population of 322 US multinationals in South Africa from 1982 to 1987. Eleven sets of variables (about five variables per set and two indicators per variable) made the theory operational. Readers, who wish to avoid the technical details in this section, may skip to the summary sub-sections for quick overviews. Chapter 7 provides details on the setting, the time frame, the population and the sets of variables to be tested. At least three sources of data existed for each variable — a main source, a source to crosscheck data and a source to resolve discrepancies. Chapter 8 provides information on the analytical procedures used to test the hypotheses including logistic regression and linear regression analyses with lagged independent variables and pooled cross-sections. These techniques reflect the time frame of the study, the population's attrition over the period under study and the diverse scales that measured the variables. The chapter highlights the significant results and discusses their generalizability.

Finally, Part 5 focuses on the theoretical and strategic implications of this research. Stakeholders, including governments, consumers and stockholders continue to use sanctions against multinationals to influence their behaviors in host states and to align these behaviors with stakeholders' values and ethics. Yet, this research reveals that stakeholders' actions did not have the desired results (indeed stockholders' resolutions seemed to have influenced multinationals to stay in South Africa) and that extraneous circumstances, such as regulation, may have greatly influenced multinationals' behaviors. Significant differences seemed to distinguish the variables that explained leaving and staying actions in periods of more and less regulation. Accumulated social legitimacy also seemed to influence strongly multinationals' actions to stay in or to leave South Africa. Chapter 9 outlines the main results of the research on multinationals in South Africa confirming the important effects of social legitimacy, profits and some competitive strategies for multinationals' strategic behaviors. In the period of no regulation, as hypothesized, more symbolic actions, higher profits and lower order backlogs influenced whether multinationals stayed in South Africa. In the period of regulation, as hypothesized, greater advertising and less product diversification influenced whether multinationals stayed in South Africa. The chapter suggests some contributions that a theory of multinationals as chameleons may make to international-business and to management theories as well as explores different policy implications and repercussions. Using stakeholders' protests against Nike's Asian operations and against Myanmar's violations of human rights as examples, this chapter highlights some circumstances in which stakeholders can influence multinationals to leave foreign countries, and other circumstances in which managers may stave off the threats.

PART II

MULTINATIONAL CORPORATIONS AS CATALYSTS

2. Multinational Corporations
as Change Agents

A catalyst is a change agent. In chemistry, the term depicts a substance that by its presence either speeds up or slows down a chemical reaction. In the process, the catalyst itself undergoes no permanent chemical change. In general, the catalyst brings an alternative path to the reaction.

Theories have generally portrayed multinationals as catalysts. For example, some theorists have argued that multinationals move resources, like capital, from places with low returns to places with high returns. Consequently, multinationals bid up the prices of abundant resources, like labor. Other theorists have posited that by making more efficient uses of global resources than domestic firms, multinationals may boost global outputs. In this fashion, theorists have shown the growth of multinationals as causing reactions in the environments from which multinationals come, and in the environments to which multinationals go. However, multinationals themselves have been portrayed as substantially unchanged by the growth: supposedly, the motivations for their behaviors alter very little. Thus, multinationals are depicted as changing stakeholders, but not as being changed substantially by them.

In this book, the variable "presence" captures a firm's or organization's structural changes — the entry, growth, and decline of that firm or organization over time. Many theories have proposed explanations for the presence of multinationals in host states. Other theories have built on these rationales to analyze their presence in broader social contexts. The second category of theories has portrayed multinationals as catalysts in host states. This chapter covers some rationales that existing theories of international business have offered for the presence and catalytic reactions of multinationals. The chapter also highlights which stakeholders the theories emphasize and critically analyzes some underlying theoretical assumptions.

Rationales for Presence

Many theories have proposed explanations for the entry, growth and decline of multinationals in host states (e.g., see Buckley and Ghauri, 1999). Most of these theories have assumed that market failures in host states prompt multinationals' behaviors. Desires to maximize profits and efficiencies, as well as to control and to coordinate operations, fuel multinationals' behaviors in imperfect markets. Multinationals' reasons for growth and decline are generally depicted as arising from their reasons for entry.

Rationales for Entry

Entry refers to a multinational's actions to produce in foreign markets. Generally, the entry of multinationals has been portrayed as a response to market failures in host states. Theories of market imperfections, internalization, strategic management, manufacturing processes and oligopolistic markets have sketched the distinctive characteristics that help multinationals to surmount entry barriers in host states.

Market Imperfections:

Market-imperfection theories trace their origins to Stephen H. Hymer. In his seminal, doctoral dissertation, Hymer (1960) argued that multinationals enter host states because they possess certain assets. Hymer (1960) presented these assets as the advantages that multinationals have over domestic firms: Hymer (1960) argued that foreign-based firms such as multinationals would have to possess some advantages to overcome domestic firms' knowledge of local product markets and conditions. Hymer (1960) contended that in perfect product markets, domestic firms with local knowledge would out-compete foreign firms. Consequently, profit-maximizing foreign firms could only exist in imperfect product markets that allow them to use their special assets.

Hymer (1970) also argued that imperfect knowledge (information) markets influence profit-maximizing multinationals' decisions to produce abroad rather than to license knowledge to host states' firms. He theorized that such imperfections arise from buyers' uncertainty (buyers of knowledge cannot assess its worth until they possess it), lack of institutionalized markets for knowledge and multinationals' desires for secrecy. In imperfect markets, multinationals cannot induce competitive bids to get full returns on their investments. Licensing may also result in extra costs like the costs of policing property rights to the knowledge (Buckley and Davies, 1980). Therefore, Hymer (1970) contended that profit-maximizing motives, like firms' desires to control knowledge, and their fears of creating competitors, cause firms to favor foreign production over licensing.

Subsequently, Kindleberger (1969), Caves (1971) and Dunning (1973; 1974; 1981) extended Hymer's arguments to highlight multinationals' intangible assets and the imperfect product and knowledge markets that allow multinationals to exploit these assets efficiently. Intangible assets may represent edges in technology (knowledge about how to produce cheaper or better products than competing firms); marketing (skills that allow multinationals to differentiate their products through styling or promotion); capital arbitrage (abilities to borrow capital in places with lower interest rates and to employ capital in places with higher interests rates); managerial talent (access to skilled and educated employees); and economies of scale (abilities to reduce costs by increasing quantities produced). For example, Kindleberger (1989) argued that multinationals possess assets in product differentiation, marketing, and administered pricing to exploit imperfect goods markets; that multinationals enjoy differential access to patented or proprietary knowledge, and to capital and skill differences, to exploit imperfect factor markets; and that multinationals use horizontal and vertical integration to exploit external economies of scale and governments' entry and output restrictions. Gorecki (1976), using Canadian data, tested and confirmed the proposition that intangible assets help multinationals to overcome entry barriers in host states' markets.

Besides efficiencies, theories on the entry of multinationals have placed critical importance on their profitability. According to the theories, anticipated profits to stockholders translate firms' abilities to enter host states into their actual desires to do so (Buckley, 1985). For example, theorists have contended that multinationals prefer to produce goods abroad (rather than to export goods) when tariff and transport-cost barriers exist, or when local production permits them to adapt products more economically to local conditions.

Other theorists discussed financial-market imperfections rather than imperfections in product and knowledge markets (e.g., Agmon and Lessard, 1977; Aliber, 1970). These theorists looked at owners' (stockholders' and investors') efforts to diversify risks and to maximize profits. For instance, Aliber (1970) argued that multinationals enjoy advantages in international financial markets over host states' firms; consequently, foreign direct investment can take place even if the markets for licensing are perfect. Aliber's (1970) analysis centered on currency premiums. Holders of debt denominated in particular currencies bear risks that will reduce their returns if those currencies depreciate in values relative to other currencies. In perfect markets, if investors are risk neutral, the rates of interest on debts denominated in particular currencies will exactly reflect expected rates of depreciation of those currencies. But investors are risk averse and demand premiums for bearing exchange-risk uncertainties. According to Aliber (1970), markets bias applications of these currency premiums. Investors are myopic in Aliber's (1970) model — they treat all the assets of subsidiaries as if they were in the same currency areas as the parent firms. An English factory is a sterling asset; but if a US company owns the factory, the market regards the factory as a dollar asset. Consequently, multinationals originate from those states that can borrow at lower interest rates. Also, markets value multinationals more highly because their earnings are capitalized at home states' currency rates.

However, investors' myopia inadequately explains the existence of multinationals. Could not speculators turn such biases into advantages and thereby eliminate the phenomena? Would not international markets recognize that multinationals are multiple currency earners and that such earnings are subject to exchange risks if converted to home states' currencies? Aliber's (1970) theory also fails to explain the distributions of foreign direct investment among industries, and simultaneous cross-investments within industries and between currency areas.

In his analyses of financial markets, Lessard (1979) pointed out that multinationals have advantages that accrue from internalizing financial transactions. These advantages stem from exchange-control arbitrage, credit-market arbitrage, and equity-market arbitrage (risk reduction through diversification). Agmon and Lessard (1977) theorized that as capital transfers between countries entail costs, multinationals provide investors with indirect means for risk reduction through diversification. Therefore, individual investors' desires to diversify their holdings may contribute to the existence of multinationals. Agmon and Lessard (1977) argued that multinationals serve as diversification vehicles when two conditions exist: first, portfolio-capital flows must cost more than direct-investment flows; and, second, investors must recognize that multinationals provide diversification vehicles. Agmon and Lessard (1977) provided some evidence that investors take the international involvement of US multinationals into account. However, Jacquillat and Solnik (1978) found that portfolios made up of multinationals' shares appear to form poor substitutes for international portfolio diversification. Also, the international involvement of firms had very little influence on their stock prices (Jacquillat and Solnik, 1978).

Internalization:

Internalization theories have depicted the entry of multinationals into host states as efforts to overcome transaction costs (Dunning, 1983) by replacing markets with hierarchies (Williamson, 1975). Social efficiencies dictate that existing knowledge should be available freely. However, firms want property rights over their knowledge, and payments from other firms for their uses of this knowledge. Internalization (transfers within firms) provides firms with low-cost channels for transfers of knowledge and prevents dissipation of knowledge, justifying foreign direct investment over alternatives like licensing (Teece, 1976).

The distinctive characteristics of some knowledge may contribute to internalization. For example, Caves (1982) argued that intangible assets, like research and development skills, often constitute public goods (goods that can be used at different locations with few extra costs or reductions in original amounts). Consequently, intangible assets tend to be priced inefficiently. Transactions in intangible assets suffer from failures like impactedness, uncertainty and opportunism in markets for information. So, managerial desires to control intangible assets may prompt firms to enter host states.

Magee's (1976; 1977) theory of appropriability enunciates the distinctive characteristics of technology that encourage internalization. Multinationals discover and develop products, production functions and markets. Therefore, Magee (1976) contended, multinationals generate technology that they wish to appropriate. Magee (1976) deduced that as competitors have more difficulties imitating sophisticated technologies than simple technologies, multinationals have more success appropriating the returns from sophisticated technologies. As multinationals can also transfer sophisticated technologies more efficiently via internal channels than through markets, Magee (1976) asserted that managers have incentives to generate sophisticated technologies — to the detriment of some users like less-developed countries.

Imperfect markets for knowledge also form the basis of Buckley and Casson's (1976) theory of multinationals. They focused on markets for intermediate products rather than markets for final products. Buckley and Casson (1976; 1985) argued that firms carry out many activities apart from routinely producing goods and services. All these activities, including marketing, research and development (R&D) and training of labor, are interdependent and related through flows of intermediate products such as knowledge and expertise. However, firms have difficulties organizing intermediate, product markets. Therefore, firms create internal markets, that is, they bring external, market activities under common control and ownership. This internalization of intermediate markets gives rise to multinationals (Hennart, 1982; Rugman, 1982).

Internalization theorists have assumed that multinationals endeavor to retain the firm-specific advantages that they generated in their home markets; so, foreign subsidiaries tend to be branch plants (miniature replicas) of parent firms (Grosse, 1982).

Strategic Management:

Information markets are imperfect and search costs are higher for foreign than for domestic investment decisions. These higher, fixed costs constitute larger barriers to entry for smaller, foreign firms (Aharoni, 1966). Consequently, many strategic-management theories have assumed that only large firms, able to make substantial capital outlays, decide to enter host states.

The exact factors precipitating the entry decisions of multinationals often seem quite random: their export markets may be threatened or their competitors may go abroad. Multinationals may see these precipitating factors as appropriate instances in which to exploit their intangible assets (Aharoni, 1966; Michalet and Delapierre, 1976).

Strategic-management theorists have argued that investment opportunities are often noticed at lower-management levels. For example, Bower (1970) contended that functional departments down the line, rather than top management, often propose entry into host states. Once proposed, such projects must gather sufficient supporters along organizational hierarchies to bring them to the notice of top managers. The control structures of multinationals influence who decides to support what projects, and the impetus that projects get as they move along hierarchies.

Manufacturing Processes:

Manufacturing-process theories revolve around the product-cycle initially proposed by Vernon (1986). Vernon (1966) concluded that all manufacturing technologies evolve through three phases: introductory or innovative phases, growth or process-development phases and finally, mature or standardizing phases. As these technological phases generate different economies, competitive firms adopt different strategies during each phase. Vernon (1966) contended that these strategies prompt the entry of multinationals into host states.

Manufacturing-process theories have proposed the following chronology (Stobaugh, 1968; Wells, 1972): Preliminary, innovative phases occur in advanced, industrialized states because of their large home markets (i.e., demand) and the resources that firms can devote to innovative activities (i.e., supply). Uncertainties in production processes and communication costs cause innovating firms to produce initially at home with home states' resources such as labor. As foreign demand rises, firms begin to export to foreign markets in other industrialized countries. In time, growth of foreign demand, diffusion of firms' technologies to foreign competitors, and rising trade barriers in foreign markets make foreign production of goods feasible and necessary. Therefore, firms decide to enter host states. During these secondary phases, manufacturing processes continue to improve. In the final phases, multinationals standardize and actually move their manufacturing processes to less-developed states. Or, multinationals may shift only the labor-intensive phases of production to less-developed states with low labor costs. Multinationals may then use the less-developed states as export platforms for global markets, including home markets (Vernon, 1966).

Manufacturing-process theories explain the entry of multinationals into Europe, Africa and Asia, through the late 19th and mid-20th centuries. For example, they provide useful frameworks to explain the post World War II expansion of US, horizontally integrated, manufacturing multinationals into other states. However, Vernon (1979) later acknowledged that the explanatory powers of product-cycles had waned. Multinationals now have global networks that allow them to develop innovations in response to threats and opportunities in various markets (see Ghauri, 1992; Haley, 1998). Besides, initial production may not occur in the areas where innovations occur. Rather, multinationals may undertake initial production in states with low labor costs. Therefore, multinationals may never utilize home states' labor. The theories also do not explain why multinationals produce abroad rather than license their products (Giddy, 1978). Nor do the theories explain the rise of multinationals, with more rudimentary technologies, in less-developed states.

Oligopolistic Markets:

Oligopolistic markets are characterized by entry barriers and therefore by small numbers of firms. Entry barriers in oligopolistic markets result from factors such as patented technology, unpatented secret know-how, large capital requirements and economies of large-scale production. Like market-imperfection theories, oligopoly theories see market structures as granting multinationals competitive advantages over domestic firms.

For instance, Knickerbocker (1973) posited that multinationals enter host states because oligopolistic markets motivate follow-the-leader behaviors in firms. Knickerbocker (1973) argued that oligopolistic firms try to increase their potential competitive actions by occupying the same markets as their competitors. These imitative efforts may cause firms to follow their competitors abroad.

Knickerbocker (1973) proposed that loose-knit (rather than tight-knit) oligopolies encourage firms to invest abroad: Firms in loose-knit oligopolies recognize their interdependence with their rivals, but lack sufficient, mutual understanding to coordinate their activities. Consequently, firms adopt simple patterns of imitative behaviors. Knickerbocker (1973) tested his notions statistically with US multinationals in 23 countries from 1948–1967. By calculating entry-concentration indices, Knickerbocker (1973) found that concentrations of entries increase with concentrations of sellers to a point, and then decline. Knickerbocker (1973) viewed these findings as confirming his propositions: high-concentration industries breed collusion; low-concentration industries lack firms' interdependence; therefore, firms in moderate-concentration industries seem most likely to follow competitors into host states.

Rationales for Growth

Growth refers to a multinational's expansion of size. Many theories have represented the growth of multinationals as attempts to retain control of firm-specific, intangible assets, and to exploit these assets profitably and efficiently. Thus, the growth of multinationals has generally been portrayed as an extension of the causes that drive them to make foreign direct investments in the first place. Theories of market imperfections, internalization, and strategic management have also dealt with growth.

Market Imperfections:

Market-imperfection theorists have reasoned that by understanding when markets fail, one can also comprehend multinationals' strategic behaviors like growth. Theorists have posited that markets fail when production techniques and commodities' properties prevent market mechanisms from allocating resources efficiently. Briefly, theorists have proposed that lumpy, technical and managerial knowledge (knowledge that has to be used in conjunction with other inputs to be efficient), or knowledge that gives rise to spillovers, contributes to market imperfections (Johnson, 1970). Johnson (1970) identified three types of market failures that contribute to imperfections: external effects, public goods and economies of scale. Theorists have concluded that the imperfections in turn hinder efficient, international production and international transfers of knowledge. Therefore, the growth of multinationals reveals efforts to surmount market imperfections.

Market imperfections have been used to explain the horizontal and vertical growth of multinationals in host states. Horizontal investments enable multinationals to function efficiently by producing similar goods in both home and host markets. Vertical investments ensure multinationals with supplies of raw materials, and other inputs, and contribute to economies of scale. Theorists' analyses of horizontal and vertical growth have emphasized firm-specific advantages such as established marketing systems, controls over transportation, managerial skills and access to capital that enable multinationals to exploit market imperfections.

Internalization:

Internalization theories have explained growth as arising from managerial needs to control and to coordinate operations. When managerial control becomes inefficient, multinationals no longer provide good replacements for markets. Then, theorists have reasoned, multinationals stop growing. Many have concluded that multinationals grow till the costs of coordination and control exceed the revenues from growth (e.g., Buckley and Casson, 1985).

Magee (1976) used technology cycles to explain growth through internalization: in young industries, firms create technologies at rapid rates. Consequently, as internal transfers are more efficient, firms expand to internalize the technologies that they produce. In more mature industries, firms create technologies at slower rates, and therefore, the optimal sizes of these firms diminish. Magee's (1976) theory implies that as industries mature, foreign direct investment should dwindle relative to licensing or exporting.

Strategic Management:

Strategic-management theories have concentrated on why the formal structures of multinationals evolve as they grow. The theories have also explained how successful managers control and coordinate their operations to extract the maximum benefits from growth. The structural growth and evolution of multinationals have occupied many strategic-management theorists. For example, Stopford and Wells (1968) discussed how multinationals alter their formal structures (from autonomous subsidiaries, to international divisions, and finally to global structures) as they develop new and complex strategies. Stopford and Wells (1968) also indicated how multinationals lose control over their destinies by including new partners, like governments, in joint ventures.

Theorists have argued that structural growth enhances managerial needs for coordination. For instance, Fayerweather (1969) contended that multinationals' diverse units face simultaneous competing pressures for unification and fragmentation. Gains to unification include headquarters' capabilities in technology, production and management; the economic and efficiency gains from integration; and, the abilities to interchange subsidiaries' capabilities to match changing environments and businesses. Gains to fragmentation stem from subsidiaries' needs to adapt to local conditions; cultural factors; nationalism; and, economic factors. According to Fayerweather (1969), multinationals' managers have to balance the competing claims in product policies, logistical plans and distributions of R&D work, financial-flow systems and operating methods.

Other researchers extended Fayerweather's (1969) framework. For example, Porter (1986) argued that successful multinationals configure (locate) and coordinate their activities nationally or globally to exploit advantages in production, procurement, service, technology, marketing and sales. The advantages may vary across industries (Porter, 1986). Similarly, Hamel and Prahalad (1983) reasoned that profitable multinationals follow national, rather than global, strategies when subsidiaries adapt products to national markets; subsidiaries cannot exploit scale economies in R&D, manufacturing, and purchasing; subsidiaries face large numbers of non-global competitors in national markets; nationally distinctive distribution channels exist; product substitutes exist; and, subsidiaries do not depend on headquarters for R&D. And, Ghoshal (1987) added that multinationals' competitive advantages stem from their abilities to coordinate national differences in input and output markets, economies of scale and economies of scope. These abilities, as well as desires to maximize efficiencies, to reduce risks and to enhance learning prompt managers of successful multinationals or transnationals (Bartlett and Ghoshal, 2000) to trade globally and nationally responsive strategies (Ghoshal, 1987).

Rationales for Decline

Decline refers to cutbacks in sizes, reductions in absolute rates of growth, and multinationals' leaving host states. The decline of multinationals in host states has often been explained as the flip side of their reasons for entry: Decline sets in when multinationals cease to operate as profit-maximizing and efficiency-driven firms or cease to coordinate their operations. Theories of internalization and strategic management have offered some rationales for decline.

Internalization:

Boddewyn (1983) extended internalization theories of multinationals to explain divestment: when multinationals lose their firm-specific assets or their abilities to internalize the assets, or when cheaper methods of servicing markets arise, then multinationals leave host states.

Shapiro (1986) also used internalization theories, along with market-imperfection theories, to depict the comparative ease with which multinationals could leave states. Shapiro's (1986) explanation enlarged the Caves–Porter analysis (Caves and Porter, 1976; Eaton and Lipsey, 1980; 1981) of the symmetrical relations between entry and exit barriers. Caves and Porter (1976) focused on domestic firms' investments in durable and firm-specific assets such as durable plant and equipment, advertising expenditures, firm-specific human capital, R&D expenditures, as well as economies of scale. Caves and Porter (1976) argued that new firms must duplicate these expensive assets, with limited, resale markets, to remain competitive. Consequently, existing firms' uses of durable and specific assets constitute entry barriers for new firms. In addition, assets' specificities limit their scrap values and increase new firms' risks of entry. However, these characteristics also make the assets exit barriers for existing firms: the committed assets, with their limited marketability, become nonrecoverable costs. Simply stated, firms become bound to their markets, unable to divest (Caves and Porter, 1976). Shapiro (1986) argued that as exit barriers seem similar to entry barriers, multinationals' subsidiaries are less restricted than domestic firms by exit barriers. Subsidiaries' intangible assets are deployed relatively cheaply, reducing multinationals' necessary, recoverable costs (Shapiro, 1986). In addition, the assets may be transferred within multinational systems, using internal, rather than external markets. Analyzing Canadian data from 1972–1976, Shapiro (1986) found that investments in technology did deter domestic firms from leaving but appeared not to deter multinationals. Therefore, he concluded that multinationals may leave industries more easily than domestic firms do.

Strategic Management:

Strategic-management theories generally explain the divestitures of subsidiaries as arising from multinationals' needs to control and to coordinate global operations, as well as to maintain system-wide profitability (Porter, 1986). Thus, subsidiaries' performances alone do not influence multinationals' decisions about leaving. For example, from case studies of eight multinationals, Tornedon and Boddewyn (1974) concluded that the divestitures of subsidiaries depended on their profitability, changes in headquarters' strategic positions, as well as various environmental influences on headquarters. Headquarters' decisions to leave host states seemed to emanate from a series of incremental, investigative decisions, rather than from conscious strategic decisions (Tornedon and Boddewyn, 1974). The next section traces the effects of multinationals' strategic behaviors on various stakeholders.

Relations with Stakeholders

This section covers theoretical rationales for multinationals' relations with stakeholders. For the most part, theories have built on multinationals' behaviors in imperfect markets. As Figure 2.1 describes, most theories have emphasized either multinationals' profit-maximizing and efficiency-driven behaviors, or their control and coordination of global operations.

Theories dealing with market imperfections, internalization, and strategic management have concentrated on multinationals' internal characteristics, portraying them as entrepreneurial firms. In the process, they have delineated owners' and managers' interests and influences. A second set of theories dealing with manufacturing processes, oligopolistic markets, redistribution, international relations, dependent development and global networks generally have specified multinationals' abilities to affect labor, governments, states, societies and the world. The second set of theories has portrayed multinationals as catalysts, or change agents: the theorists have assumed for the most part that as multinationals possess certain characteristics, their presence brings about catalytic reactions.

Owners & Managers

Theories of market imperfections have depicted multinationals' relations with owners; theories of internalization and strategic management have portrayed some of multinationals' relations with managers.

Figure 2.1   Reviewing multinational corporations' effects on stakeholders.

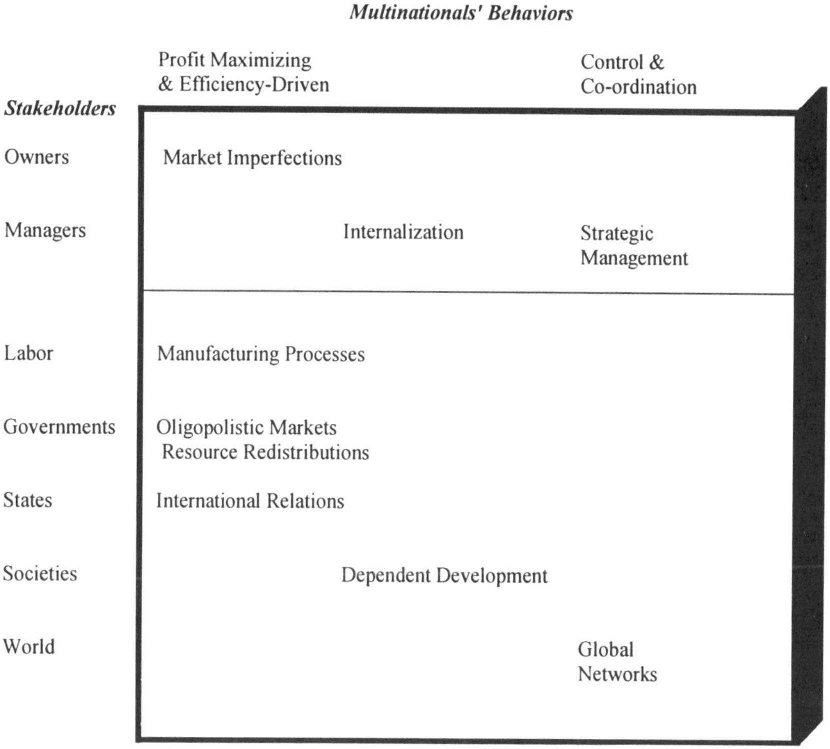

Multinationals' Behaviors

Stakeholders	Profit Maximizing & Efficiency-Driven	Control & Co-ordination
Owners	Market Imperfections	
Managers	Internalization	Strategic Management
Labor	Manufacturing Processes	
Governments	Oligopolistic Markets Resource Redistributions	
States	International Relations	
Societies	Dependent Development	
World		Global Networks

Market Imperfections:

Market-imperfection theories have painted multinationals as entrepreneurial firms that strive to maximize profits and efficiencies. Consequently, the theories have granted owners' (stockholders' and investors') interests paramount importance. The theorists have generally ignored other stakeholders' interests.

As market-imperfection theories have explained the presence of multinationals as arising from their abilities to exploit market imperfections, many have highlighted the advantages that multinationals provide to stockholders and to investors. For example, Caves (1971) depicted multinationals' behaviors in host states as arising from their profit-maximizing efforts to utilize efficiently their intangible assets. Similarly, Aliber (1970) and Agmon and Lessard (1977) argued that multinationals' behaviors constitute efforts to diversify and to reduce the risks of stockholders' portfolios.

Internalization:

Internalization theories have explained some of multinationals' relations with managers. Like market-imperfection theorists, internalization theorists have assumed that managers exist to pursue owners' interests through maximizing profits and efficiencies. However, many of the theories also deal with how managers recoup transaction benefits by common governance of separate but inter-related activities located in different states. That is, the theories explain why managers control and coordinate operations. Many of the theorists have assumed that subsidiaries are miniature versions of headquarters. Consequently, subsidiaries' and headquarters' managers are portrayed as having similar interests and views.

Strategic Management:

Strategic-management theories have focused on how headquarters' managers may control subsidiaries to maximize profits. When the theories have explained labor's or governments' behaviors (Bartlett, 1986; Doz, 1986; Encarnation and Wells, 1986; Mahini and Wells, 1986), they have concentrated on the circumstances under which the stakeholders hinder or help managers' coordination and control activities.

Many theories have focused on multinationals' needs to integrate subsidiaries' managers into global operations (such as Ghauri, 1992). For example, through empirical studies of six Swedish multinationals, Hedlund (1980; 1981) concluded that subsidiaries' and headquarters' managers often develop divergent views of realities that hinder headquarters' efforts to maintain multinational systems. Similarly, Bartlett and Ghoshal (1987) discussed how simultaneous global and national strategic pressures evoke divergent views from headquarters' and subsidiaries' managers. To maintain profitability, Bartlett and Ghoshal (1987) advocated more sophisticated, management controls based on headquarters' cooptation of subsidiaries' managers.

Strategic-management theorists have often discussed the most efficient types of management controls in multinational systems. For example, through a series of field studies, Prahalad and Doz (1981), and Doz and Prahalad (1981), concluded that various organizational mechanisms enhance the abilities of headquarters' managers to elicit valid, reliable information from subsidiaries' managers. These include data-management mechanisms such as information systems, measurement systems, resource-allocation procedures and strategic-planning and budgeting processes; managerial mechanisms such as choices of key managers and career paths, reward-and-punishment systems, management-development programs and socialization patterns; and conflict-resolution mechanisms such as decision-responsibility assignments, task forces, issue-resolution processes, coordination committees, integrators and business teams (Doz and Prahalad, 1981).

Labor

Manufacturing-process theories have related multinationals' growth and expansion to technological developments. They have derived multinationals' effects on home and host-states' labor from their profit-maximizing and efficiency-driven behaviors.

Manufacturing Processes:

Manufacturing-process theorists have generally assumed that technological developments for multinationals occur in developed countries with high labor costs. Consequently, multinationals utilize labor-saving, capital-intensive technologies. When multinationals eventually move production to less-developed states, the theorists have posited that they continue to use the same factor proportions in production — to the detriment of labor-rich, host states. For the most part, theorists have ignored the possibilities that by initiating labor-intensive innovations of their own, host states could make multinationals less competitive. For example, Davidson (1982) showed that innovations in European countries seem substantially less capital-intensive than those in the USA; also Haley (2000a) identified several examples of process innovation in the Asia-Pacific developing countries that have forced multinationals from industrialized countries to respond.

Vernon, and other theorists (e.g., Wells, 1972), also used manufacturing processes to explain multinationals' effects on domestic labor. As multinationals' technologies evolve, their operations may utilize foreign rather than domestic labor. Efficiency and profit considerations may prompt multinationals to export labor-intensive jobs from home to less-developed states. In effect, multinationals may snatch jobs from home states' labor. Thus, theorists explained social phenomena, such as the antagonistic behaviors of home states' labor towards multinationals.

Governments

Oligopoly and political-economy theories have portrayed some of multinationals' effects on governments. They have derived the effects from multinationals' profit-maximizing and efficiency-driven behaviors.

Oligopolistic Markets:

Oligopoly theorists have argued that multinationals may prevent the growth of domestic firms. Therefore, oligopoly theories have strong implications for governmental roles in industries in general, and in the regulation of multinationals' activities in particular.

In many oligopoly models (e.g., Knickerbocker, 1973), multinationals' behaviors become defensive strategies in response to competitors' price cuts and maneuvers. Graham (1978) referred to the relations between oligopolistic multinationals as exchange-of-threat motivations. Oligopoly theorists have often concluded that as multinationals increase their response potentials, they concurrently reduce domestic and global competition and stabilize markets.

Oligopoly theories imply that multinationals' comparative advantages and global strategies often preclude domestic firms from competing successfully in the same markets. Assumptions about governmental roles in oligopoly theories derive directly from classical and neoclassical economic assumptions: Social relations between economic actors, such as a few multinationals, constitute frictional drags that impede competitive markets. For example, Adam Smith (1776/1979:232) complained "people of the same trade seldom meet together, even for merriment and diversion, but the conversation ends in a conspiracy against the public, or in some contrivance to raise prices". Consequently, the theorists assume that governments should intervene to maintain competitive markets, and to promote social welfare, by correcting the imbalances perpetuated by multinationals.

Redistribution:

Political-economy theories have depicted redistributions of powers and resources between multinationals and governments. Early political economists utilized bilateral-monopoly models to analyze the relations between multinationals and governments: Multinationals control capital, technology, management and marketing skills to launch economic projects; governments control access to states before multinationals invest, and control conditions for operation afterwards. Multinationals and governments were generally represented as struggling over the distributions of benefits from economic projects. For example, Penrose (1959) argued that at first, multinationals receive just enough benefits to induce them to commit investments; later, they receive just enough to prevent them from withdrawing.

Kindleberger (1965) contended that Penrose's formulation constituted the lower limits that multinationals receive. He posited that the scarcity values of multinationals' investments to governments decide the upper values of the benefits that multinationals receive from governments. The upper values then constitute the prices at which governments would rather forego the investments. The distance between, upper and lower values affords opportunities for negotiations (Kindleberger, 1965).

Vernon (1971) introduced the concept of the obsolescing bargain to add dynamism to the static, bilateral-monopoly models. Risks and uncertainty formed central tenets of Vernon's (1971) theory. According to Vernon (1971), before multinationals invest in foreign states, production costs and markets determine their perceptions of risks and uncertainties. To induce foreign investments, governments structure contracts to reward multinationals handsomely for successful projects. Consequently, initial contracts tilt heavily in favor of multinationals. However, if projects prove successful, risks and uncertainties dissipate. Hostage effects also take place, as multinationals cannot credibly threaten to exit once they have invested heavily in states. Besides host states may move up learning curves of bargaining and managerial skills, drive harder bargains with multinationals and threaten to replace them if they fail to renegotiate contracts. Whatever the causes, the obsolescing bargain predicts that initial agreements favoring multinationals are likely to be renegotiated in favor of host governments.

Bennett and Sharpe (1985) sketched a bargaining model to explain multinationals' powers vis-à-vis the Mexican government. They argued that governments' cohesion and organizational unity greatly influenced their relative powers vis-à-vis multinationals. They also highlighted institutional environments that limit multinationals' and governmental powers. Bennett and Sharpe (1985) contended that firms' behaviors (firms' incorporation of local content, exports and pricing behaviors) shape policies on industrial structures (questions regarding the numbers of firms and of foreign ownership) by setting decision-making agendas. Governmental powers to act on these agendas depend on their planning capacities, their administrative abilities to monitor and to control foreign capital, and the technical knowledge that governmental officials have about industries; multinationals' powers depend on their knowledge of local markets and political systems, and their administrative abilities to negotiate with governments (Bennett and Sharpe, 1985). Bennett and Sharpe (1985) portrayed multinationals as homogeneous entities with common, internal interests; and, they confined their analyses of institutional restraints to market structures.

Political-economy theories have generally depicted subsidiaries' behaviors as strategies to exploit intangible assets and to extend parent firms' abilities to extract oligopoly rents. For the most part, the theories have concentrated on just a few ways in which governments influence multinationals: by creating or heightening market imperfections through tariffs and trade barriers, by restricting financial and factor markets, by restricting know-how, by containing sellers' markets and by widening international-tax differentials.

Generally, the theories have focused on how multinationals influence governments. Theorists have argued (e.g., Parry, 1980) that multinationals cause efficiency and equity effects in states. Efficiency effects deal with multinationals' abilities to increase states' outputs: As multinationals move resources like capital from places where returns are low, to places where returns are high, they bid up the prices of abundant resources, like labor, in host countries. By their more efficient uses of global resources, multinationals may increase global outputs. By increasing market competition, multinationals may also boost domestic firms' efficiencies. Equity effects deal with the distribution of the incremental outputs between governments and multinationals. Equity effects generally take place through host states' taxes, lower prices for consumers and increased profits for multinationals.

Political-economy theorists often viewed governments and multinationals as antagonists, arguing over allocations of incremental outputs through taxes or repatriated profits. Yet, governments and multinationals sometimes form networks to distribute benefits as in Singapore (Haley, 2000a; Haley, Low and Toh, 1996). Generally, however, the only other stakeholders that theorists have acknowledged — labor forces — often lose in these theories: Multinationals' strivings for increased efficiency, together with their flexibility, cause labor forces to lose their bargaining powers.

Kindleberger and Hymer developed the efficiency and equity effects implied by imperfect-market theories into contradictory critiques of multinationals' and governmental roles in states' economies. Kindleberger (1969), argued that multinationals propel states towards greater efficiency and prosperity. He acknowledged that multinationals may swallow domestic competitors. However, he also reasoned that multinationals increase efficiencies by increasing global, competitive interactions, breaking up domestic monopolies, and surmounting national barriers to free competition. Therefore, Kindleberger (1969) concluded that governments should not hamper multinationals. Hymer (Hymer, 1970; 1971; Hymer and Rowthorne, 1970; Rowthorne and Hymer, 1970) argued that multinationals' advantages give them certain powers vis-à-vis governments. These powers enable multinationals to channel wealth and power away from peripheral (less-developed) states to central (industrialized) states. Consequently, he concluded that governments should regulate multinationals.

States

For the most part, international-relations theories have drawn on neoclassical, economic propositions about multinationals' profit-maximizing and efficiency-driven behaviors. The theories have highlighted multinationals' effects on nation states and global, economic and political orders.

International Relations:

Many international-relations theorists have assumed that from the early 1900's until World War II, the USA constituted the world's dominant military and economic power. As the dominant power, the USA greatly contributed to creating and to maintaining the international economy through institutions like multinationals (e.g., Gilpin, 1975; 1987). After World War II, the USA, Western Europe and Japan formed the dominant powers. Today, this triad, and the economic order it maintained, is in disarray. International-relations theorists have offered at least two contradictory explanations for multinationals' roles in the aftermath of this hegemonic collapse.

One explanation was initially proposed by Vernon (1971) in his influential book *Sovereignty at Bay*. Vernon (1971) argued that economic inter-dependence, and technological advances in communication have undermined the traditional, economic rationales for states. World efficiencies and domestic, economic welfares will continue to decrease states' powers vis-à-vis multinationals and other international institutions (Vernon, 1971).

Sovereignty-at-bay differentiates between the USA's creation of a world economy, and the subsequent dynamics of its maintenance. Vernon and other theorists subscribing to this theory have argued that rather than hegemonic powers, interdependent, international, economic interests, and the benefits from the interdependencies now bind international orders together. States have joined in economic relations with multinationals and other states from which they cannot easily escape, and from which they derive great benefits (see Haley, 1998). States' citizens, the theorists have argued, would not tolerate the sacrifices in economic well-being that would follow if states hamper multinationals' operations. Governments therefore, dare not forego employment and regional-development opportunities by sanctioning multinationals (Johnson, 1970).

Sovereignty-at-bay deduces that the flexibility and vast resources of multinationals grant them advantages in confrontations with states (Vernon, 1971). If multinationals move production facilities elsewhere, states lose employment, corporate resources and access to world markets. Thus, the theorists have argued that multinationals often escape states' controls and emerge as powers to change international, political relations (Huntington, 1973).

Obversely, the theorists have contended that states often face the possibility of losing control over economic affairs to multinationals. States may not be able to retain traditional sovereignty and to meet their citizens' rising economic demands. Therefore, the sovereignty-at-bay model views states' efforts to enhance security and power as incompatible with an interdependent world economy that generates absolute gains. The theorists have contended that economic forces will eventually contribute to the end of nationality as we know it (Huntington, 1973). The sovereignty-at-bay world consists of interdependent economies with voluntary cooperative relations that accelerate everyone's economic growth and welfare. In this world, multinationals, freed from nation states, form critical transmission belts of capital, ideas and growth.

Another explanation revolves around the mercantilist theories. Mercantilist theorists have painted the interplay of states' interests as the primary determinants of the international economic order's future. They generally relegate multinationals to peripheral places, or regard them as states' instruments. According to these theorists, the interdependent world economy that provided an extremely favorable environment for multinationals has come to an end. In the wake of the relative decline of the USA's power, and of the growing conflict among capitalist economies, a new international order, less favorable to multinationals, is coming into existence (Calleo and Rowland, 1973; Gilpin, 1987). This emergent world order is characterized by intense, international, economic competition for markets, investment outlets, and sources of raw materials.

In the new order, states manipulate economic arrangements to maximize their own interests, even at the expense of stakeholders. States' interests concern domestic matters (like employment and price stabilities), as well as foreign-policy matters (like security and independence). Thus, mercantilist theories have granted priority to states' economic and political objectives over global economic efficiencies. In pursuit of economic objectives and national interests, states attempt to control actors within their realms, including multinationals (Krasner, 1978).

Mercantilist theorists have argued that international competition has intensified because the USA has lost its technological lead in products and manufacturing processes. The US multinationals must now increasingly compete on the bases of prices and a devalued dollar. Thus, the USA can no longer draw on the technological rents associated with its industrial supremacy and the supremacy of US multinationals in the economic order has come to an end. Consequently, US multinationals play greatly diminished roles in maintaining the USA's hegemonic rule. States will now increasingly form regional, trade and monetary alliances to advance their own interests. This regionalization will replace the USA's emphases on multilateral free trade, the dollar's international role and the US multinationals' supremacy. In the wake of the Asian Crisis, and the subsequent dominance of US multinationals and management (Haley, 2000a; 2000b), many of the mercantilists appear anachronistic.

Statist theorists have not explicitly built theories of multinationals but have discussed states' efforts at influencing multinationals. For example, Krasner (1978), recognized that multinationals' managers have reasons to cooperate with states. However, Krasner (1978) did not build his arguments into a theory of when and why multinationals cooperate with states. For the most part, Statists focus on the characteristics that give states powers over other actors in economic and political systems. They have argued that the strengths of states in societies range from weak to strong depending on their abilities to resist private pressures, to change private behaviors, and to change social structures (Krasner, 1978). The weakest states are totally vulnerable to interest groups, including multinationals; the strongest states can remake societies and cultures. According to Krasner (1978), most states fall somewhere in between those two extremes.

Statists have proposed that even the strongest states enjoy uneven powers across policy areas. For example, Katzenstein (1978) distinguished between strategies open to Japan and to France that can apply policy instruments at industry-sector levels, and to Britain and to the USA that must rely on macroeconomic manipulations of fiscal and monetary parameters. Therefore, Statists have contended that complete analyses of states' powers require examinations of the organizations and powers of states, of socioeconomic interest groups such as multinationals and of other societal actors. Statists have depicted multinational-state relations from states' viewpoints as states' efforts to influence multinationals; they have not attempted to build a coherent theory of multinationals, or of their influences.

In a critique of international-relations theories, Nye (1986) concluded that hegemonic theories offer inadequate explanations for multinationals' roles in the 1980's. Nye (1986) argued that relationships between the spread of multinationals and of the USA's military power have never been established. Similarly, sovereignty-at-bay seems jaded and dated: Incidences of nationalizations and protests in developing countries have declined dramatically since the 1970's, reflecting changes in multinationals' and states' bargaining powers. Nye advised against generalizations. He predicted (Nye, 1986) that states and multinationals would muddle through as in the past, with bilateral agreements, weak multilateral measures, some sectoral closures, and a great deal of flexibility and adaptation. Different industries, sectors and firms may present different patterns; but, the patterns have yet to be discovered (Nye, 1986).

Societies

Multinationals' effects on societies are largely depicted in sociological studies dominated by the Marxist, dependency school. Dependency theorists have generally accepted neoclassical, economic propositions about multinationals' desires to maximize profits and to coordinate and to control operations. They have focused primarily on processes of societal development, and secondarily on multinationals' roles in development (Biersteker, 1978; Chase-Dunn, 1975).

Dependent Development:

A variety of contentions, some contradictory, have emerged from the dependency theorists. Drawing on Hymer's characterizations of multinationals, dependency theorists have argued that multinationals distort economic development in less-developed states by forcing them into associated or "dependent development" relationships (Evans, 1979). They have charged multinationals with creating branch-plant economies of small, inefficient firms that are incapable of propelling overall development. They have argued that foreign subsidiaries exist as appendages of their home firms, and as enclaves in states' economies, rather than as engines of self-reliant growth (Rosen and Kurth, 1974). They have accused multinationals of introducing inappropriate, technological developments and of employing capital-intensive, production techniques that cause unemployment and prevent the emergence of domestic technologies. They have asserted that multinationals add skewness to the income distributions among classes in less-developed states (Evans, 1981). And, because of their repatriation of profits and their superior access to local capital, they have contended that multinationals prevent the rise of indigenous enterprises (Hirschman, 1969).

Dependency theorists have also concluded that multinationals have negative, political consequences for less-developed states (Breton, 1964; Johnson, 1965; 1967; Vernon, 1967). For example, theorists have asserted that multinationals require stable, host governments that are sympathetic to capitalism; therefore, dependent development encourages authoritarian regimes in host states and creates alliances between multinationals and domestic, reactionary elites. They have contended that multinationals' home governments sustain these exploitative alliances by intervening in the internal affairs of less-developed states. In this fashion, multinationals tend to make host states politically dependent upon home, industrialized states.

Other dependency studies have concentrated on how multinationals perpetuate social and economic inequalities by distorting employment opportunities and labor-force structures (Evans and Timberlake, 1980). The studies generally have drawn on Marxists' beliefs that capitalist systems increase inequalities. For example, Robinson (1976) suggested that multinationals' effects on inequalities are mediated by their penetration of societies. Multinationals are more likely to penetrate states with weak, national apparatuses; therefore, weak states have more inequalities (Robinson, 1976). Similarly, Bornschier and Ballmer-Cao (1979) argued that multinationals weaken the power of labor and middle-class groups and strengthen the hands of traditional, power holders.

Still other dependency theorists have concentrated on multinationals' negative effects on societies and cultures (Evans, 1981). They have argued that states may lose control over their culture and social development. Therefore, multinationals may contribute to cultural imperialism or CocaColaization of less-developed societies. The theorists have proposed that multinationals undermine societies' traditional values by introducing new values and tastes through advertising and business practices. These new values often create demands for goods that do not meet the masses' true needs.

In an incisive article, Moran (1978) demonstrated that every societal threat is also a societal opportunity. The dependency theorists have drawn on neoclassical economic propositions about multinationals' capabilities that can be turned on their ears to show the benefits that multinationals provide to states. For the most part, dependency studies have provided evidence of associations rather than theories of the ways in which multinationals affect capital formation, labor-force structures and power distributions in host states. Studies testing propositions that multinationals distort the development of states have yielded mixed results (Bornschier, Chase-Dunn and Rubinson, 1978): some studies used flows of foreign direct investment and others used firms' equities to gauge effects on Gini indices and similar distributional measures of income. Dependency theorists have been unable to distinguish between the effects of multinationals and of general economic growth. Economic growth itself creates disparities of wealth (Frank and Freeman, 1978; Ruggie, 1983). As manufacturing multinationals often invest in rapidly growing economies, their impacts appear inseparable from other growth processes (see Haley and Haley, 1997 for a discussion of the contradictory effects of foreign direct investment in Vietnam).

The World

Anthropological theories have analyzed multinationals' attempts to control and to coordinate their operations by managing global environments. The theories have emphasized how multinationals de-emphasize profit-maximizing criteria as they forge global, social networks.

Global Networks:

Changes in political and economic systems threaten multinationals' abilities to predict, to plan, to manage, and to economize. To help control their destinies, multinationals generate large-scale regularities and interdependencies through means other than centralization (Gerlach and Palmer, 1981). Anthropological theories show how political and economic networks develop as multinationals create branch offices, merge, and cooperate with other firms, with political groups and with governmental agencies. Thus, multinationals develop political-control networks that serve as socially integrating mechanisms for them. The networks bind multinationals, states and families into supranational structures with ambiguous boundaries — analogous to acephalous, segmentary, social systems (Wolfe, 1967). But, as multinationals extend their spheres of influence through participating in the networks, and as they increasingly adopt policies that slow growth, they also de-emphasize their market-exchange functions and increasingly emphasize redistributive functions with respect to states and societies (Gerlach and Palmer, 1981).

Haley, Tan and Haley (1998) documented how the Overseas Chinese companies form global networks to enhance the distribution of information while not necessarily maximizing profits or efficiencies. Wolfe (1977) also described how multinationals bind together in global networks that channel reciprocities. He isolated two types of decision rules that multinationals use: maximization rules in which behaviors are contingent upon anticipated returns; and, reciprocity rules in which behaviors are contingent upon assessing others' needs and wants. Wolfe (1977) argued that often multinationals follow reciprocity rules just to keep some stakeholders in the system. According to Wolfe (1977), multinationals in mining frequently deviate from maximization rules when dealing with their subsidiaries or with their partners in joint ventures. For example, multinationals may loan money and sell products to each other at prices well below the market. One multinational may sell another a raw material that is in such short supply as to be unavailable to firms unaffiliated with the system. In this fashion, multinationals may control and coordinate their operations at global levels, while not necessarily maximizing profits or efficiencies.

Theoretical Assumptions

Generally, theorists have argued that the reasons for the entry of multinationals into host states also explain their subsequent growth and decline. Multinationals bring new, scarce resources that they strictly control — capital, technology, management and marketing skills; their strategic uses of these resources change stakeholders for better or for worse. Consequently, many of the theories have implied that multinationals behave as catalysts in states. To depict these catalytic effects, theories of multinationals have incorporated certain assumptions about their behaviors. In particular, most theorists have assumed that multinationals use static, analytical schemes, coordinate and control operations efficiently, and enjoy relatively stable relations with stakeholders.

Static Analytical Schemes

Most theories have implied that multinationals use certain analytical schemes to analyze environments. When environments change, multinationals note the changes and then apply the same, analytical schemes to the new environments. Most of the theories have emphasized efficiency criteria. Regardless of the complexities that multinationals face, most theorists have assumed that historical processes eliminate managerial decision rules that do not solve joint-optimization problems. Most theorists have also assumed that multinationals act as profit maximizers. Consequently, most of the theories have portrayed multinationals as using only performance criteria, like profits and sales, to gauge their environments.

Most theories also fail to distinguish between multinationals' initial investment decisions and subsequent, incremental investment flows. Yet, as Kogut (1986) pointed out, incremental investments in established subsidiaries form the predominant shares of foreign direct investments' flows. In the light of these trends, existing theories of multinationals provide incomplete explanations for multinationals' behaviors (Kogut, 1986).

Efficient Control and Coordination

Some theories of multinationals have emphasized headquarters' need to control and to coordinate multinationals' operations. The theorists have argued that multinationals can exploit intangible assets efficiently only when organizational forms are efficient, i.e., when headquarters can control and coordinate operations for optimal benefits. Most of the theorists have posited that headquarters control multinationals' operations to increase efficiencies, to add to social welfare, to increase adaptability and therefore to increase profits. For example, according to internalization theories, multinationals grow so long as the benefits from growth exceed the costs of coordination and control. Conversely, internationalization theories imply that multinationals divest when they no longer benefit from internalization. Consequently, the theories grant internal-market efficiencies more importance than external-market efficiencies.

Stable Relations with Stakeholders

Most theories of multinationals have taken the stability of relations with stakeholders for granted, presumed the recurrence of environmental conditions and stated that multinationals can improve performances by building cumulatively on past experiences. Externally, most of the theories have focused on relationships with established publics. Theories have examined the relations between multinationals, labor, governments, societies and states. Generally, the relationships have been depicted as antagonistic and conflict ridden.

However, multinationals' behaviors towards their stakeholders demonstrate more than conflict and competition (Gladwin and Walter, 1980; Haley,

2000a; Hawkins and Walter, 1981; Walter, 1982). For example, multinationals' behaviors often include collaboration, accommodation and avoidance (Gilpin, 1987; Gladwin and Walter, 1980; Haley and Haley, 1996). The next chapter re-evaluates some assumptions that theories of multinationals make.

3. Reassessing Theories of Multinational Corporations

Most theorists would agree that multinationals have characteristics that distinguish them from domestic firms. Fewer theorists would agree that multinationals change only in preset and anticipated ways, operate efficiently, rarely deceive their stakeholders, and rarely make mistakes. Yet most theories of multinationals have included only these behaviors. Thus, as Chapter 2 indicated, multinationals' strategic behaviors in host states are largely derived from their reasons for entries.

This chapter argues that contrary to most theories, multinationals' reasons for entries may not explain their subsequent growth and decline or relations with stakeholders: multinationals and environments change. In particular: multinationals' analytical schemes change; control and coordination of operations by multinationals often prove illusory; and multinationals' relations with stakeholders change.

Dynamic Analytical Schemes

Kogut (1986) pointed out that incremental investments in established subsidiaries constitute the predominant shares of foreign direct investment flows. No evidence indicates that the evaluation criteria that multinationals' managers use remain the same across these decisions. Yet, most theories of multinationals have failed to distinguish between multinationals' initial investment decisions and subsequent decisions on growth.

According to the simple, neoclassical, one-period model, firms operate in highly competitive industries in static, certain environments. Production functions relate various input possibilities to outputs. Optimum inputs can be inferred from input and output prices, from the outputs obtainable from input combinations and from goals of profit maximization. Firms maximize net profits — incomes from sales less the costs of inputs. In this one-period model, firms' strategies maximize the resources available for firms' consumption in later periods. At profit-maximizing solutions, three powerful conditions hold. First, any two inputs or any two outputs can substitute for each other in proportion to the ratios of their prices. Second, additional revenues obtained by using more of any inputs equal the costs of additional inputs. Third, additional costs of producing more outputs equal the selling prices of the additional outputs (Carter, 1981).

The one-period model outlined appears simple, but its implications permeate theories of multinationals. Succinctly, the model implies that prices trigger multinationals' resource-allocation decisions and therefore their presence. For example, the model implies that headquarters move subsidiaries out of some states, and establish subsidiaries in others, because managers expect higher sales in the new states. Similarly, headquarters support those goods, services and subsidiaries that grant the greatest probable returns on investments.

Economic and financial models have provided many insights into how managers should behave in order to allocate resources efficiently, into how managers do behave and into how managers' behaviors can be modeled — whether or not they consciously act as the models posit. The models often do very well in explaining average firms' as opposed to specific firms' behaviors in particular situations (Gladwin and Walter, 1980; Walter, 1982). It is on these grounds that researchers have both praised and criticized the economic and financial models of firms, including multinationals.

Most of the economic and financial models of multinationals assume large amounts of information and they abstract firms' attributes. Yet, behavioral processes are rarely efficient. Most neoclassical economic models of multinationals assume omniscience on the part of at least one person who knows input and output prices, income and cost streams, and production functions (Carter, 1981). For the most part, this assumption is invalidated by multinationals' vast sizes, personnel's opportunistic behaviors (Williamson, 1975), and bounded rationality (Simon, 1945). Managers may also fall prey to systematic biases that permeate decision processes (Haley and Stumpf, 1989). These factors often preclude multinationals from behaving as theories say they should.

Evidence indicates that sometimes multinationals' behaviors deviate from expectations inspired by theories. For example, Hawkins and Walter (1981) pointed out that multinationals' efforts to set feasible goals for subsidiaries, to disaggregate planning targets and to allocate funds for efficient expansion among competing units often prove futile. Also, Hout, Porter and Rudden (1982) argued that multinationals operate in diverse, geographical environments that cause subsidiaries' profit horizons to vary. Consequently, subsidiaries often have to re-establish profit-maximizing criteria (Hout, Porter and Rudden, 1982). Multinationals have to make, and to digest, complex arrays of economic, financial and political forecasts to operate efficiently. Yet, managers frequently do not know all the options that exist. Haley and Haley (1998) described how managers in developing countries have to compete effectively under conditions of high uncertainty with unreliable statistical and market information. Typical measures of performance — such as accounting profits or accounting costs — may prove notoriously deficient as planning aids in multinational contexts (Hawkins and Walter, 1981; Walter, 1982). Consequently, multinationals' analyses about political, economic and social changes are often based on criteria no more rigorous than the subjective and judgmental estimates of subsidiaries' managers (Haley, Tan and Haley, 1998; Hawkins and Walter, 1981; Schollhammer, 1971). As headquarters' and subsidiaries' managers receive new information, they often re-evaluate old criteria.

Behavioral concepts have shed light on how specific firms make decisions. For example, Simon (1955) contended that managers do not actively seek out all alternatives and then select the alternatives that maximize utility. Rather, managers often satisfice, choosing alternatives that are available and appear reasonable (Simon, 1955). One can argue that satisficing constitutes a sophisticated form of optimization that allows for the costs of search. Extending this analysis to organizations, Simon (1964) emphasized the hierarchical level of decisions. Participants' (or stakeholders') perceptions and expectations form important constraints for managers. Organizations remain viable so long as participants such as labor, consumers and stockholders perceive that the inducements they receive from firms exceed the contributions required of the participants. Therefore, firms' goals include those of their participants. Simon (1964) argued that goals pursued and decisions reached at higher organizational levels become constraints that managers at lower organizational levels must satisfy. Lower-level managers' final goals then satisfy all the constraints imposed upon them.

In an excellent survey of the behavioralists, Machlup (1967) cataloged the various deviations of managers from profit maximization, and then asked how significant and effective these deviations were. He argued that an enlarged view of economic marginalism can accommodate most behavioralists' concepts. Thus, if stimuli trigger actions, as Cyert and March (1963) have argued, the marginalists can claim that these behaviors are consistent with long-run, profit maximization. Machlup (1967) contended that tests analyzing researchers' predictions against actual events verify marginalists' models — regardless of divergences between the thinking marginalists impute to managers and managers' actual thought processes. Machlup (1967) suggested that various plausible objectives for maximizing exist, several of which link directly to profits, and all of which have various constraints that may apply. Stressing that many concepts of the firm exist, Machlup (1967) said that economists should not be blinded by false concerns that only one economic view could be correct. Where there are large groups of firms and one wishes to predict directions of change rather than absolute levels, Machlup (1967) said the marginalists' focusing upon long-run profit-maximization proves most useful. For explaining particular firms' behaviors with numerical answers, Machlup (1967) acknowledged that behavioral incrementalism appears more relevant.

Most theories of multinationals have not adequately represented their pursuits of these multiple, short-term goals, instead of long-term, profit-maximizing goals. Yet, empirical studies show that managers operating on general-preference functions do not single-mindedly pursue profits in the short run (Lanzilotti, 1958; Shubik, 1961). Rather, multinationals' behaviors may reflect adherence to some minimal profit constraints (Aharoni, 1966; Bower, 1970; Williamson, 1963). The minimal profit constraints may vary from very high to very low, depending on the industry and stakeholders' pressures (Rhenman, 1973). Minimal profit constraints do not imply that multinationals are not profit-seeking entities. Institutional pressures exist and managers can consistently ignore stakeholders' demands, such as high price-to-earnings ratios, only by raising risks of hostile takeovers, reshuffling of management teams, and pruning of corporate leadership (Gladwin and Walter, 1980). Rather, minimal profit constraints imply that in the short-run, multinationals as complex organizations pursue multiple goals that include the pursuit of profits. Consequently, some behaviors of multinationals may be better understood by incorporating the shorter-term goals that multinationals pursue.

Some empirical studies have indicated that large corporations, characterized by absentee ownership, do seem to maximize functions that include multiple goals. For example, Shubik (1961) studied public and private statements by officers of 25 corporations to determine corporate goals. Shubik (1961) ranked these corporate goals by frequencies of managerial responses. The goals included duties and responsibilities to personnel (21 responses), society (19 responses), consumers (19 responses), and stockholders (16 responses); pursuit of profits (13 responses); quality in products (11 responses); and, technological progress (9 responses).

Managers often get rewarded for attending to the demands of organizational stakeholders (Baumol, 1962; 1967; Berle and Means, 1932; Galbraith, 1967; 1973; Haley, 1991; Marris, 1967; Starbuck, 1965; Williamson, 1963). For example, managerial status, prestige, salaries and security seem to correlate with increases in sales, assets, staff and risk-averse policies, as well as profits (Dahrendorf, 1959; Herman, 1981; McEachern, 1975; Monsen and Downs, 1965). Therefore, managers may pursue a variety of short-term goals that reflect responses to stakeholders' interests and values. In the process, multinationals' analytical schemes may change.

Illusory Control and Coordination

Some theorists have explained the growth and decline of multinationals and their relations with stakeholders as arising from efficient control and coordination of operations. However, in large corporations, the separation of ownership from management creates opportunities for divergent motives and strategies for deception (Starbuck, 1965). This section offers some reasons why formal control and coordination in multinationals may prove illusory.

Some theorists have tackled the organizational problems of bounded rationality and opportunism in multinationals by assuming that institutions replace trust. For example, internalization theorists (e.g., Buckley and Casson, 1985) have argued that actors in semi-competitive markets thoroughly internalize normative standards of behavior so as to guarantee orderly transactions. Malfeasance is averted because clever institutional arrangements make it too costly. Conversely, institutional arrangements have evolved to discourage malfeasance (Hennart, 1982). In these theoretical arguments, institutional arrangements do not produce trust but substitute for it. For example, explicit and implicit contracts reduce employees' shirking on jobs and absconding with proprietary secrets. Thus, the theories have emphasized organizational control and coordination.

By emphasizing control and coordination, theories, such as internalization, have incorporated the assumption that internal markets for information operate more efficiently than external markets for information (Granovetter, 1985). The theorists assume that hierarchically structured firms can transmit accurate information about proprietary knowledge and employees better than markets can. For example, internalization theories have portrayed multinationals' internal markets as having auditing advantages that translate to fair prices for assets such as technology. The auditing advantages are supposed to be felt most strongly in activities such as transfer pricing. Yet, in an ethnographic study of a large chemical plant, Dalton (1959) showed that cost accounting of all kinds is arbitrary and highly politicized, rather than technically sound and efficient. In a study of transfer-pricing practices, Eccles (1982) reached similar conclusions. After interviewing 150 managers in 13 companies, Eccles (1982) concluded that no cost-based method can be carried out in a technically neutral way: no universal criterion for costs exists. "Problems often exist with cost-based methods when the buying division does not have access to the information by which the costs are generated. . . Market prices are especially difficult to determine when internal purchasing is mandated and no external purchases are made of the intermediate good . . . There is no obvious answer to what is a markup for profit" (Eccles, 1982:21).

Eccles (1982) argued that political elements in transfer pricing strongly affect whose definitions of costs are accepted. "In general, when transfer pricing practices are seen to enhance one's power and status they will be viewed favorably. When they do not, a countless number of strategic and other sound business reasons will be found to argue for their inadequacy" (Eccles, 1982:21). Eccles (1983:28) also noted the "somewhat ironic fact that many managers consider internal transactions to be more difficult than external transactions, even though vertical integration is pursued for presumed advantages".

Theorists that stress coordination and control have assumed that employees internalize firms' interests, suppressing any conflict of their own (Hennart, 1982). Consequently, the theories imply that orders given within corporate hierarchies elicit easy obedience. Yet, many empirical studies have presented evidence to reassess these theories, if not to contradict them (Granovetter, 1985). Personal and divisional resistance to overarching organizational interests seems rampant. Pursuits of these divergent interests also seem to require extensive networks of coalitions (Granovetter, 1985). Indeed, Dalton (1959:49) asserted that the level of cooperation achieved by divisional chiefs in evading central audits involved joint action "of a kind rarely, if ever, shown in carrying on official activities".

In reality, firms can drift for long periods of time, with decreasing performance, before external constituents or competitive forces come into play (Hirschman, 1970). Institutional arrangements allow firms to pick and to choose practices and policies that grant legitimacy and survival independent of their contributions to firms' effectiveness. For example, managers may erect facades (or false fronts) and increase symbolic actions to stave off control by other stakeholders (Meyer and Rowan, 1978). Managers can maintain facades of responsibility by ritual conformity with approved practices that bear only tenuous relationships to firms' operations. In effect, firms may define and implement policies to reassure stakeholders, rather than to influence economic operations (Feldman and March, 1981). Formal structures and lines of communication, and social controls, like performance and accounting measures, often seem weak and inappropriate (Meyer and Rowan, 1978). Therefore, formal control and coordination may inadequately explain the presence of multinationals or relations with stakeholders.

Shifting Relations with Stakeholders

Most theories of multinationals have emphasized their behaviors in large conflict systems — markets — without realizing that multinationals themselves function as conflict systems. Yet, multinationals are composed of groups that disagree with one another, whose relationships change over time, and who express their interests by forming unstable coalitions with other stakeholders (Hawkins and Walter, 1981). In the short-run, multinationals rarely seem to exhibit stable relationships with stakeholders. Many occurrences involve real conflicts of interests and values between multinationals' stakeholders; and multinationals' actions reflect compromises, collaborations and deceptions (Gladwin and Walter, 1980).

Assumptions about stable relationships have often led to simplifications about multinationals' behaviors. For example, some researchers have assumed that subsidiaries' behaviors in states reflect headquarters' interests and values. Subsidiaries may begin as appendix organizations that extend headquarters' goals (Rhenman, 1973). Yet, Prahalad and Doz (1981) showed how headquarters lose control over subsidiaries as subsidiaries gain access to independent resources. Prahalad and Doz (1981) argued that as multinationals grow and age, subsidiaries' interests might diverge from those of headquarters. A great deal of evidence indicates that established subsidiaries may start functioning as institutions — organizations with internal and external goals and values of their own (Ghauri, 1992; Haley, 2000a; Hawkins and Walter, 1981).

Theorists have argued that multinationals want to maximize repatriated profits and states want to maximize taxes, social development, etc. Because of these divergent interests, multinationals and states appear as competitors in most theories. But, Gladwin and Walter (1980) showed through a series of case studies that such portrayals often misrepresent subsidiary–state relations. Subsidiaries and states behave in diverse fashions with each other. For example, the Sperry Rand Corporation and Dresser Industries behaved differently when affected by the Carter Administration's decisions to curb trade with the Soviets. In 1978, the US government denied Sperry an export license to ship a $6.8 million computer system to the Soviet Union. In 1978, the US government also placed under its control US exports of oil-field technology to the Soviets, thus affecting Dresser, a diversified supplier to the energy industry. Sperry cooperated with the Carter administration's decisions. Dresser combated the administration's decision, proceeding with a $150 million contract to build a drill-bit plant in the Soviet Union (Gladwin, 1982). Haley (1998; 2000a) and Haley, Low and Toh (1996) also identified how the Singapore government cooperates with multinationals to aid national development as well as to implement its policies on regionalization. However, the environmental forces and firms' characteristics that induce collaboration or competition between states and subsidiaries have not been systematically identified.

As Etzioni (1988) pointed out, governments sometimes augment firms' market powers. Governments may provide firms with effective ways of capturing and holding on to market shares, of curbing competitors' entries, and of collusion. Etzioni (1988:223) termed this governmental power interventionist. The term calls attention to multinationals' abilities to control large shares of markets, without being the dominant firms; to block competitors from entering markets regardless of market concentration; and to generate excess profits by controlling input prices rather than by raising market prices. Etzioni (1988) argued that firms can use political means to achieve the aforementioned effects — effects that economic theories have generally attributed to concentrations of economic power. Etzioni's (1988) theorem contradicts the Marxist notion that political power merely reflects economic power: Economic power may precede, follow or remain uncorrelated with political power. However, theories of multinationals have largely ignored the political forces that cause governments to intervene on behalf of multinationals.

Social context assumes an important place in theories of political power like Etzioni's (1988). Yet, social contexts, and attendant notions such as multinationals' legitimacy, have largely been ignored by theories of multinationals. Multinationals' behaviors considered entirely legitimate in one state may be deemed socially irresponsible in another (Hawkins and Walter, 1981; Walter, 1982). For example, most multinationals originate in advanced industrialized states, such as the UK or the USA. These states encourage private firms' proactive behaviors. However, the states also counter firms' attempts to restrict competition with antitrust legislation and other measures. Unfair attempts to exploit markets have brought forth regulatory agencies like the US Food and Drug Administration, and the US Federal Trade Commission. The agencies have sometimes proven unable to restrict firms, leading to the emergence of other organizations such as the Securities and Exchange Commission, labor legislation and pressure groups representing various causes from pollution control to shareholders' rights. Consequently, multinationals' home states often have webs of social control to constrain firms' behaviors that conflict with some social goals. Simultaneously, political processes, including party systems and private ownership of capital and technology, tend to foster some proactive behaviors among firms in Western industrial democracies. Periodic excesses may exist on all sides, but balancing, and counterbalancing forces in the economies generate proactive behaviors that create dynamic, social equilibriums (Hawkins and Walter, 1981).

When multinationals from advanced industrial states produce abroad, they often face social controls quite different from those at home (see Haley, 2000a for some of the controls that Western multinationals may encounter in the Asia Pacific). Host states' social controls may sometimes be stronger; they are often weaker. Multinationals, with managerial attitudes and practices substantially transferred from home, may remain proactive in certain areas (Hawkins and Walter, 1981). States with undeveloped social controls may judge such proactive behaviors from multinationals as illegitimate. For example, in 1972, ITT attempted to enlist the US Central Intelligence

Agency's (CIA's) help in preventing Allende from ascending to the Presidency of Chile. This corporate attempt to affect a country's social and political fabric proved unacceptable to the Chilean government of 1972 (Gladwin and Walter, 1980). In such contexts, multinationals may try various means to establish social legitimacy and host states' preferences may shift (Hawkins and Walter, 1981). Dynamically, if significant differences between home and host states' attitudes become visible, and host and home states' social controls clash, subsidiaries may espouse preferences distinct from headquarters. Thus, multinationals' behaviors mirror the complex and changing relationships between various influential stakeholders including subsidiaries, headquarters, governments, interest groups, dominant coalitions, the media and the military. The next chapter uses existing theories to explain the presence of multinationals in South Africa.

4. Applying the Theories to South Africa during Apartheid

Theories about multinationals have revealed the unique skills and abilities that grant them competitive advantages over domestic firms. The theories have also elegantly analyzed the welfare implications of multinationals. However, the elegance has come at the cost of many organizational realities and the existing theories fail to explain many of the multinationals' behaviors in host states. This chapter surveys the specific behaviors of some US multinationals in the 1980s in South Africa when diverse stakeholders from home were clamoring for their leaving the host state. This particular era in South Africa's business history was chosen as never before or since have so many multinationals' diverse activities, as well as those of their stakeholders, been so thoroughly documented. The chapter also assesses if existing theories could effectively predict and explain the multinationals' behaviors. Finally, it provides case studies to recategorize the multinationals' behaviors in South Africa in particular, and in host states in general.

Explaining Multinationals' Behaviors

Apartheid-practicing South Africa in the 1980s (prior to 1989 when F. W. de Klerk assumed the Presidency, leading to Nelson Mandela and the previously abolished African National Congress assuming power) provided the most organized and publicized focus of diverse stakeholders' actions against multinationals. During the period of stakeholders' actions, 1987 constituted the last year when US multinationals could operate in South Africa without governmental regulations adversely inhibiting their production or repatriation of profits: in 1988, in an effort at sanctioning multinationals, the US government abolished credits for taxes paid in South Africa. Consequently, multinationals' operations in 1987 have been chosen to illustrate the explanatory power of existing theories. Table 4.1 draws on 1987 data for five US multinationals' subsidiaries in South Africa, their performance on five-year Returns on Investment (ROIs) which indicate long-term profitability (Channon, 1974; Hawkins and Walter, 1981), their representative behaviors and whether they stayed or left. Thumbnail sketches of the subsidiaries were compiled from various issues of the *New York Times* (1987), *Wall Street Journal* (1987), and *Business Week* (1987). Each of these subsidiaries accounted for between one and two percent of global sales. Brief sketches of the subsidiaries' behaviors follow.

Table 4.1   US multinational corporations' behaviors in South Africa.

Multinational	5-Year ROI	Behavior
► Union Carbide	Steady profits	Stayed and maintained size; Increased public-service contributions
► GM	Steep losses	Left by selling to local management
Revlon	Increased profits	Left by selling to South African firm
IBM	Increased profits	Left by selling to local management
Goodyear	Steady losses	Grew through investment by headquarters

►: Theories of multinationals adequately explain these behaviors.
Sources: *New York Times*, 1987; *Wall Street Journal*, 1987; *Business Week*, 1987

Union Carbide

Union Carbide enjoyed steady profits for five years in South Africa. The multinational planned to invest the dividends from its South African operations in local social projects. In this fashion, it hoped to alleviate the plight of established publics such as black communities and black workers.

General Motors (GM)

GM had been experiencing steady losses for five years in South Africa. Unit sales and production dropped by half in two years; market share fell by one-third. Layoffs took place. GM left South Africa by selling its operations to local management. Managers said the sale would relieve the company of most of its debt, giving it the best balance sheet it had in 15 years.

Revlon

Revlon's profits had been rising steadily in South Africa for five years. Revlon left South Africa by selling its operations to a South African competitor. African-American consumers in the USA had boycotted Revlon products to protest a Revlon executive's remark about inefficient, US minority-owned businesses.

International Business Machines (IBM)

IBM had been consistently profitable in South Africa, and had twice the market share of its nearest competitor. The multinational left South Africa by selling its operations to local management; it also agreed to honor its social commitments of about $15 million to South African blacks. IBM's announcement came on the heels of social protests against its links to the South African military.

Goodyear

From 1982 to 1987, Goodyear's profits in South Africa fell by 18 percent, and sales fell by one percent. Yet, in 1987, headquarters was planning a $20 million expansion to Goodyear's $100 million plant in Johannesburg.

Conclusions

From the cases outlined, most theories of multinationals would provide adequate explanations for only Union Carbide's and GM's behaviors. Union Carbide sustained high profits and the multinational's size probably enabled managers to control and to coordinate operations efficiently. Union Carbide therefore maintained its size and consolidated its position. Conversely, GM seemed unable to generate profits for several years; the steady decline in profits probably occurred because of market changes in South Africa. As headquarters' managers seemed unable to integrate efficiently GM's South African and global operations, the multinational left.

However, the theories offer few insights into the other multinationals' complex behaviors in the changing South African business environment. For example, why did Revlon and IBM leave despite generating high profits in high-growth markets? Why did they undertake their particular forms of leaving? Why did headquarters' managers increase investment in Goodyear despite low profits in a low-growth market? The theories also fail to differentiate between forms of leaving. For example, why did some multinationals sever ties with their subsidiaries in South Africa? Why did other multinationals sell to local management but maintain production ties? Additionally, the theories cannot explain intra-industry differences in declines. For example, in the same South African industries, when profitability remained stable, why did some multinationals leave and others stay? Additionally, the theories do not distinguish between different types of growth in South Africa. For example, when did headquarters undertake incremental investments in subsidiaries? When did subsidiaries finance their growth through retained earnings? But, useful theories should aid in understanding how multinationals adapt to changing environments, deal with discontinuities, exploit new opportunities and deal with failures. They should be able to isolate the interactive processes by which multinationals mold environments and abandon them.

Leaving or Staying in South Africa

We need new theories to explain why multinationals left or stayed in South Africa and whether these reasons prompt similar behaviors in other host countries. Great public interest focused on the US multinationals with direct investments in South Africa: Researchers and policy makers analyzed the multinationals' efforts, or lack thereof, to dismantle apartheid through enlightened labor practices, contributions to black-community development and political activism. The vociferous anti-apartheid movement had great success on some issues: The number of multinationals that left South Africa rose steadily in the 1980s (Paul and Duffy, 1988). Many assumed that their leaving brought about the downfall of apartheid in South Africa and the stakeholders' actions could be emulated elsewhere with similar results.

However, both researchers and policy makers ignored several issues revolving around the multinationals' leaving. One key set of ignored issues concerns the multinationals' modes of leaving. How did the US multinationals sell their assets? Did the multinationals' leaving consolidate economic power in white South Africans hands at a crucial time in the country's development? Did the power shifts occur at the expense of the black workers and progressive organizations that benefited from the US corporate commitment to the Sullivan Principles?

Another set of issues revolves around economic ties like licensing, franchising, and distribution that continued between many US multinationals and their former subsidiaries. Roughly half the multinationals that left South Africa in the 1980s maintained economic ties to the country (Kibbe and Hauck, 1988). These issues have raised new questions both for stakeholders' activism, as well as for university trustees, city and state officials and company shareholders. How should these stakeholders define leaving? Should they continue to demand an end to direct investment when economic ties remain intact? Can the multinationals' leaving reduce the US governments' and other stakeholders' powers? Can the success of stakeholders' activism (in getting multinationals to leave) ensure its failure (in the ensuing loss of control over companies)? Existing theories of multinationals fail to provide answers to these questions or even avenues in which answers can be provided.

Sources like the Investor Responsibility Research Center, Reports to US Congressional Requesters, and newspaper reports have carefully cataloged how US multinationals left and stayed in South Africa. The multinationals used at least six distinct modes to leave and to stay. This section outlines the six modes.

Total Liquidation and Piecemeal Sales of Assets

From January 1986 to April 1988, 13 US multinationals left South Africa by liquidating their subsidiaries and selling their assets piecemeal (Kibbe and Hauck, 1988:7). About 12 percent of the US multinationals left in this fashion from 1986 to 1988, and they included only three percent of the total number of employees that worked for the leaving multinationals (Kibbe and Hauck, 1988:7). Generally, the multinationals that chose this method of leaving had only small sales offices or representative offices with very few employees. The multinationals often received low prices for their assets and their employees were put out of work.

Eastman Kodak's leaving captures some characteristics of this mode. Eastman Kodak liquidated its subsidiary and left South Africa in November 1986. The multinational employed 466 people — about 41 percent of the total number of people employed by the 13 disinvesting firms. After Polaroid in 1977, Eastman Kodak became only the second US multinational to close its operations and to ban the sale of its products. These actions were undertaken by the multinational to protest the South African government's apartheid policies. Eastman Kodak offered its subsidiary's employees ten months severance pay. Yet, its leaving engendered much bitterness among its black African employees, many of whom remained unemployed in 1988 (Kibbe and Hauck, 1988). Also, Eastman Kodak's sales ban proved relatively ineffective: Several South African dealers continued to obtain the multinational's products through dealers in other countries.

Sale to South African or European Company

From January 1986 to April 1988, 48 US multinationals left South Africa by selling their subsidiaries to European or South African companies (Kibbe and Hauck, 1988:7). About 45 percent of the US multinationals left in this fashion from 1986 to 1988 and they included 50 percent of the total number of employees that worked for the leaving multinationals (Kibbe and Hauck, 1988:7). The multinationals that used this mode of leaving seemed unable to secure ongoing equity agreements or to protect their technology; however, they received higher prices for their assets than those that sold to local management. The foreign companies also paid at least part of the purchase prices in foreign currencies, thereby circumventing the influences of the financial and commercial rand rates.

General Electric's leaving in 1986 seems typical of this mode. After five years of declining sales and profits, General Electric sold its three subsidiaries to Genwest Industries — an existing company, created previously by the managers of General Electric's South African subsidiaries among others. The financing came from local banks. The sale agreement called for an initial payment to General Electric followed by subsequent payments depending on Genwest's profitability.

Genwest had not signed the Sullivan Principles, but as part of the sale contract, agreed to heed General Electric's fair employment practices. However, General Electric retained no mechanism to review Genwest's compliance with its former employment practices and stated it had no control over Genwest's other labor practices as well.

In the year before General Electric's leaving, the General Electric Foundations, Inc. gave one million rand (about $500,000 at that time) to endow a South African educational trust for black South Africans. The endowment's continuing benefits were unaffected by the leaving and were used to fund such programs as the US–South Africa Leader Exchange Program (USSALEP), READ, TOPS, PACE, several secondary schools and day centers.

Under the sale agreement, General Electric licensed Genwest to continue producing the same light industrial products that the subsidiaries had been manufacturing at the time of the sale. The licensing agreements ran from two to five years, depending on the products. General Electric also signed distribution and marketing agreements with Genwest for General Electric products made in the USA. In addition, Genwest continued to manufacture and to distribute non-General Electric products. General Electric also agreed to provide independent services and parts to its past customers.

Sale to another US Company

From January 1986 to April 1988, six US multinationals left South Africa by selling their subsidiaries to other US companies (Kibbe and Hauck, 1988:7). About five percent of the US multinationals left in this fashion from 1986 to 1988 and they included only two percent of the total number of employees that worked for the leaving multinationals (Kibbe and Hauck, 1988:7).

Fairchild's leaving in July 1986 captured some characteristics of this mode. Fairchild sold its South African subsidiary, Cardkey Systems, to EyeDentify Inc. of Canoga Park California. Fairchild retained no agreements or contracts with its former South African subsidiary.

Sale to Local Management

From January 1986 to April 1988, 25 US multinationals left South Africa by selling their subsidiaries to local management (Kibbe and Hauck, 1988:7). The subsidiaries then became independent companies under the old local management. About 23 percent of the US multinationals left in this fashion from 1986 to 1988 and they included 17 percent of the total number of employees that worked for the leaving multinationals (Kibbe and Hauck, 1988:7). The purchase prices were financed through a combination of managerial assets, commercial bank loans backed by the subsidiaries' assets, unsecured loans from investment banks, and financing arrangements with the parent companies. The local managers almost always entered into nonequity and supply arrangements with the parent companies. The parent companies also exercised formal and informal controls over technology and personnel practices (Kibbe and Hauck, 1988).

Coca-Cola's leaving in November 1986 captured some characteristics of this mode. Through the Johannesburg branch of the Coca-Cola Export Corporation (a wholly-owned subsidiary), Coca-Cola owned a concentrate operation in Durban, a 30 percent equity stake in Amalgamated Beverage Industries (that owned three of the 40 Coca-Cola bottling franchises in South Africa and Namibia), and a 55 percent equity stake in Amalgamated Beverage Canners (ABC), a canning company. In the fall of 1987, Coca-Cola closed its concentrate plant in Durban and opened a new one in Swaziland — a black homeland bordering on South Africa. Thereby, Coca-Cola complied with its worldwide policy of maintaining control over the concentrate-production process as well as with its new policy of having no investments in South Africa.

Coca-Cola sold its remaining South African assets to National Beverage Service Industries (NBS) in September 1986. NBS, owned by the former management of the Export Corporation's Johannesburg branch, paid a portion of the purchase price and Coca-Cola took back a note for the remainder. The purchase was concluded before the Comprehensive Anti-Apartheid Act's prohibition on the extension of new credit to South African entities went into effect. Coca-Cola began to sell concentrate directly from the Swaziland plant to independent bottlers. NBS, the main holder of the Coca-Cola franchise, sublicensed to the bottlers and assumed responsibilities for protecting the Coca-Cola trademark in South Africa. NBS also started providing a variety of services to the bottlers, including marketing, quality control, advertising, financing and technical services.

Under the terms of the sale agreement, NBS agreed to maintain Coca-Cola's employment practices and to follow the employment code contained in the Comprehensive Anti-Apartheid Act — a code similar to the Sullivan Principles. Although this agreement did not contain formal reporting requirements, NBS voluntarily supplied Coca-Cola with information on its employment practices; it also met with independent franchise bottlers to discuss employment practices. Coca-Cola remained an endorser of the Sullivan Principles, though NBS did not sign the Principles.

In 1986, Coca-Cola established the Equal Opportunity Foundation (EOF) to support education, housing, and business development in South Africa.

After leaving South Africa, Coca-Cola retained its commitment to provide $10 million over five years to the EOF which was managed by an independent board of trustees comprised mainly of black South Africans.

Formation of Trust

From January 1986 to April 1988, seven US multinationals formed trusts to leave South Africa (Kibbe and Hauck, 1988:7). Only seven percent of the US multinationals left South Africa in this fashion from 1986 to 1988 but they included over 25 percent of the total number of employees that worked for the leaving multinationals (Kibbe and Hauck, 1988:7). The multinationals created either offshore (outside South Africa) or onshore (in South Africa) trusts. Trusts generally gave the parent multinationals more leeway to set prices for South African assets. Trusts also almost always specified how the parents would be repaid, what would happen to the South African assets after repayment, and how the South African operations would be overseen, thereby granting the parents substantial control over future operations.

Exxon's leaving seems typical of this mode. On December 30, 1986, Exxon announced that it would leave South Africa. Exxon sold the shares of its two subsidiaries to an offshore trust that it established to continue operations. One of the terms of the sale agreement dealt with brand names: Exxon disallowed its two former subsidiaries from using the Exxon/Esso brand names. Consequently, Esso South Africa (Pty.), a petroleum-products marketing company, became Zenex Oil (Pty.) Ltd; and, Exxon Chemicals (Pty.) Ltd., a chemical marketing company, became Aktol Chemicals (Pty.) Ltd..

Exxon did not disclose the names of the three trustees it chose to run the trust. However, the multinational acknowledged that it chose a trust company on the Channel Islands of Jersey and two others for business and financial guidance. The trustees, that neither worked for nor were under contract to Exxon, assumed sole responsibility for selecting subsequent trustees.

The Channel Islands of Jersey provided Exxon with the dual advantages of not taxing the trust's earnings and of allowing the multinational to appoint a protector in addition to the trustees. The offshore trust also constituted a non-South African entity. Therefore, Exxon could lend the trust money to buy the South African subsidiaries without contravening the Comprehensive Anti-Apartheid Act's ban on new loans to South Africa. The trust agreement did not grant Exxon a buy-back option.

The trust's beneficiaries consisted of unnamed charitable organizations that served black, colored and Asian communities in South Africa. While the trust repaid Exxon's loan, charitable organizations that the multinational supported when it operated in South Africa received undisclosed portions of current pretax profits. After the trust repaid Exxon's loan, as the terms of the sale dictated, all the trust's profits went to the South African charitable organizations that the trustees selected.

The trust required that the trustees set up employees' profit-sharing programs that distributed cash bonuses of 2.5 percent of the average of the prior two years' pretax profits. The trust also required that the trustees continue Exxon's nondiscriminatory employment practices. The two, former Exxon subsidiaries were not signatories to the Sullivan Principles.

Exxon granted Zenex and Aktol the licensing rights to use the technologies currently used in-house to produce lubrication additives and blended petroleum products. Exxon waived rights to royalties or other future income from Zenox or Aktol for the use of these technologies. These rights formed parts of the sale prices of the subsidiaries. The sale agreements did not commit Exxon to provide future licensing for new technology. Exxon also agreed to sell chemicals to Aktol on spot bases; consequently, contractual obligations bound neither Exxon nor Aktol.

No Additional Investment by US Headquarters

US foreign direct investment refers to the ownership or control of ten percent or more of a foreign business by a US company. Historically, about 80 percent of all foreign direct investment in South Africa came from reinvesting subsidiaries' profits and borrowing from South African sources rather than from additional investments by headquarters (GAO/NSIAD-88-165:29). Several factors encouraged this practice. For example, the South African rand declined sharply between 1982 and 1987 and most multinationals found reinvesting profits more lucrative than repatriating them.

In October 1986, The Comprehensive Anti-Apartheid Act became law. The act prohibited new investments by US headquarters in South African subsidiaries but affected neither reinvestments of profits from existing investments with majority US ownership, nor secondary market sales of South African stocks and bonds (issued prior to the Act).

Some evidence indicates that the bulk of foreign direct investment in South Africa resulted from reinvestments of profits. For example, the book value of US direct investment in South Africa declined from $2.28 billion in 1982 to $1.14 billion in 1986; almost the entire decline resulted from the devaluation of the South African rand (GAO/NSIAD-88-165:29). If one controls for exchange-rate changes on the value of US direct investment, the data show a reduction of only about ten percent from $2.32 billion in 1982 to $2.10 billion in 1986 (GAO/NSIAD-88-165:29); yet, about half the US multinationals withdrew from South Africa during that period. The correspondingly small reduction in the value of US direct investments in South Africa strongly indicates that the remaining multinationals continued to reinvest their profits in South Africa and to borrow from local sources.

Increased Investment by US Headquarters

Before 1987, some US multinationals did inject additional amounts of capital into their South African subsidiaries. Although no comprehensive figures exist for that period, a maximum of 20 percent of the growth of US direct investments in South Africa seems to have come from headquarters (GAO/ NSIAD-88-165:29).

Goodyear's investment seems typical of this mode. Goodyear, with about one hundred million dollars of direct investments in South Africa, employed nearly 2,500 people in 1987 and ranked among the top half-dozen employers in South Africa. In 1986, headquarters invested $20 million in its South African subsidiary through an additional plant to produce radial truck tires.

Summary

Table 4.2 outlines the five major modes of leaving South Africa that US multinationals undertook. The next chapter sketches some organizational realities that most theories of multinationals ignore.

Table 4.2   How US multinational corporations left South Africa.

Multinational	Mode of Leaving	Percent of Total Multinationals (%) & Total Employees Using Mode (%)
Eastman Kodak	Total liquidation & piecemeal sale of assets	12 & 3
General Electric	Sale to South African or European company	45 & 50
Fairchild	Sale to another US company	5 & 2
Coca-Cola	Sale to local management	23 & 17
Exxon	Formation of trust	7 & 25

Source: Investor Responsibility Research Center

PART III

MULTINATIONAL CORPORATIONS AS CHAMELEONS

5. The Development of Multinational Corporations

As organizations, multinationals are continually changing. Following Child and Keiser (1981), "development" refers to changes in the conditions of multinationals. Multinationals may develop over time towards greater innovativeness, size and higher growth rates, or towards decline and extinction. Little evidence indicates that periods of growth, consolidation and decline for organizations (including multinationals) form life cycles or that large organizations grow out of small ones (Penrose, 1952; Starbuck and Nystrom, 1981). However, considerable evidence indicates that systematically different internal processes distinguish organizations that are growing rapidly from those that are either consolidating their positions or declining (e.g., Lodahl and Mitchell, 1980; Starbuck, 1965; Whetten, 1987).

This chapter isolates some of the forces that affect organizational development. It highlights how these forces may cause multinationals to grow, to consolidate their positions and to decline and how they affect relations with stakeholders over time.

Forces for Organizational Development

No theoretical consensus exists as to which forces generate or hinder organizational development. Fundamental debates in economics and organization theory have ranged over the significance of environmental forces versus managerial actions, of organizational dependence versus organizational autonomy (Astley and Van de Ven, 1983). Some theorists have interpreted organizational development largely as the product of external forces rooted in economic and social systems. Other theorists have seen organizational development mainly as arising from key organizational decision makers' purposeful behaviors. Still other theorists have portrayed organizational development as stemming from power and bargaining between stakeholders. The outlined approaches have several variants.

Environmental Determinism

Some economic theories portray environments as ultimately determining the development of multinationals and other firms that must succumb to the market's invisible hand. The environment's discernible features assume importance in these theories. For example, industrial and niche characteristics may pose obdurate constraints for multinationals and their managers (Karakaya and Stahl, 1991; Porter, 1980; 1998a; 1998b). Other economists have employed the biological analogy of natural selection to external environments (e.g., Alchian, 1950) to explain how multinationals may develop over time through adaptation. Similarly, some natural-selection models in organization theory depict environments as selecting organizations for survival and growth. Environmental selection thereby tailors organizational activities and structures to specific environmental characteristics (Aldrich and Pfeffer, 1976; Hannan and Freeman, 1977).

Theories of environmental determinism have largely emphasized the technical-efficiency forces that prompt organizations to develop. Technical efficiencies correspond to efficient, profit-maximizing production by firms (Shen, 1981) and include decisions about combinations of labor and capital that may affect the market performance of multinationals. These theories imply that decision makers within multinationals largely confine their purposeful actions to recognizing, exploiting and conforming to externally imposed requirements. The theories scantily cover or skip strategies aimed at changing or controlling the environments.

Environmental-determinism approaches apply to the development of populations of organizations or of industries (e.g., Tushman and Romanelli, 1985). As indicated in Chapter 4, the theories often fail to explain why specific multinationals, and not others, adopt certain organizational characteristics and structures. The theories also fail to explain why specific multinationals may find protected environmental niches (Haley, 2000a); or why some managers may negotiate with or dominate external parties through deliberate strategies (Haley, Tan and Haley, 1998).

Purposeful Actions

Theories of purposeful actions complement those on environments by drawing attention to their deficiencies. Theorists using this approach focus on the actions that organizational decision makers, like managers and administrators, take to generate new conditions (Child, 1972; Cummings and Worley, 1997; Galbraith, 1973; Haley, 2000a). These theories emphasize that individuals and organizations can choose in decision-making situations: managers can construct, eliminate or redefine environmental features, thereby purposefully creating their own realities and restricting their decisions (Weick, 1979).

Penrose (1952:818–819) supplied a rationale for the purposeful-action approach when she argued "to treat innovations [in firms] as chance mutations not only obscures their significance but leaves them essentially unexplained, while to treat them directly as purposive attempts of men to do something makes them far more understandable". Examples of the approach in organization theory include examinations of how organizations manage their dependence on external resource providers (Pfeffer, 1972a; 1972b; 1997), and create their environments (Starbuck, 1976) as well as political-economy models of interorganizational relationships (Benson, 1975; Wamsley and Zald, 1973).

Purposeful-action theories highlight some of the ideologies and motivations that may lie behind multinationals' decisions. Ideological forces refer to the important beliefs of organizational stakeholders especially about causal relationships between courses of actions and outcomes (Beyer, 1981). Consequently, the theories may help in deducing some strategies of multinationals for managing or adapting to environments. For example, ideologies could explain in part the circumstances under which stakeholders, including managers, believe that they can influence multinationals.

Power

Classifying the development of multinationals as either environmentally or managerially determined may often prove misleading. For instance, using Emery and Trist's (1965) environmental classifications, Hrebiniak and Joyce (1985) provided examples of turbulent environments in which organizational development may reflect both high environmental and high managerial determinism. Conversely, in placid environments, organizational development may reflect both low environmental and low managerial determinism (Hrebiniak and Joyce, 1985). This contradiction could result because organizational employees and outsiders often cannot identify when organizations end and environments begin (Starbuck, 1976). Consequently, Astley and Van de Ven (1983:267) advised that research questions about complex organizations should admit both deterministic and voluntaristic views, juxtaposing them to study interactions and reciprocal interdependencies over time. Similarly, Weick (1979:52) exhorted researchers "to think in circles" of mutual causation when investigating organization-environment relations.

Studies on power have concentrated on some of the interdependencies between organizations and environments (e.g., Dahl, 1963; Haley, 2000a; Jacobs, 1974; Pfeffer and Salancik, 1978). In these theories, the underlying dependencies and relative vulnerabilities of organizations and environments interact to create tensions and to change both. Studies on power have focused on its bases, loci, attendant processes and measurement (Mowday, 1978; Pfeffer, 1997; Salancik and Pfeffer, 1974). The theories concentrate on organizational and individuals' influences and countervailing powers and link to environmental uncertainty and resource control. External stakeholders constitute organizational environments in these theories (Hrebiniak and Joyce, 1985). Consequently, some theorists argue that multinationals' and external stakeholders' relative powers over time may explain when choice or determinism influence the development of multinationals. For example, high power for multinationals may indicate greater choice for managers and high power for external stakeholders may result in greater environmental determinism. When a powerful multinational confronts powerful stakeholders, high choice and high determinism may coexist. Typical studies include those on attributions of politicization and perceived organizational politics (Gandz and Murray, 1980), interorganizational power relations (Salancik and Pfeffer, 1974), coalitions (Bacharach and Lawler, 1980) and business-government interactions (Baysinger, 1984; Haley and Low, 1998; Haley and Richter, 2001).

Theories of power have relied on political forces to explain organizational development. Pfeffer (1981:7) defined political forces in organizations as activities "to acquire, develop and use power and other resources to obtain one's preferred outcomes in a situation in which there is uncertainty or dissensus about choices." Political models view organizations as pluralistic and divided into various subunits, interests and cultures. Actions result from games among players who view different faces of issues and differ in the actions they prefer (Allison, 1971; Haley, Low and Toh, 1996). Political forces deal with stakeholders' powers within organizations as well as distribution of organizational resources, outputs and benefits among stakeholders (Cyert and March, 1963; March, 1962; Simon, 1945). When preferences collide, the players' relative powers determine the outcomes: those with the greatest power will receive the greatest rewards (March, 1966). The next section draws on environmental, purposeful-action and power approaches to present arguments for the development of multinationals.

Rationales for Organizational Development

Environmental, purposeful-action and power approaches suggest that technical-efficiency, ideological and political forces may affect the development of multinationals. As argued in the previous section, technical-efficiency forces derive from the external environment, ideological forces stem from purposeful actions, and political forces emanate from power.

Rationales for Growth

Growth encapsulates relative measures of organizational size over time including expansions in size, employees and assets (Starbuck, 1965; Whetten, 1987). Those rationales for organizational growth that can also apply to multinationals are discussed here.

Theories have generally attributed motives for organizational growth to senior managers and administrators who make decisions on organizational policies (Child *et al.*, 1975). These key decision makers form the dominant coalitions in organizations. To the extent that other relevant stakeholders' goals are supported by organizational policies, the composition of the dominant coalition remains the same.

Technical-Efficiency Forces:

Theories of multinationals have shed much light on the relation between the performance of multinationals and their growth (see Chapter 2). Managers may pursue growth because technical-efficiencies enhance performance: growth can increase profits, sales and market power as well as reduce costs. As multinationals grow, they can also specialize their production to exploit factor efficiencies and economies of scale (Walter, 1982).

Second, as profits provide managers with the means to reward and to influence stakeholders, a desire for higher performance may indirectly fuel the growth of multinationals (Starbuck, 1965). Managerial remunerative influence over stakeholders often rests on distributing material resources and rewards including dividends, wages, commissions and fringe benefits (Etzioni, 1961).

As increased size can increase complexity and cause coordination problems, growth may not always increase profits. Nevertheless, the major components of profits, costs and revenues, may independently become reasons for growth (Starbuck, 1965). Managers seem to believe that as firms grow, costs fall through efficiencies, specializations, and economies of scale; consequently, the pursuit of reduced costs may prompt growth. For oligopolistic firms subscribing to minimum profit constraints rather than to profit-maximizing criteria (Baumol, 1962; Starbuck, 1965), higher revenues, through sales often become ends in themselves.

Fourth, managers may pursue growth to increase market power. For example, several US multinationals pursued growth in South Africa to keep pace with growing consumer markets in Africa. Despite managerial strategies, social fears about unfair competition in oligipolistic markets may constrain the market power of multinationals. For example, regulation and other social retaliations may prevent large multinationals from exploiting their market power (Gladwin and Walter, 1980).

Ideological Forces:

The growth of multinationals may have strong ideological justifications because stakeholders associate growth with vibrant values. Two main reasons exist for organizational growth as a goal in itself (Starbuck, 1965).

First, stakeholders may value growth as a symbol of achievement. As intraorganizational stresses and external forces hinder organizational growth, organizations and societies often bestow prestige and admiration upon people who bring it about. These people may also receive personal rewards through feeling success and pride in their achievements.

Second, increased organizational size may constitute an operational goal, benchmarking progress. Relatively easy to measure and to talk about, size often forms a good operational goal for multinationals. Many multinationals use rates of return on assets (ROAs) and growth rates, rather than rates of return on investments (ROIs) as indicators of performance (Czechowicz, Choi, and Baveshi, 1982). However, such performance measures do not necessarily mean that stakeholders value the growth of multinationals per se. Growth may simply assist the attainment of more relevant goals for stakeholders or of more immediate interest for organizational subunits (Starbuck, 1965).

Political Forces:

The growth of multinationals may maintain dominant coalitions, help stakeholders' goals, and enhance managerial benefits.

First, growth may provide job security to the dominant coalitions. Larger firms, with more local prestige than smaller firms, may have easier access to capital and to other resources. Consequently, when profits dip, larger firms may obtain financial support more readily than smaller firms do (Starbuck, 1965). In larger firms, jobs enjoy more permanence, and relations with consumers and suppliers enjoy more durability, contributing to managerial job security (March and Simon, 1958) and restraining managerial transfers within multinationals (Edstrom and Galbraith, 1977). Consequently, growth, by assisting the multinationals' survival and stable relations with stakeholders, may maintain the dominant coalitions, including top managers, in power.

Second, growth may also facilitate achieving what Cyert and March (1963) called the quasi-resolution of conflict. Managers of growing multinationals may find stakeholders' demands easier to satisfy if the growth does not incur diminishing returns or disproportionately rising costs. Stakeholders may also try to achieve their own goals through organizations (March and Simon, 1958; Pfeffer and Salancik, 1978) and these stakeholders' actions for self-realization may fuel the growth of multinationals. Newman and Logan (1955) listed some instances in which stakeholders' actions for self-realization cause growth: Customers demand more complete services; divisions attempt to master technologies; and, research labs develop products outside established lines. Satisfied stakeholders may also endorse and thereby maintain the dominant coalition of managers in multinationals. Newman and Logan (1955) argued that if firms do not grow, they do not remain the same, but contract.

Third, managerial desires for more benefits may result in growth. For example, Gordon (1945) stated that managerial power and status, including greater prestige, higher salaries and more job security, constitute important, nonfinancial motives for the growth of firms. In addition to the prestige of supervising a successfully growing firm, managers attain prestige through supervising employees. As subordinates are usually more dispensable than superiors, managerial power and job security may increase with the number of employees they supervise (Gordon, 1945). Williamson (1963) extended this proposition into a formal theory of managerial slack: managers take some of their compensation as staff functions that are larger than necessary for efficient production. Executive salaries also seem to correlate with the growth of their companies. For example, with the aid of anecdotal evidence, Simon (1957) argued that higher managerial salaries are associated with greater spans of control (measured by more subordinates and hierarchical levels).

Rationales for Consolidation

Consolidation refers to relatively long time spans of incremental change and adaptation by organizations that elaborate structures, systems, controls, and resources towards increasing coalignment (Tushman and Romanelli, 1985). Organizations may try to consolidate their positions through enacting favorable environments (Starbuck, 1976). In particular, organizations try to maintain economic viability and legitimacy among key stakeholders (DiMaggio and Powell, 1983; Haley, Low and Toh, 1996; Meyer and Rowan, 1978; Pfeffer and Salancik, 1978; Pfeffer, 1981). High performance grants economic viability and slack to organizations and symbolic behaviors grant them legitimacy. Their efforts to consolidate their environmental positions may contribute to the development of multinationals. Those rationales for organizational consolidation that can also apply to multinationals are discussed here.

Aldrich and Mindlin (1978) have pointed out that organizational efforts to cope with environmental uncertainty and dependence contribute to organizational development. Uncertainty and dependence form two conceptually distinct dimensions in organization-environment relations. Forestalling, forecasting and absorption serve to reduce uncertainty or information-processing burdens on organizations (Pennings, 1981). Studies have examined the information-processing roles of regulation, personnel transfers and interlocking boards of directors (Burt, 1980a; 1982; Galbraith, 1973; Pfeffer, 1972a; 1973). Strategies to reduce resource dependence on exchange partners can also affect organizational development. First, organizations can adapt to the demands of exchange partners by changing their operations. Second, organizations can reduce dependence by finding alternate partners or by acquiring means to exercise greater control over existing partners (Aldrich,

1971; Pfeffer and Salancik, 1978). The protection of economic viability by reducing dependence constitutes another force generating organizational development.

Dependence and uncertainty can originate simultaneously from various environmental sectors. Organizations may reduce uncertainty and dependence in some sectors through policies aimed at growth, profitability or improvements in performance only to incur new or additional dependencies or uncertainties in other environmental sectors. Also, organizations may never reduce dependence or uncertainty despite their objectives. Insufficient capacity (Metcalfe, 1974), bounded rationality (Simon, 1945), and stakeholders' conflicting interests (Cyert and March, 1963) may hinder organizational objectives.

As organizations consolidate their positions, they may start catering to wider ranges of internal and external stakeholders. Both journalists and academicians have commented on the corporatism that characterizes organizational interdependence (Galbraith, 1967; 1973; Pahl and Winkler, 1974). For example, labor unions and governmental agencies may assume greater influence as organizations cope with uncertainty and dependence (Child and Keiser, 1981). Previous organizational goals emphasizing service and quality may be replaced by managerial goals of career advancement that require cultivating certain external stakeholders (Michel, 1962). For example, Moyer (1970) and Pfeffer and Salancik (1978) argued that managers might deliberately disperse shareholdings to pacify external stakeholders. Yuchtman and Seashore (1967) identified how managers cultivate suppliers of scarce resources: In their theory, managers and organizations remain effective to the extent that they maintain supplies of scarce resources. By satisfying suppliers, managers indirectly satisfy all other stakeholders (Yuchtman and Seashore, 1967). Organizations may also adapt to dominant social institutions. For example, several case studies have observed that reform-orientated governmental agencies transform their liberal goals and flexible open structures as they associate with established groups (Lipset, 1950; Selznick, 1949).

Despite their efforts, organizations may never actually satisfy any stakeholders, no matter how influential (Crozier, 1974). For example, multinationals' subsidiaries may ignore clear instructions from headquarters or pursue policies more forcefully than originally intended. Organizational goals, and the goals of the individuals in them, change as organizations take actions to reduce uncertainties or dependencies. Actions affect the preferences that initiated them; and discoveries of new intentions sometimes follow intentional behaviors (Starbuck, 1985). As multinationals consolidate their positions, gaps may develop between headquarters' plans and subsidiaries' behaviors and some evidence indicates that multinationals tend to drift away from planned courses (Gladwin and Walter, 1980).

Technical-Efficiency Forces:

Multinationals try to arrange their social and technical resources to produce efficiently some desired outputs. Efficient production often requires dividing strategic initiatives between headquarters and subsidiaries. In particular, subsidiaries may have to solicit funds, to find appropriate contractors, to open new markets, to hire qualified personnel, to establish effective procedures and so forth. The more these solutions deviate from those planned by headquarters, the more unanticipated the development of multinationals is likely to be.

Strategic decisions about production lack structure; novelty, complexity and open-endedness characterize strategic decision processes (Mintzberg, Raisinghani, and Theoret, 1976). Managers may use long-range plans as filtering and organizing devices, thereby reducing the complexities of decision situations. By limiting the information that firms process, long-range plans may serve as heuristics or rules of thumb that managers use to improve decisions (Haley, 1997; Haley and Stumpf, 1989; Tversky and Kahneman, 1982).

Long-range plans may also carry the seeds of their own destruction. March (1981a) listed some classical complications in long-range-planning. As organizations try to anticipate futures, they often note that many very unlikely future events would change their action's consequences, and therefore, their present choices. However, too many, very unlikely future events can be imagined; as each is very improbable, managers sometimes consciously exclude them from careful forecasts and plans. Consequently, organizational plans may hinge on futures that managers know with certainty can never be realized. More generally, the most favorable outcomes of particular alternatives may often depend on the occurrences of very unlikely events; under those circumstances, the expected values of those alternatives would be low and sensible organizations would not choose them. Therefore, rational planning processes may sometimes not recommend the best alternatives (March, 1981a). Indeed, Grinyer and Norburn (1975) found no evidence that consensus about objectives, well-defined roles, or formal planning correlated positively with financial performance across 21 companies. Instead, financial performance correlated positively with reliance on informal communications, and with the diversity of information used to assess corporate performance (Grinyer and Norburn, 1975). As multinationals operate in highly diverse environments, headquarters may not know the best strategic alternatives and long-range plans and expectations may not synchronize with the demands of local situations (Hawkins and Walter, 1981; Walter, 1982).

Subsidiaries, conscious of the weaknesses of long-range plans, may undertake many contingent strategies to control their performance: for example, many organizations attempt to structure their environments through cementing economic dependencies on sellers and buyers. In particular, contracting or coalescing with governmental agencies seems to have a strong positive effect on organizational performance (Olsen, 1981; Pfeffer and Salancik, 1978; Thompson 1967). Governments can control much of a multinational's environment through regulating aggregate demand, assuring sales, controlling costs and insulating subsidiaries from competition with rank-and-file members and control from headquarters. Governmental abilities to influence multinationals heighten if they assume prominent roles as suppliers, consumers or partners (Haley, 1998; Levine and White, 1961; Litwak and Hylton, 1966; Pfeffer and Salancik, 1978).

Governments may help organizations to negotiate their environments rather than to anticipate environmental actions, to buffer themselves from uncertainties through growth, to reduce risks and conflicts by creating stable environments and to carve out domains (Starbuck, 1976). Although governmental links can help multinationals to reduce uncertainties and to enhance their chances of survival, they may also introduce inertia. Managers may find that their decision periods become longer, that they cannot break contracts unilaterally, exploit new opportunities or disagree with governmental policies and interests except in constrained and limited ways (Olsen, 1981).

Ideological Forces:

As social institutions, multinationals reflect their stakeholders' and especially their dominant coalitions' important beliefs. As multinationals consolidate their positions, new personnel may join, and new work methods and practices may emerge. These changes in ideology may lead to the further development of multinationals.

First, organizational development occurs as mixes of stakeholders change (Stinchcombe, Dill, and Walker, 1968; White, 1970). Turnover may produce new stakeholders with dissimilar attitudes, abilities and goals. Internal processes for ideological change include the influences of younger, unsocialized employees, new work practices, technological innovations, new methods of evaluation, and laxer managerial controls. External forces reflect the pressures to imitate key organizations in environments (DiMaggio and Powell, 1983), economic changes in environments, technological revolutions (Hedberg, 1974) and the pressures to conform to new stakeholders' expectations (Meyer and Rowan, 1978).

Second, organizations may undertake a number of solutions to maintain their legitimacy with stakeholders. To survive in historical and cultural environments, organizations manipulate meanings, structures, and social processes to legitimize their operations as well as to influence stakeholders (Selznick, 1957; Stinchcombe, 1965). For example, Kamens (1977) and Meyer and Rowan (1978) identified legitimating myths that organizations create for themselves; Lee (1971) and Perrow (1961) examined how organizational elites manipulate external referents of prestige; Lentz and Tschirgi (1963) described how firms publicize their commitments to ethics of corporate social responsibility; and DiMaggio and Powell (1983) argued that imitation of other organizations enhanced legitimacy. Among these legitimating strategies, public service by organizations has received considerable attention (Haley, 1990a). Charitable contributions seem to form effective means to demonstrate organizational goodwill and to placate problematic and hostile elements in environments (Fry, Keim and Meiners, 1982; Haley, 1990a; Useem, 1984). Hawkins and Walter (1981) pointed out that multinationals' subsidiaries often do substantial public service in the communities in which they locate.

Cultural symbols figure prominently in managerial efforts to legitimize their policies to stakeholders (Edelman, 1964; March and Olsen, 1983). Symbols focus attention on organizational activities consistent with social norms, values and expectations (Pfeffer, 1981). Symbols may thereby ensure the continued survival of multinationals operating in turbulent environments. Social ideologies influence symbols by informing multinationals about important dimensions in social settings, environmental values along those dimensions, and general affective reactions that multinationals can expect from certain strategic actions (Hawkins and Walter, 1981).

Sometimes, the symbolic values of organizational policies may dominate other factors in decision situations (Dunbar and Wasilewski, 1985; Feldman and March, 1981). For example, in turbulent environments, organizations may adopt facades or false fronts to exploit symbolic meanings and to placate stakeholders by decoupling organizational operations from their public stances (Haley, 2000c; Meyer and Rowan, 1978).

Political Forces:

Because legislative environments significantly affect them, organizations attempt to use governmental and societal powers to control legislation (Olsen, 1981) through the politics of distribution (Palamountain, 1955). Miles and Cameron (1982:23) described the politics of distribution when they stated that "organizations and elements of society may be found constantly engaged in efforts to insert their interests into the mainstream of societal values, and hence to create or safeguard the legitimacy of their definition of the 'right' social order". The political objectives of organizations vis-à-vis governments encompass obtaining special monetary favors from governments, managing uncertainty revolving around governmental threats to organizational objectives or resisting governmental efforts to intrude on traditional managerial authority (Baysinger, 1984). Multinationals strive hard to impact regulatory policies because regulation bears on virtually all aspects of their behaviors in markets including decisions on pricing, product qualities, disposition and repatriation of profits, labor relations, acquisition of finance capital, and health, safety and environmental standards (Pugel and Walter, 1985).

One organizational strategy to reduce uncertainty, includes recruiting prestigious people to their boards of directors, and having their executives recruited by correspondingly prestigious boards (Provan, Beyer and Kryutbosch, 1980; Thompson, 1967). Evidence indicates that organizations engage in board interlocks with governmental agencies to promote their interests by allowing opportunities for co-opting government officials and influencing regulatory policies (Pennings, 1981; Pfeffer, 1997). Co-opted government officials may grant organizations autonomy, discretion and economic viability. For example, co-opted governmental agencies may offer organizations influence over policies, cartelization benefits, legitimacy, public recognition and participation in public success, thereby increasing their chances of growth and survival (Jones and Walter, 1982; Olsen, 1981; Nordlinger, 1981; Stephan, 1978).

Conversely, co-optation may also introduce inertia into organizations, reduce requisite variety, exaggerate the importance of local events, hinder standardization and limit mechanisms to select which variations to generate or to perpetuate (DiMaggio and Powell, 1983; Pfeffer, 1997). Organizations may become associated with governmental actions, lose freedom in their own actions and be blamed for the policy failures of governments (March and Olsen, 1983; Olsen, 1981; Pfeffer, 1997). Strategies of co-optation may also extend the political demands that organizations have to satisfy. For example, subsidiaries represented on governmental boards may be forced to reevaluate headquarters' goals, and the distributions of benefits among stakeholders.

Flows of personnel may affect the relations between organizations and states (Pfeffer and Salancik, 1978). Organizations can co-opt governmental agencies through representing them on their boards of directors (Pennings, 1981; Pfeffer and Salancik, 1978). Also, employees of states' regulatory agencies can become employees of the organizations they used to regulate.

In particular, some researchers have found that expectations of future employment may lead governmental officials to treat the organizations involved more favorably (Galaskiewicz, 1985). Consequently, cooptation may lead to controlled change, as possible opponents are socialized and provided with modest successes.

The basic rationale for co-optation — to strip leadership from opposition groups by inducing opposition leaders to accept more legitimate roles — may also lead to unexpected problems. One conspicuous complication lies in the extent to which offers of co-optation provide incentives to resist, and thereby increase, rather than decrease opposition. Also, if the regulated organizations provide possible employment as incentives for favorable treatment, they risk producing patterns of unfavorable turnover in the regulatory agencies. For example, friends may leave governmental agencies, and only those unfriendly to organizational interests may remain, prompting new offers of co-optation from organizations!

Rationales for Decline

Organizational decline can assume at least two aspects: stagnation, and cutbacks (Whetten, 1980). Stagnation reflects decreases in the absolute rates of expansion; cutbacks denote decreases in the sizes of organizational assets, workforces, budgets, etc. Research on the effective management of declining organizations has shown that issues associated with shrinking economic resources and moral support differ qualitatively from issues associated with growth (Cameron, Whetten and Kim, 1986; Haley, 2000c). Those rationales for organizational decline that pertain to multinationals are discussed here.

Conditions of decline involve restricted resources and pressures to retrench. Researchers (e.g., Hermann, 1963; Levine, 1978; 1979; Whetten, 1980) have noted that conflicts intensify and attempts to protect turf dominate as stakeholders fight over smaller resource bases. Managers may use slack resources to suppress conflict and to raise morale, thereby reducing redundancy within the organizational system. Pluralism, or the development of organized and vocal special interest groups, increases as organizations become politicized (Pfeffer, 1981; Pfeffer and Salancik, 1978; Whetten, 1981).

For example, in times of high unemployment and economic difficulties, vested interests in organizations become apparent as labor unions and other employee groups become increasingly vocal. Governmental assistance at this juncture may also signify a stakeholder group's attempt to participate (Whetten, 1987).

Technical-Efficiency Forces:

The decline of organizations can stem from inabilities to achieve and to maintain economic efficiencies in market transactions. When economic environments change to where they no longer support efficient operations, organizations can find other ecological niches or scale down their operations (Cyert, 1978).

Second, decline may follow when organizational adaptations do not keep pace with environmental changes. Managers may ignore environmental changes because they are new, or because organizations are incapable of absorbing them, or because their effects in the past have been benign. In particular, successful past strategies may desensitize organizations to environmental changes (Hedberg, Nystrom and Starbuck, 1976). For example, successful multinationals may adopt heuristic programs to deal with recurring situations. Unfortunately, situations may appear equivalent so long as the same programs can handle them, and programs may remain in use after the situations they fit have vanished (Hedberg, Nystrom and Starbuck, 1976). Organizational inertia may result and the most successful multinationals may become vulnerable to failures.

Young, not-so-successful organizations may also fail to adapt adequately because of less organizational slack. Tornedon and Boddewyn (1974) in a study of divestitures found that young, aggressive companies can overextend themselves by acquiring overseas subsidiaries before establishing growth policies. When environments change, the companies find they have little adjustment potential, and rapid divestitures may take place (Tornedon and Boddewyn, 1974). Fast-growing organizations seem no more adept at handling decline than slow-growing ones (Kotter and Sathe, 1978). While the former's inertia lies in failure to recognize sagging performance as a problem, the latter's lies in inability to generate responses because of little organizational slack (Kotter and Sathe, 1978).

Ideological Forces:

The inability of multinationals to achieve and to maintain an ideological base in society may contribute significantly to their decline. For example, Hawkins and Walter (1981) described cases where hostility in host states seriously impairs multinationals' operations by causing considerable structural and legislative barriers. Other theorists have noticed that societies have to accept organizational goals for organizations to survive (Rhenman, 1973). For instance, Rothman (1972) linked the rise and fall of various criminal-justice programs to shifts in societal ideologies. As the prevailing views shifted from incarceration to rehabilitation of criminals, organizations gained or lost public funding, depending on their values.

In his classic work on life cycles, Stinchcombe (1965) argued that newly established organizations seem particularly vulnerable to failures; he called this symptom the liability of newness. Similarly, Starbuck and Nystrom (1981) and Kaufman (1976) concluded that younger organizations face much higher death rates than older ones. These theorists argued that lack of social support and connections, and inability to get funding, often bring about organizational decline. Newly established organizations have to cope with new work methods and environments and organizational inexperience may lead to failure. Although failure characterizes organizational operations, most newly established organizations have not had sufficient time to establish reputations or to build social acceptance and this lack of legitimacy may lead to greater failure (Stinchcombe, 1965).

Second, changes in personnel, work-practices and technologies may bring about ideological changes. The inability of multinationals to achieve and to maintain legitimacy among new strategic stakeholders can contribute to their decline. Benson (1975) noted that declining organizations often overemphasize the acquisition of economic resources, and underemphasize the value of social acceptance. Multinationals already in decline may accelerate this development by ignoring new stakeholders' beliefs and values.

Figure 5.1   Reviewing rationales for organizational development.

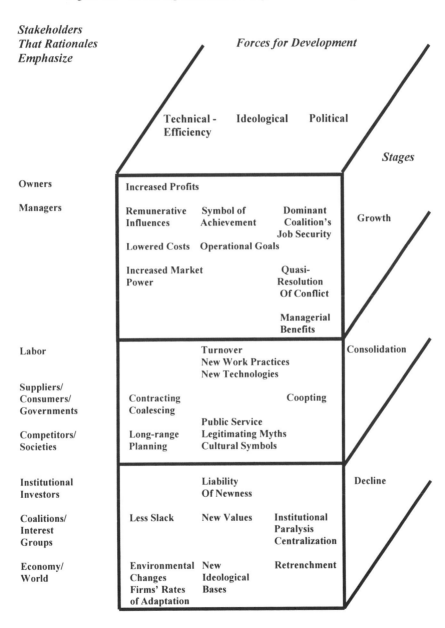

Political Forces:

Internal political considerations may also contribute to organizational decline. For example, Yarmolinsky (1975) pointed out that when no interest group has sufficient power to implement strategies or to alter organizational courses, stagnation or institutional paralysis sets in.

Changes in work practices, like conservatism and short-term orientations, may also result from political forces in declining organizations. As efficiency takes priority over effectiveness with stakeholder groups, centralization of decision making in top managerial echelons may increase (Cameron, 1983; Staw, Sandelands and Dutton, 1981). As scarce resources make mistakes more costly, participation of other stakeholders in decision-making may decrease (Staw, Sandelands and Dutton, 1981). Centralization also restricts communication channels and increases the likelihood that frustrated organizational stakeholders who feel uninformed will scapegoat leaders. Managerial credibility may suffer, leading to high managerial turnover and leadership anemia (Greenhalgh and Rosenblatt, 1984; Whetten, 1981). When forced to retrench, and faced with conflicting demands, managers in declining organizations may prefer across-the-board cutbacks to selective cutbacks: across-the-board cutbacks may hurt more stakeholders but would probably minimize political fall-outs as some stakeholders would not appear to suffer more than others (Boulding, 1975; Cyert, 1978; Whetten, 1980). Figure 5.1. provides an outline of some rationales for organizational development that may apply to multinationals. The next section highlights relations with stakeholders over time.

Relations with Stakeholders over Time

The previous section presented a panorama in which multinationals as organizations operate continuously under conditions of uncertainty and with some degree of dependence on outside stakeholders. Stakeholders within multinationals also demand benefits and rewards. Managers make decisions based upon their perceptions of all of the foregoing forces, and upon their own motivations, to arrive at strategies. These strategies are then implemented in various stages of the development of multinationals. Consequently, one way to understand the development of multinationals over time is to analyze the ways in which they are supposed to satisfy some or all of the interests of key stakeholders.

Goals, priorities and appropriate criteria of effectiveness shift as multinationals grow, consolidate and decline. For example, the structural properties and internal processes observed in rapidly growing organizations differ from those observed in declining organizations (Whetten, 1987). Different power configurations arise at different portions of the development of multinationals, giving rise to different patterns. For example, Mintzberg (1984) argued that as organizations develop, their power structures become more diffuse, more complex, more ambiguous, and at some point less functional even though more stable. Strong managerial leadership seems often to prevail at the outset, enabling organizations to establish themselves. Established organizations seem more responsive to external stakeholders, either directly by catering to identifiable groups, or indirectly through organizational mission. As organizations continue to develop, they may turn inward and tendencies to serve the elite members' interests may become prominent. Societal and public service organizations may extract a great deal from managers at these junctures of development in return for prestige and social acceptance. However, conflict may arise between various internal and external stakeholders who wish to use the organizations to advance their own interests. This conflict may displace organizational service to external stakeholders to the detriment of performance and organizational decline may follow.

This book assumes that stakeholders become involved with multinationals to advance their interests and that criteria evaluating the effectiveness of multinationals reflect these interests. This view of effectiveness allows for multiple evaluations from multiple stakeholders (Freeman, 1984). For example, a focal multinational may be rated highly effective on various dimensions by labor unions, somewhat effective by consumers and quite ineffective by regulatory agencies (Connolly, Conlon and Deutsch, 1980).

This book proposes a political-action framework to fuse technical-efficiency, ideological and political forces and to understand the development of multinationals. The framework draws attention to the environments that may facilitate or constrain growth, consolidation and decline. Simultaneously, the framework pays attention to the criteria by which decision makers assess the performance of multinationals, and to the policies that they adopt to affect development. The framework also deals specifically with multinationals' relationships with internal as well as external stakeholders, the major strategies that managers utilize to foster development, the circumstances under which they are adopted and consequences for the restructuring of multinationals.

The behavioral theory of the firm offers some relevance for such a political-action framework to understand organizational development (Cyert and March, 1963). The theory suggests the quasi-resolution of conflicts in real life, avoidance of uncertainty until crises develop, orientation of search processes towards known problems and iteration. However, for predictive validity, the behavioral theory needs to be coupled with a more holistic and long-term view of organizations that throws into perspective key, strategic decisions in organizational development. The theory also fails to explain long-term directions of development unless political dynamics are incorporated, particularly the goals and values of managers and other stakeholders.

Child *et al.* (1975) sketched a model that analyzed organizational development in the terms offered by the behavioral theory of the firm. The iterative decision model was derived in large part from business-policy analyses. Child *et al.* (1975) singled out managers as the key vehicles for the formulation of organizational strategies. Managers' personal characteristics, both psychological (like flexibility) and social (such as stake in ownership), influence their general orientations towards organizational objectives. Social and professional values that managers possess, and reward structures available to them, mediate their decisions. In addition, other stakeholders such as stockholders, sponsors and labor unions express their expectations of the organization in return for their support. Organizational objectives reflect managers' perceived pressures from these stakeholders. Objectives become strategies through processes whereby environmental information, including assessments of past organizational performance, is assimilated. This information passes through various organizational filters before managers evaluate it. Even then, managerial perceptions of implications influence the strategies they may choose for the further development of their organizations. Child *et al.* (1975) concluded that the types of structures through which management works influence managerial success in implementing strategies. Stakeholders receive organizational outputs and their responses largely determine organizational performance and potential for development.

Tushman and Romanelli (1985) proposed a punctuated equilibrium model that analyzes managerial efforts to juxtapose long periods of incremental, adaptive change, with short periods of discontinuous change in which organizational strategy, power, structure and control fundamentally transform into new coalignments. They argued that middle managements' decisions dominate convergent periods and top managements' decisions dominate reorientations. The next chapter incorporates some of these theories in a political-action framework.

6. Why Multinational Corporations Leave Host States

The chameleon is a lizard with the legendary ability to adapt to its external environment by changing colors. Changes in the chameleon's colors take place through both reflexive and purposeful actions. The chameleon changes colors through pigment-bearing, contractile cells at various depths in its skin. Its central nervous system controls the contractions and dilations of these cells. This capability to change colors increases the types of environments that the chameleon can inhabit, and the natural enemies with which it can deal. In effect, the chameleon has a repertoire of solutions for environmental problems. Contrary to folklore, the chameleon does not respond to external environments per se, but to changes in internal and external factors such as emotions, light and temperatures. Its abilities to adapt and to change colors have also been greatly exaggerated. In reality, the chameleon adapts to a relatively small band of colors, displaying less adaptability and flexibility than many other lizards. When its repertoire of solutions proves inadequate, the chameleon may be forced to make structural changes like dropping its tail or moving to another environment. This chapter likens the development of multinationals over time to the changes that chameleons undertake.

Like chameleons, multinationals fluctuate and respond to internal and external forces all the while constrained by its resources and environment. Like chameleons, structural changes in multinationals stem from reflexive and purposeful actions. And as they have for chameleons, reports have greatly exaggerated the ability of multinationals to generate new solutions and to maintain their integrity in different environments. This chapter offers a political-action framework to capture multinationals' behaviors as chameleons and includes sets of testable hypotheses for why multinationals may leave host states.

A Political-Action Framework for Multinationals

As discussed in Chapters 2 and 3, theories have generally portrayed multinationals as catalysts, changing host states but remaining relatively unchanged themselves. In contrast, this book proposes that multinationals behave as chameleons, changing in relation to their environments. This section examines internal and external sources for inertia and metamorphic change in multinationals, as well as for the impact of managers on multinationals' behaviors over time. It argues for a political-action framework to explain how managers implement strategies for the development of multinationals through acting on their perceptions and motivations (Child and Keiser, 1981; Tushman and Romanelli, 1985). The framework in this chapter provides a new perspective for why multinationals may leave host states.

Multinationals must allocate internal resources efficiently and maintain workflows by effectively producing goods and services for external economies (Katz and Kahn, 1966). Multinationals also require external legitimacy to prevent stakeholders from challenging their operations as well as internal legitimacy to maintain personnel and behavioral cycles (Haley, Low and Toh, 1996; March and Simon, 1958; Rhenman, 1973). Competitive and noncompetitive strategies provide stakeholders with inducements, thereby providing multinationals with a repertoire of solutions to enhance legitimacy and to tackle unforeseen problems. Concomitantly, competitive and noncompetitive strategies may change multinationals.

Many theorists have recorded how organizations change and when they change. For example, Tushman and Romanelli (1985) argued that organizational development consists of relatively long periods of convergence, and relatively short periods of reorientation or metamorphic change. In convergent periods, organizations progress through incremental change and adaptation that elaborate structures, systems, controls and resources towards increasing co-alignment. Effective performance may or may not attend these convergent periods. Reorientations, when strategies, power, structures and systems fundamentally transform towards a new basis of alignment, demarcate convergent period.

In Tushman and Romanelli's (1985) model, during convergent periods, middle managers translate structures and systems. Conversely, top managers initiate, shape and direct strategic reorientations by mediating between internal and institutional forces for inertia and competitive forces for metamorphic change (Tushman and Romanelli, 1985). Similar patterns seem to exist for multinationals. Subsidiaries' managers generally implement headquarters' long-range plans by adjusting to local demands and fluctuations and by engaging in noncompetitive strategies (Hawkins and Walter, 1981; Kriger, 1988). Conversely, headquarters' managers generally decide on fundamental issues of competitive strategy such as technology, markets and products (Hawkins and Walter, 1981). The theory of multinationals as chameleons proposes that sometimes headquarters' actions on a subsidiary's presence bring about strategic reorientation or metamorphic change in the multinational, including their leaving host states.

Homeostatic equilibrium forms one way to frame metamorphic change in social systems like multinationals (Ashby, 1956; Mesarovic, Macko and Takahara, 1970). Homeostasis, a concept borrowed from physiology, refers to systemic processes to control and to counteract variations which when uncontrolled beyond limited ranges can destroy systems. Wallace (1956) defined homeostasis in social systems as consisting of coordinated actions, including cultural actions, by all or some of a social system's parts. In homeostatic equilibrium, a multinational's technical-efficiency, ideological and political forces are coordinated. Coordinated actions preserve the integrity of the multinational by maintaining minimally fluctuating, life-support matrices for its stakeholders. When stakeholders challenge some of these actions, managers may have to take emergency measures to preserve the multinational's life-support matrices.

This homeostatic equilibrium of multinationals is neither static nor moving. Moving equilibrium resembles physicists' concepts of dynamic equilibrium in which mass and velocity remain the same as in a moving top. Homeostatic equilibrium in multinationals does not depend on notions of constant social mass moving at constant velocity. In homeostatic equilibrium, multinationals can absorb new actors into their systems of action and alter rates of functional interaction with them. In homeostatic equilibrium, as against either static or dynamic equilibrium, the integrity of the multinational depends solely on the existence and stability of various technical-efficiency, ideological and political forces. These forces solve problems that arise, and that managers can predict, within cultural settings. Stakeholders' value structures or rationalized, normative preferences for systems of actions and outcomes, form one major characteristic of multinationals as defined here (Beyer, 1981; Guth and Macmillan, 1986; Guth and Taguri, 1965). Stakeholders' value structures symbolically legitimate, i.e., make morally acceptable, patterns of interaction and stratification within firms (Hirschman, 1970; Rhenman, 1973). Therefore, homeostatic equilibrium allows for certain types of structural change so long as the multinationals' solutions and their stakeholders' value structures change in harmony. For example, a subsidiary's growth and decline may occur without disturbing the multinational's homeostatic equilibrium because the changes maintain harmony between work practices and resource allocations. However, routine solutions may sometimes fail to accommodate stakeholders' changed value structures and re-equilibration has to occur for the multinational to survive: the multinational may leave the host state, and to maintain harmony in the multinational system, the form of that leaving should reflect dominant stakeholders' current value structures.

The theory of multinationals as chameleons proposes that two broad categories of stakeholders' actions capture changes in stakeholders' value structures: voice actions that strive to elicit structural changes in multinationals as well as to avoid violence, and exit actions that serve only to change. Voice actions take place through established, legitimate, organizational channels (Hirschman, 1970). Exit actions occur through extra-organizational channels and constitute efforts to destroy the multinational system (Hirschman, 1970). Managerial responses to voice actions may directly influence whether stakeholders resort to exit actions (Hirschman, 1970).

The theory of multinationals as chameleons maintains that in multinational systems, headquarters provide the life-support matrices to maintain homeostatic equilibrium. Headquarters channel and transform the strategic contributions of some stakeholders into inducements for others (March and Simon, 1958). Headquarters also coordinate technical-efficiency, ideological and political processes to provide the inducements that maintain stakeholders' participation and counteract variations through mechanisms to regulate it. A regulator is a mechanical contrivance for regulating or equalizing the movement of machinery, the flow of liquids, etc., and in organizations, regulatory mechanisms often involve structural changes (Miller and Friesen, 1984). In this book, headquarters' actions to decrease or to increase a subsidiary's presence in South Africa form regulatory mechanisms. This chapter explores the range and intensity of the regulatory mechanisms and the conditions that prompt them.

To a large extent, multinationals' actions result from top managers' core values (Guth, 1976; Guth and Taguri, 1965). Top managers' core values constrain where, how and why a firm competes (Normann, 1971). Managers' core values set parameters for decisions on products, markets, technology and timing, thereby defining multinationals' competitive domains and setting basic premises for their competitive strategies (Stahl and Grisby, 1997). The premises influence allocations of power and benefits to top managers and other stakeholders that, in turn, constrain structures and control systems within multinationals. Changes in top managers' core values generally result in cascading changes in strategy, power, structure and controls. Subsequent strategic orientations may also develop through unintended or emergent interactions among subsections and subactivities of multinationals (Mintzberg, 1979).

To summarize, two conflicting tendencies may spark the development of multinationals, including their leaving: internal and institutional forces for incremental change and inertia; and pressures emerging from misalignments with environments that necessitate metamorphic changes. This section proceeds to examine the two sources in more detail.

Sources for Inertia

As previously argued, the performance and legitimacy of multinationals flow from satisfying technical-efficiency, political and ideological requirements consistently and across subactivities. However, as webs of interdependent relationships with consumers, suppliers and financial investors grow stronger, commitments to these stakeholders form institutional patterns of culture and ideologies. Emergent social and structural processes constrain multinationals' behaviors and enact inertia by enforcing rules and norms. These processes may facilitate high performance as subsidiaries competently execute existing strategic orientations. However, the convergent social and structural processes may also impede environmental reassessment and necessitate metamorphic change (Tushman and Romanelli, 1985). Like chameleons, multinationals become constrained in their abilities to generate novel solutions.

Technical-efficiency forces, as outlined in Chapter 5, dominate sources for organizational inertia from competitive strategies (such as advertising, R&D, vertical integration, diversification and order backlogging) and from some noncompetitive strategies (such as contracting) (Khandwalla, 1981). In multinationals, competitive strategies generally originate at headquarters while subsidiaries engage in noncompetitive strategies (Hawkins and Walter, 1981). Technical-efficiency forces induce system-wide incremental and consistent decisions regarding products, processes, materials, labor and vertical integration. Several researchers (Grinyer and Spender, 1979; Lodahl and Mitchell, 1980; Miller and Friesen, 1980; Smith, 1982) have described linkages between technical and structural complexity and organizational inertia. For example, Abernathy (1978) argued that as firms tailor production processes to product lines, social and technical systems become increasingly coupled and specific; these developments create inertia by permitting only incremental elaboration of existing strategies. Similarly, Kimberly's (1980) study of an innovative medical school demonstrated how incremental decisions bolstered the school's strategy, systems, procedures and values. Once in place, these complex structural and social linkages resist forces that may change them. External forces for reliable outputs and performance accountability also generate complex standard operating procedures that block major changes in organizations (Hannan and Freeman, 1977).

Political forces, as outlined in Chapter 5, contribute to organizational inertia because coalitions, or stable, self-perpetuating groups, form vested interests in the status quo. For example, in large companies, the dominant coalition of top managers may institutionalize strategies that provide benefits to them (Galbraith 1973; Monson and Downs, 1965). Similarly, some noncompetitive strategies, such as co-opting, may create coalitions that institutionalize strategies. Noncompetitive strategies aim at agreements with other organizations on explicitly or tacitly agreed bases (Child and Keiser, 1981) and include co-opting, coalescing (Thompson, 1967) and public service (Child and Keiser, 1981; Haley, 1990a). In multinationals, noncompetitive strategies are generally implemented by subsidiaries (Hawkins and Walter, 1981; Kriger, 1988). As multinationals develop, managers coordinate operations through formal routines rather than through feedback (Crozier, 1964; Merton, 1968). Despite increasing performance, the formal routines may also stunt multinationals' abilities to handle new situations (Hedberg, Nystrom and Starbuck, 1976). Political processes within and between interest groups may therefore dominate nonroutine decision-making in such multinationals. When political processes dominate, managers make important decisions slowly and with highly pruned information (Downs, 1967; Olson, 1982; Wilensky, 1967). Consequently, multinationals may not generate novel solutions to handle new environmental problems.

Ideological forces, as outlined in Chapter 5, contribute to inertia from strategies to maintain legitimacy among stakeholders. These strategies include multinationals' symbolic actions and efforts to placate stakeholders. As environments become more structured, these strategies may generate coercive, mimetic and professional dynamics that homogenize and constrain organization-environment relations (DiMaggio and Powell, 1983; Stinchcombe, 1965). For example, Meyer and Rowan (1978) described the myths, ceremonies and incremental decisions that arise in educational systems from external institutional factors. Similarly, Tolbert and Zucker (1983) depicted how civil service agencies adopted administrative structures as a consequence of rationalized, institutionalized patterns. Organizations that adopt socially sanctioned practices and structures generally attract other resources from their environments (Dowling and Pfeffer, 1975; Meyer and Rowan, 1978). Such organizations are also more likely to maintain stakeholders' continued participation and identification (Rhenman, 1973). By identifying themselves with socially valued and accepted methods of operation, ideological forces can provide legitimacy to subsidiaries in host states. However, this legitimacy may impede subsidiaries from harmonizing their values and actions with prevailing expectations at home.

Multinationals' selection, socialization and promotion practices may accentuate the emergent social and normative processes that lead to inertia (Daft, Sormunen and Parks, 1988; Miles, 1982). Organizations often attempt to control human variability by attracting and selecting individuals whose personal values synchronize with organizational values (Katz and Kahn, 1966; Sigelman, 1977). Once selected, recruits are inculcated with expectations, beliefs and decision-making premises (Van Maanen, 1975). For example, multinationals often choose and socialize top managers through training and transfers (Edstrom and Galbraith, 1977; Sarason, 1972). Top managers then transmit these organizational norms and values through ideology, myths and sagas (Barnard, 1948; Selznick, 1957). Many researchers have confirmed that top managers' symbolic behaviors shape work environments (Martin, 1980; Pettigrew, 1979).

This section has described how external requirements for accountability and predictability, and internal coordination requirements, increase structural complexity, interdependence and convergence around strategic orientations for multinationals; concomitantly, multinationals resist fundamental change. Inertial processes at individual, group and organizational levels interact to cut the dominant coalition's range of responses (Keisler and Sproull, 1982; Staw, Sandelands and Dutton, 1981). For example, managers' prior commitments and self-justification may affect information acquisition and interpretation thereby bolstering the status quo (Guth and Macmillan, 1986). Similarly, top managers reinforce history, precedent and commitment to the status quo when stability and incremental change advance their career interests (Morison, 1966). The systems, procedures and structures that supported existing strategic orientations, work to focus attention and to filter information in support of the status quo (Wildavsky, 1964; Wilensky, 1967).

These inertial tendencies increase as dominant coalitions become more stable (Allen and Panian, 1982; Zaleznick and Kets de Vries, 1975). As tenure and team homogeneity increase, top managers converge on sets of norms, values and decision-making procedures while informational and resource diversity tend to decrease. Dominant coalitions may place greater emphasis on cohesion and conformity, become more committed to prior courses of action (Janis, 1972; Shambaugh, 1978) and resist strategic change. Whether labeled congealment (Boswell, 1973), ossification (Downs, 1967) or momentum (Miller and Friesen, 1980), inherent convergent processes pull multinationals and other organizations towards inertia.

Sources for Metamorphic Change

When incremental modifications to values, structures and controls fail to establish or to maintain consistency, multinationals and other organizations will not achieve sustainable levels of performance and legitimacy. Continued low performance and loss of legitimacy brought about by major changes in competitive, social and political conditions seriously endanger their survival. When systemic disequilibria become apparent in multinationals, headquarters may have to disrupt old networks of interdependent resource relationships and value structures to re-establish equilibrium. Regulatory mechanisms, such as headquarters' actions on a subsidiary's presence, provide means to re-establish equilibrium and multinationals may leave host states.

Performance pressures pose primal threats for multinationals and may necessitate metamorphic change. For example, technical-efficiency considerations, such as changes in industry-wide, long-run demand growth, provide basic forces driving product-class changes (Hannan and Freeman, 1977; Porter, 1980). Demand growth rates may additionally affect technological progress, scale economies, choice of suppliers and entry/exit barriers (Baysinger, Meiners and Zeithaml, 1981; Chandler, 1977; Schmookler, 1966).

Political forces may also result in redefinitions of performance criteria and key strategic contingencies, thereby compelling metamorphic change, including leaving. Multinationals and other organizations form negotiated orders composed of different interest groups (Pettigrew, 1973). These negotiated orders remain stable so long as performance fluctuates within some zones of indifference and distributions of power and inducements remain stable (March, 1962). When a multinational's performance dips drastically, inertial forces may contribute to further decreases in performance as well as increases in internal turbulence. Turbulence often results in erratic decisions, intraorganizational conflict and political behavior. Prolonged incremental change in support of inappropriate strategic orientations may lead to further crises and to internal pressures for metamorphic change (Grinyer and Spender, 1979; Mintzberg and Waters, 1982; Miller and Friesen, 1980).

Ideological forces also fuel metamorphic change by altering stakeholders' assessments of multinationals' operations. For example, fundamental changes in legal and social conditions may provoke crisis in a multinational by threatening external legitimacy (Kaufman, 1960; Miles, 1982; Mintzberg and Waters, 1982). Again, given the pervasiveness of inertial, organizational forces, metamorphic change, such as leaving, may be necessary to respond to stakeholders' changed demands.

Regulatory mechanisms, such as headquarters' actions on a subsidiary's presence, include metamorphic change in internal and external relations. Structures, systems, processes and commitments may need fundamental transformation and rebuilding. A multinational's history and relationships form inertial forces that resist implementing new strategies and systems. For example, in the case of South Africa, headquarters' actions to decrease a subsidiary's presence could have been deflected if the subsidiary made profits as high profits sow the seeds of extraordinary resistance to fundamental change (Biggart, 1977; Morison, 1966). The intensity of headquarters' actions on a subsidiary's presence therefore depends on how widely inertia prevails. Only the dominant coalitions in multinationals can regulate them by intervening between institutional forces for inertia and metamorphic change.

In multinationals, the dominant coalitions generally consist of headquarters' and subsidiaries' top managers (Gladwin and Walter, 1980). The dominant coalitions' perceptions of opportunities and constraints guide headquarters' actions on a subsidiary's presence. Perceptions include the dominant coalitions' assessments of the strength of stakeholders' actions as well as potential effects on their benefits (Finkelstein and Hambrick, 1989). These perceptions vary systematically with the stability of the dominant coalitions, their personal commitments and interdependencies, affecting their recommendations for metamorphic change. Consequently, headquarters may drastically decrease a subsidiary's presence after sustained performance declines and changes in the dominant coalition.

Figure 6.1 provides a political-action framework of a multinational as a hierarchical system regulated by headquarters' actions on a subsidiary's presence. Stakeholders contribute resources and services in exchange for inducements of money, goods and satisfaction from the multinational.

Figure 6.1   A multinational corporation as a hierarchical system.

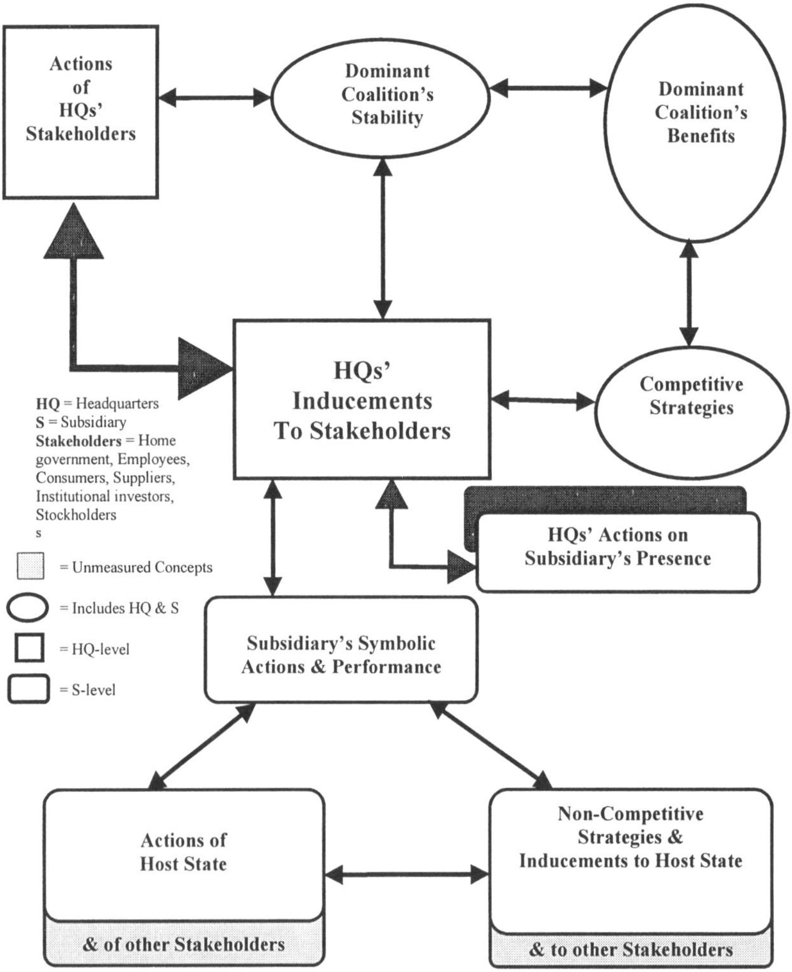

The multinational's inducements also stem from stakeholders' contributions and the system channels a steady flow of resources, money, services and satisfaction to all its stakeholders. The inducement-contribution balance (as described by March and Simon, 1958) maintains stakeholders' participation in the multinational system. Figure 6.1 has one subsidiary; however, the theory can extend to *n* subsidiaries.

Headquarters' inducements redistribute output from the subsidiary's operations while coordinating technical-efficiency, political and ideological forces, thereby maintaining the dominant coalition's stability. Competitive and noncompetitive strategies provide the multinational with the direction and meaning from which it fashions inducements. Like the chameleon's cells that provide the solutions, the multinational's strategies provide the inducements with which it solves problems. When the inducements prove inadequate, the multinational cannot maintain homeostatic equilibrium in its existing structural form. This book proposes that headquarters' actions on a subsidiary's presence in South Africa maintained homeostatic equilibrium in the multinational system by realigning technical-efficiency, political and ideological forces for a new inducement-contribution balance. The next section provides some tests of this theory of multinationals.

Hypothesizing Why a Multinational May Leave

Headquarters' actions on a subsidiary's presence forms the primary dependent variable. In this study, *headquarters' actions on subsidiary's presence* is a dichotomous variable to capture leaving and staying in South Africa. Leaving includes total liquidation, sale to a South African or European company, sale to a US company, sale to local management and the formation of a trust. Staying includes no additional investment by headquarters in the subsidiary, and increased investment in the subsidiary by headquarters. Some hypotheses on the variables affecting headquarters' actions on subsidiary's presence, on possible intervening variables, and on key linkages between environmental variables, are now proposed. Figure 6.2 summarizes the main hypotheses regarding headquarters' actions to maintain a subsidiary's presence in South Africa.

Figure 6.2   Hypothesized main influences on subsidiary's presence.

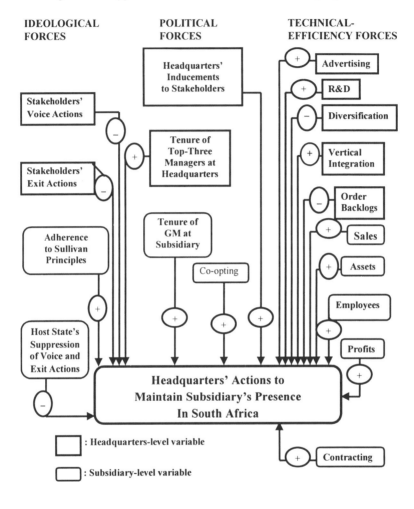

Headquarters' Inducements to Stakeholders

In the case of US multinationals in South Africa, *headquarters' inducements to stakeholders* would have incorporated payments of money to headquarters' stakeholders including dividends, interest expenses, federal taxes and cost of goods sold.

Links to Headquarters' Actions on Subsidiary's Presence:

As headquarters' inducements to stakeholders increase, the dominant coalition's ability to engage in quasi-resolution of conflict among stakeholders may increase. Effective resolution of conflict may have helped to maintain the subsidiary's presence in South Africa. Headquarters' inducements also indicate some profitability on the part of the multinational. Researchers have noticed, that in profitable organizations, inertia and commitment to prior courses of action increase disproportionately (O'Reilly, 1978; Wilensky, 1987). As headquarters' inducements increase, the dominant coalition's potential to receive or to process adverse information may also decrease. In the case of US multinationals in South Africa, headquarters' inducements to stakeholders may have decreased the likelihood that headquarters would have acted to decrease the subsidiary's presence in South Africa. For instance, Goodyear's CEO, Mercer, justified increased investment in the South African subsidiary around the high dividends that Goodyear offered American stockholders (Kessler, 1985). Consequently,

H1: The greater headquarters' inducements to stakeholders, the less likely that headquarters would have acted to decrease the subsidiary's presence in South Africa.

Voice and Exit Actions of Headquarters' Stakeholders

Hirschman (1970) identified two types of actions that stakeholders may take to change social systems: voice and exit. Voice occurs when stakeholders express their dissatisfaction through established organizational channels (Hirschman, 1984a). Exit occurs when stakeholders leave the social system altogether (Hirschman, 1984b). In the case of US multinationals in South Africa, *voice actions of headquarters' stakeholders* would have included stockholders' resolutions, and US government legislation that prevented governmental purchasing from multinationals with operations in South Africa. *Exit actions of headquarters' stakeholders* would have included stockholders' divestitures and legislation that forced state and municipal funds to divest stocks and bonds in multinationals with South African operations.

Links to Headquarters' Actions on Subsidiary's Presence:

Voice and exit actions of headquarters' stakeholders reflected stakeholders' value structures and the degree to which they bequeathed legitimacy to the multinational's operations in South Africa. Consequently, headquarters' actions on the subsidiary's presence should have reflected stakeholders' voice and exit actions. One can hypothesize,

H2a: *The greater the voice actions of headquarters' stakeholders, the more likely that headquarters would have acted to decrease the subsidiary's presence in South Africa.*

H2b: *The greater the exit actions of headquarters' stakeholders, the more likely that headquarters would have acted to decrease the subsidiary's presence in South Africa.*

Headquarters' Inducements to Stakeholders as a Mediator:

Hirschman (1984a) argued that in firms, the pull of managerial skills and strategies could alter the push of voice and exit. In the case of US multinationals in South Africa, headquarters' inducements to stakeholders could have interacted with stakeholders' voice and exit actions to alter headquarters' actions on the subsidiary's presence in South Africa. Headquarters inducements to stakeholders would have included dividends, interest expenses, federal taxes and cost of goods sold. For instance, in spite of stakeholders' voice and exit actions, US multinationals that paid out high dividends seemed to maintain a higher presence in South Africa than those that paid out low dividends (GAO/NSIAD-88-165). By maintaining legitimacy with some stakeholders, headquarters' inducements may have muffled other stakeholders' actions that could have adversely affected the subsidiary's presence in South Africa. Consequently,

H3a: *The greater headquarters' inducements to stakeholders, the less likely that the voice actions of headquarters' stakeholders would have caused headquarters to decrease the subsidiary's presence in South Africa.*

H3b: The greater headquarters' inducements to stakeholders, the less likely that the exit actions of headquarters' stakeholders would have caused headquarters to decrease the subsidiary's presence in South Africa.

Links between Voice and Exit Actions of Headquarters' Stakeholders:

Dynamically, stakeholders' perceptions of their abilities to change multinational systems can affect their actions (Baysinger, Keim and Zeithaml, 1985; Kolarska and Aldrich, 1980). For example, Hirschman (1970; 1984a) postulated that the existence and effectiveness of voice, directly affected the existence of exit. Similarly, in the case of US multinationals in South Africa, the US Senate justified the Comprehensive Anti-Apartheid Act of 1986 on the grounds that milder protests did not seem to affect their behaviors. If stakeholders' voice actions seemed to have no impact on the subsidiary's presence in South Africa, the actions could have intensified or changed with stakeholders moving from voice to exit actions. One can hypothesize,

H4: The greater the voice actions of headquarters' stakeholders, the more likely that headquarters' stakeholders would have engaged in exit actions.

Dominant Coalition's Stability

The dominant coalitions in multinationals generally consist of headquarters' top managers and the subsidiaries' general managers (Gladwin and Walter, 1980; Hawkins and Walter, 1981). In the case of US multinationals in South Africa, the dominant coalitions would generally have included headquarters' top three managers and the South African subsidiary's general manager. The dominant coalition's stability is measured by the *tenure of headquarters' top three managers and of the subsidiary's general manager.* Tenure indicates if the dominant coalition remained the same from the previous year or was changed and is measured from 1982.

Links to Voice and Exit Actions of Headquarters' Stakeholders:

Research has shown that stakeholders' voice and exit can adversely affect managerial tenure (Kolarska and Aldrich, 1980). For example, some top managers may be fired as scapegoats when stakeholders seem persistently or chronically dissatisfied with operations (Hedberg, Nystrom and Starbuck, 1976). Other researchers argued that when significant organizational problems persist, stakeholders' support for top managers diminishes and the managers' voluntarily or mandatorily resign (Salancik, Staw and Pondy, 1980; Thompson, 1967; Zald, 1965). In the case of US multinationals in South Africa, the voice actions of headquarters' stakeholders directed against the multinational's South African subsidiary included stockholders' resolutions, and purchasing legislation by US state, city and county governments. Exit actions of headquarters' stakeholders directed against the multinational's South African subsidiary included stockholders' divestitures and legislation forcing state and municipal funds to divest interests in multinationals with South African operations. These stakeholders' actions would probably have shortened the tenure of headquarters' top three managers and of the South African subsidiary's general manager. Consequently,

H5a: *The greater the voice actions of headquarters' stakeholders, the shorter the tenure that headquarters' top three managers and the South African subsidiary's general manager would have had.*

H5b: *The greater the exit actions of headquarters' stakeholders, the shorter the tenure that headquarters' top three managers and the South African subsidiary's general manager would have had.*

Links to Headquarters' Actions on Subsidiary's Presence:

Research suggests that inertial processes at individual, group and organizational levels interact to constrain the dominant coalition's ability to change the status quo (Keisler and Sproull, 1982; Staw, Sandelands and Dutton, 1981). These inertial tendencies increase with managerial tenure (Allen and Panian, 1982; Zaleznick and Kets de Vries, 1975). As their tenure increases, top managers may place greater emphasis on cohesion and conformity, become more committed to prior courses of action and resist strategic changes that disrupt the status quo (Janis, 1972; Shambaugh, 1978). For example, in a case study of major divestment decisions, Gilmour (1973) found that replacement of top managers preceded each divestment decision. In the case of US multinationals in South Africa, headquarters' actions to decrease the subsidiary's presence in South Africa could have disrupted the status quo and broken with precedent. When top managers enjoyed longer tenure, headquarters may have been less likely to change the status quo in South Africa. For example, Goodyear, with a stable dominant coalition of headquarters' and subsidiary's managers, increased its investments in South Africa despite other multinationals divesting (Kessler, 1985). Consequently,

H6: The longer the tenure of the top three managers at headquarters and of the South African subsidiary's general manager, the less likely that headquarters would have acted to decrease the subsidiary's presence in South Africa.

Links to Dominant Coalition's Benefits:

Stable dominant coalitions may indicate that managers share stakeholders' goals. Rational compensation schemes should capture this commonality of goals by offering greater benefits to the dominant coalition (Finkelstein and Hambrick, 1988; March, 1984; Norburn and Birley, 1988). Conversely, unstable dominant coalitions may reflect that managers do not share stakeholders' goals and the dominant coalition's benefits would decrease (Gamson and Scotch, 1964; Salancik, Staw and Pondy, 1980).

The dominant coalition may also co-opt stakeholders such as compensation committees and the media, to increase their salaries, status and prestige (Mace, 1971). The more stable the dominant coalition, the higher the probability that such a co-optation would occur. However, Finkelstein and Hambrick (1989) concluded that a curvilinear relationship might exist between the dominant coalition's stability and benefits.

In the case of US multinationals in South Africa, *the dominant coalition's benefits* would have included rewards to the top three managers at headquarters and to the South African subsidiary's general manager. As subsidiaries rarely disclose managerial salaries, in this study, measures of benefits include prestige and status accruing to managers from positive coverage of the South African subsidiary in the American press. Therefore,

H7: *The longer the tenure of the top three managers at headquarters and of the South African subsidiary's general manager, the greater the benefits that the managers would have received.*

Multinational's Competitive Strategies

Multinationals' competitive strategies reflect attempts to control market-related performance. Competitive strategies generally determine appropriate values for *advertising, R&D, vertical integration, diversification and order backlogs* (Khandwalla, 1981). In the case of US multinationals in South Africa, competitive strategies would have been measured by advertising expenditures, R&D expenditures, vertical integration between the South African subsidiary and the US multinational, product diversification based on Standard Industrial Classification (SIC) codes and changes in order backlogs demonstrating changes in inventory.

Links to Dominant Coalition's Benefits:

Competitive strategies help multinationals to exercise greater control over market structures, to extract stable performance and to diversify risk (Scherer, *et al.*, 1975; Ferguson, 1960; Jacquemin and de Lichtbuer, 1973; Marris and Wood, 1971; Miller, 1998; Singh, 1971). Competitive strategies may also satisfy the dominant coalition's need for higher salaries, prestige and power (Roberts, 1956; 1959; Simon, 1957). For example, high advertising and low order backlogs may indicate greater sales, higher profits and more efficient production management, factors that may increase the dominant coalition's salaries, job security and prestige (Williamson, 1963). Similarly, competitive strategies may build a larger firm, thereby indirectly increasing the dominant coalition's salaries and benefits (Ciscel, 1974; Finkelstein and Hambrick, 1989). Conversely, potential benefits to the dominant coalition may serve to motivate certain competitive strategies (Finkelstein and Hambrick, 1989).

Competitive strategies may also increase the dominant coalition's benefits by increasing managerial independence and decreasing the importance of short-term performance criteria. Consequently, differences in the dominant coalition's benefits often correlate with differences in divisional autonomy (Berg, 1969; 1973). Similarly, studies have concluded that more diversified firms, with more elaborate plans, reward managers on the basis of more rigid financial criteria, thereby reducing managerial discretion over their own benefits (Salter, 1973; Pitts, 1974). Less diversified firms tend to maintain more entrepreneurial atmospheres, with more flexible reward specifications for managers (Kerr, 1985). Less diversified firms also seem to encourage more independent actions from division managers in R&D, marketing and production. On vertical integration, using qualitative and operating indicators, Lorsch and Allen (1973) found that vertically integrated firms linked managerial benefits with overall performance. Kerr (1985) also found some evidence that the dominant coalition may institutionalize strategies that provide benefits. In the case of US multinationals in South Africa, the dominant coalition's benefits represented the rewards accruing to the top three managers at headquarters and to the South African subsidiary's general manager. Consequently,

H8a: The greater the advertising, the greater the benefits that the top three managers at headquarters and the South African subsidiary's general manager would have received.

H8b: The greater the R&D, the greater the benefits that the top three managers at headquarters and the South African subsidiary's general manager would have received.

H8c: The greater the order backlogs, the less the benefits that the top three managers at headquarters and the South African subsidiary's general manager would have received.

H8d: The greater the vertical integration, the greater the benefits that the top three managers at headquarters and the South African subsidiary's general manager would have received.

H8e: The greater the product diversification, the less the benefits that the top three managers at headquarters and the South African subsidiary's general manager would have received.

Links to Headquarters' Actions on Subsidiary's Presence:

Researchers have shown that by increasing structural complexity, specialization and dependence, competitive strategies may increase structural inertia in firms. For example, R&D in large firms often comes with dedicated professional staff, increased specialization of skills and functions, greater delegation of technology, and therefore, structural inertia (Dewar and Hage, 1978; Khandwalla, 1974; Scherer, 1970). By putting more eggs into the same end-product basket, vertical integration also increases dependence on particular lines of activity, suppliers and customers leading to some loss of strategic flexibility for firms (Ansoff, 1965; Duhaime and Grant, 1984). Physical facilities shared with other healthy businesses, goodwill and loyalty in distribution relationships, and manufacturing and technological factors such as durable and highly specific capital assets also heighten exit barriers and constrain firms from divesting assets (Caves and Porter, 1976; Duhaime and Grant, 1984; Harrigan, 1980; 1985; Porter, 1976).

In the case of US multinationals in South Africa, R&D and advertising created product reputations that could have discouraged headquarters' actions to decrease the subsidiary's presence in South Africa. Large order backlogs indicate small inventories and headquarters could have been more likely to decrease the subsidiary's presence in South Africa when order backlogs were large. Vertical integration could also have discouraged headquarters' actions to decrease the subsidiary's presence in South Africa by increasing interdependencies within the multinational. The more diversified the multinational, the less likely that switching costs and economies of scale are perceived as very high, that intangible assets can only be used in conjunction with each other, and that capital requirements are highly specialized (Harrigan, 1981; Hatten, Schendel and Cooper, 1978). Consequently, in more diversified multinationals, headquarters may have been more likely to act to decrease the subsidiary's presence in South Africa. Therefore,

H9a: The greater the advertising, the less likely that headquarters would have acted to decrease the subsidiary's presence in South Africa.

H9b: The greater the R&D, the less likely that headquarters would have acted to decrease the subsidiary's presence in South Africa.

H9c: The greater the order backlogs, the more likely that headquarters would have acted to decrease the subsidiary's presence in South Africa.

H9d: The greater the vertical integration, the less likely that headquarters would have acted to decrease the subsidiary's presence in South Africa.

H9e: The greater the diversification, the more likely that headquarters would have acted to decrease the subsidiary's presence in South Africa.

Subsidiary's Symbolic Actions

Symbols, such as social programs, generate support for subsidiaries, and assure their continued presence, by making operations and outcomes appear consonant with prevailing social values (Edelman, 1977). In the case of US multinationals in South Africa, the subsidiary's symbolic actions for headquarters' stakeholders would have included its *adherence to the Sullivan Principles*. The Sullivan Principles, promulgated by the International Council for Equality of Opportunity in 1977, stated that signatories support an end to apartheid. The multinational as a signatory therefore took an explicit stand opposing South Africa's proclaimed national interests. The Sullivan Principles endeavored to end apartheid by integrating blacks into the labor force and by improving the quality of blacks' work lives and often constituted a litmus test to judge US multinationals' social responsibilities in South Africa (Paul, 1987). Arthur D. Little of Cambridge, Massachusetts collected and disseminated all the data on the Sullivan Principles. Little evidence indicates that multinationals changed their work places in response to the Sullivan Principles. However, the Sullivan Principles became symbolic because the subsidiary went through periodic, public justifications and interpretations of its stance vis-à-vis the South African government: it informed employees that it remained a signatory; informed employees of its Sullivan ratings; reviewed its progress with representative groups of employees several times a year; and subjected its progress to independent audits from outside accounting firms.

Links to Headquarters' Actions on Subsidiary's Presence:

Edelman (1964; 1977) illustrated how social programs provide primarily symbolic values that perpetuate organizations by legitimizing them to employees, stockholders and other stakeholders. In the case of US multinationals in South Africa, the subsidiary's adherence to the Sullivan Principles maintained its legitimacy with some stakeholders in the USA (Paul, 1987); consequently, adherence to the Sullivan Principles probably made it less likely that headquarters would have acted to decrease the subsidiary's presence in South Africa.

H10:   The greater the South African subsidiary's adherence to the Sullivan Principles, the less likely that headquarters would have acted to decrease the subsidiary's presence in South Africa.

Headquarters' Inducements to Stakeholders as a Mediator:

Stakeholders often judge organizations by what they attempt to do and by the inducements that they offer (Pfeffer, 1981). For examples, stakeholders at home may reason that a multinational providing the best and most plentiful resources to its stakeholders can hardly be faulted for what these resources do not accomplish in faraway social settings. In the case of US multinationals in South Africa, headquarters' inducements to stakeholders would have included dividends, interest expenses, taxes and costs of goods sold. As these inducements increased, the subsidiary's adherence to the Sullivan Principles may have proven less important to US stakeholders. Consequently,

H11:   The greater headquarters' inducements to stakeholders, the less likely that the subsidiary's nonadherence to the Sullivan Principles would have caused headquarters to decrease the subsidiary's presence in South Africa.

Subsidiary's Profits and Importance in Global Operations

Multinationals use a variety of long-term measures to evaluate subsidiaries' performance (Hawkins and Walter, 1981). Generally, profit-related measures, such as rates of return on assets (ROAs), indicate local performance. Sales, assets and employees reflect a multinational's relative performance pressures better than ROAs and also classify a subsidiary's performance relative to a multinational's other global operations (Czechowicz, Choi and Baveshi, 1982). In the case of US multinationals in South Africa, the South African subsidiary's performance measures would have included *profits, sales, assets, and employees.*

Links to Headquarters' Actions on Subsidiary's Presence:

Firms' performance often reflects the demands of stakeholders that share in the distribution of performance-based outcomes. Consequently, high economic performance offers multinationals the opportunity to pursue the quasi-resolution of conflict by providing greater inducements to stakeholders (Cyert and March, 1963). High performance also maintains a subsidiary's legitimacy with stakeholders, thereby contributing to its continued existence (Meyer and Rowan, 1978; Rhenman, 1973). On the other hand, sustained low performance may result in loss of legitimacy, depletion of resources and curtailment of headquarters' inducements to stakeholders. Therefore, a subsidiary's low performance may prompt headquarters' actions on the subsidiary's presence. In the case of US multinationals in South Africa, headquarters may have been less likely to decrease the subsidiary's presence in South Africa, if it maintained high profits, sales, assets and employees. As indicated earlier, while profits indicated a subsidiary's performance in South Africa, sales, assets and employees indicated a subsidiary's importance in the multinational's global operations. One can hypothesize,

H12a: *The greater the subsidiary's profits, the less likely that headquarters would have acted to decrease the subsidiary's presence in South Africa.*

H12b: *The greater the subsidiary's sales, assets and employees the less likely that headquarters would have acted to decrease the subsidiary's presence in South Africa.*

Subsidiary's Noncompetitive Strategies with Host State

Noncompetitive strategies refer to organizational attempts to reach agreements on explicitly or tacitly agreed bases through nonmarket activities (Child and Keiser, 1981). Thompson (1967) argued that firms' noncompetitive strategies include contracting and co-opting. Contracting refers to the subsidiary's agreements for the exchange of performances in the future; and, co-opting refers to processes of absorbing outside elements into leadership or policy-determining structures of the subsidiary. In the case of US multinationals in South Africa, *contracting* would have included the proportion of the subsidiary's sales and purchases from South African governmental agencies. *Co-opting* would have included the number of South African governmental agencies represented on the subsidiary's boards of directors, and vice versa.

Links to Subsidiary's Symbolic Actions:

Multinationals form systems of patterned activities. Managers try to develop causal explanations and rationalizations for these patterns of activity (Pfeffer, 1981) and to develop meanings for cycles of interlocked behaviors. Very strong symbolic overtones and meanings permeate subsidiaries' noncompetitive strategies. For example by co-opting representatives from governmental agencies' boards to subsidiaries' boards, or vice versa, both sets of organizations proclaim their affiliations publicly to the world and symbolically demonstrate their presumed support of each others' activities (Pfeffer, 1987). The symbolic involvement of distinct constituencies, such as host governments, in decision-making and implementation may also develop a subsidiary's commitment and motivation for actions (Salancik, 1977). In the case of US multinationals in South Africa, mutual identification between the subsidiary and the South African government may have lead to expectations and labeling effects that reinforced their association. Sometimes, a multinational's activities may create conflicts among stakeholders' value structures. For example, in the case of US multinationals in South Africa, a subsidiary's adherence to the Sullivan Principles provided symbolic reassurance to headquarters' stakeholders but also symbolized a protest of the South African government's policies on apartheid. Noncompetitive strategies may force subsidiaries to moderate, suppress or camouflage their values and ideologies (Blankenship and Elling, 1962; Peterson, 1977; Wolman, 1972) and if a subsidiary's stakeholders proclaim conflicting values, it may avoid symbolic behaviors that placate some and antagonize others. Consequently,

H13: The more the subsidiary contracted and co-opted South African governmental agencies, the lower the subsidiary's adherence to the Sullivan Principles would have been.

Links to Subsidiary's Profits:

Subsidiaries' noncompetitive strategies may contribute to high profits by serving the same purpose as economic efficiency (Pfeffer, 1987). For example, contracting may diminish the uncertainty and waste caused by competition (Child and Keiser, 1981). Through an empirical analysis of 200 corporations in the postwar, Canadian economy, Richardson (1987) also provided some support for the argument that some noncompetitive strategies may contribute to higher profits through increasing efficiency. Other theorists have proposed reverse causal relationships between directorship interlocks and profits. For example, co-optation theories propose that interlocks constitute co-optive mechanisms that fuel relatively profitable performance for the nonfinancial organizations involved (Burt, 1980a; 1983; Pennings, 1980).

Noncompetitive strategies may also contribute to higher profits by reducing costs and ensuring above-normal profits. For example, co-optation may allow organizations secure and easy access to resources and thereby control costs (Pfeffer, 1973; Pfeffer and Salancik, 1978). Also, restrictive practices and cartels, contracts that characterize oligopolistic industries, offer placid and secure operating environments that control costs for member organizations. A contracted monopoly constitutes a particularly attractive arrangement for firms since it provides a negotiated environmental niche that may provide above-normal profits (Sampson, 1973). In the case of US multinationals in South Africa, one can hypothesize,

H14: The more the subsidiary contracted and co-opted South African governmental agencies, the higher the subsidiary's profits would have been.

Links to Headquarters' Actions on Subsidiary's Presence:

A multinational may consist of coalitions of interest but also produces activities that do not fit any stakeholder's interests (Pfeffer, 1987). Once created such activity patterns persist through institutionalization (Pfeffer and Salancik, 1978). For example, subsidiaries' requirements for survival and acquiring resources probably change them (Pfeffer and Salancik, 1978). Headquarters' actions may then express more than the dominant coalitions' views by enunciating activity patterns emerging from negotiations between subsidiaries and major environmental actors (Glasberg and Schwartz, 1983). In the case of US multinationals in South Africa, a subsidiary's noncompetitive strategies with the host state probably reduced headquarters' capacity to decrease the subsidiary's presence in South Africa because of interdependent relationship webs and commitments. Consequently,

H15: The more the subsidiary contracted and co-opted South African governmental agencies, the less likely that headquarters would have acted to decrease the subsidiary's presence in South Africa.

Suppression of Voice and Exit Actions by Host State

Hirschman (1984b) identified two types of actions that states may take vis-à-vis stakeholders: the suppression of voice and the suppression of exit. In the case of US multinationals in South Africa, the South African government's *suppression of voice actions* would have included legislation demanding the subsidiary's financial support and legislation restricting information that the subsidiary could release to headquarters' stakeholders; the South African government's *suppression of exit actions* would have included legislation restricting the subsidiary's sale and the National Key Points Act that allowed confiscation of the subsidiary's property.

Links to Subsidiary's Symbolic Actions:

When questioned by external stakeholders, managers may invest more effort in making sense of and legitimating a firm's actions, creating greater correspondence between the firm's and the state's symbolic actions (Salancik and Conway, 1975). In the case of US multinationals in South Africa, the subsidiary's adherence to the Sullivan Principles represented symbolic actions that directly countered the South African government's actions on apartheid. Consequently, suppression of voice and exit actions by the South African government could have discouraged the subsidiary's adherence to the Sullivan Principles (Kaempfer, Lehman and Lowenberg, 1987; Lenway, 1988). One can hypothesize,

H16: The greater the South African government's suppression of the subsidiary's voice and exit actions, the lower the subsidiary's adherence to the Sullivan Principles would have been.

Links to Subsidiary's Profits:

A host state's suppression of voice and exit actions can affect a subsidiary's profits by altering market structures, constraining supply and demand of resources, imposing foreign exchange restrictions, limiting the transfer of information and thereby altering economies of scale, economies of scope and operating synergies (Krasner, 1978). In the case of US multinationals in South Africa, one can hypothesize,

H17: The greater the South African government's suppression of the subsidiary's voice and exit actions, the lower the South African subsidiary's profits would have been.

Links to Subsidiary's Noncompetitive Strategies with Host State:

Several researchers have argued that subsidiaries' noncompetitive strategies reduce the intervention of states in subsidiaries' operations (Kim, 1988; Olsen, 1981). For example, in a study of 104 subsidiaries' noncompetitive strategies, Poynter (1982) found that intervention by host states in subsidiaries' operations ranged from expropriation to foreign-exchange harassment to requests for political contributions. The subsidiaries that engaged in more frequent informal contacts with host governments experienced significantly less intervention. Poynter (1982) argued that subsidiaries' noncompetitive strategies altered host states' perceptions of multinationals and of subsidiaries' bargaining powers. The subsidiaries could also identify intervention measures before they became realities and assess governmental desires to enforce the intervention policies (Poynter, 1982). Similarly, in a random sample of 80 large corporations, Pfeffer (1972a) found that the proportion of inside directors was negatively related to both national and local regulation: corporations with more outsiders on their boards of directors seemed to encounter less governmental intervention. In the case of US multinationals in South Africa, the subsidiary's noncompetitive strategies would have included co-opting and contracting. Consequently,

H18: The more the subsidiary co-opted and contracted South African governmental agencies, the less likely that the South African government would have acted to suppress the subsidiary's voice and exit actions.

Links to Headquarters' Actions on Subsidiary's Presence:

Hirschman's (1984b) theories suggest that if a host state's suppression of voice and exit actions could affect a multinational's performance, these circumstances would encourage that multinational to leave. In the case of US multinationals in South Africa, the host state's suppression of the subsidiary's voice and exit actions could adversely affect the subsidiary's performance, by, for example, constraining its divestitures, as well as antagonizing headquarters' stakeholders, thereby increasing the likelihood that headquarters would act to decrease the subsidiary's presence in South Africa. One can hypothesize,

H19: The greater the host state's suppression of the subsidiary's voice and exit actions, the more likely that headquarters would have acted to decrease the subsidiary's presence in South Africa.

Subsidiary's Inducements to Host State

In the case of US multinationals in South Africa, *subsidiary's inducements to the host state* would have included taxes and fees paid to the government.

Links to Subsidiary's Symbolic Actions:

Subsidiaries often strive for some consensus between their ideologies and those of the states in which they operate (Asch, 1958; Gladwin and Walter, 1980; Katzenstein, 1985; Krasner, 1978). Importantly, degrees of ideological dissension with host states may distinguish subsidiaries from domestic firms, and lay subsidiaries open to dissatisfaction, regulation and punitive measures (Hawkins and Walter, 1981). Consequently, symbolic dissension may induce the subsidiaries to offer greater inducements to host states. In the case of US multinationals in South Africa, the subsidiary's adherence to the Sullivan Principles constituted a symbolic action that opposed the South African government's espoused ideology of apartheid; consequently, the subsidiary may have expended more on taxes and fees to placate the South African government.

Conversely, multinationals strive to shrink their overall tax burdens, and to increase their overall profitability for stockholders (Gladwin and Walter, 1980). However, when inducements to the host state increase, profits may dip. Consequently, subsidiaries may have to legitimize their operations to headquarters' stakeholders through symbolic behaviors. In the case of US multinationals in South Africa, if the subsidiary expended more money on taxes, it may have had to demonstrate deliberately greater adherence to the Sullivan principles to placate headquarters' stakeholders. One can hypothesize,

H20: The greater the subsidiary's inducements to the South African government, the greater the subsidiary's adherence to the Sullivan Principles would have been.

Links to Suppression of Voice and Exit Actions by Host State:

States may be less likely to enforce punitive measures and sanctions on subsidiaries that contribute to the national welfare by paying taxes and training local labor (Gladwin and Walter, 1980; Krasner, 1978). Conversely, payment of taxes and training of local labor may deflect host states' hostile or punitive actions (Hawkins and Walter, 1981). In the case of US multinationals in South Africa, the South African government's punitive actions included suppression of the subsidiary's voice and exit actions. Consequently,

H21: The greater the subsidiary's inducements to the South African government, the less likely that the South African government would have acted to suppress the subsidiary's voice and exit actions.

Summary

This chapter has provided sets of hypotheses to test the theory of multinationals as chameleons. Specifically it has tried to isolate and to provide hypotheses for testing when a subsidiary would have left South Africa, and what economic and political circumstances as well as stakeholders' actions would have prompted it to do so. Figure 6.2 has summarized the main hypothesized influences on leaving or staying. The next chapter provides details of the methodology and variables used to test the hypotheses.

PART IV

DATA, ANALYSES AND RESULTS

7. Methodology

The empirical part of this study deals with US multinationals in South Africa. Specifically, this study analyzes influences such as stakeholders' actions, competitive strategies and noncompetitive strategies on headquarters' actions to maintain a subsidiary's presence in South Africa from 1984 to 1987. Assuming time lags between environmental events and headquarters' actions, the study examines the effects of stakeholders' actions as well as multinationals' strategies and performances from 1982, on leaving or staying behaviors from 1984 to 1987. This chapter provides information on the setting, the time frame for the study, the population, the variables, data sources and measurement issues.

The Setting

Apartheid-practicing South Africa provided the setting for this study. The setting included competitive and noncompetitive external environments, as well as a variety of stakeholders' actions. The external environments also ranged from relatively benevolent to relatively threatening, offering many opportunities to observe multinationals in political environments.

First, settings with a range of environments grant opportunities to observe a variety of strategies from multinationals. For example, multinationals in benevolent, external environments may not have to adapt in order to survive while those in threatening, external environments may be forced to do so (Miles and Cameron, 1982; Miles and Snow, 1978). In the case of South Africa, despite historically high profits, a report to congressional requesters (GAO/NSIAD-88-165) disclosed that many US multinationals admitted to facing increasing pressures from stakeholders to leave apartheid-practicing South Africa, indicating exposure to diverse values and ethics, which may have influenced their leaving or staying.

Second, one can identify the initiation, nature and timing of the threats that the multinationals faced and the major events upon which they bore. Consequently, one can make operational the threatening external environment for multinationals as a trend line of discrete events with a definite starting point. Such information would help to discard rival hypotheses about environmental events and multinationals' strategies (Miles and Cameron, 1982). Reports to US congressional requesters and the US State Department's documents helped to identify some of the environmental threats and events. The reasons most cited by multinationals for leaving South Africa included forecasts of decreased business opportunities and selective-purchasing laws by US state and local governments restricting business with multinationals that had South African operations (GAO/NSIAD-88-165:30-31). Shareholders' actions, the President's Executive Order of 1985, and the Comprehensive Anti-Apartheid Act of 1986 appeared less significant as reasons for leaving (GAO/NSIAD-88-165:32). Newspaper reports suggested that perceptions of threats seemed to vary both within and across industries.

Third, the setting provided an opportunity to identify clearly the South African governments' influence on multinationals. Multinationals often encounter ambiguous and confused influences when they coalesce with or co-opt governmental agencies which generally encompass many opposing, influential interests (Krasner, 1978). In this study, governmental interests refer to clear and abiding social and national values enshrined in laws and bureaucratic norms (Krasner, 1978). Governmental interests fall into two categories, policy objectives and policy instruments (Katzenstein, 1978).

Policy objectives reflect choices among values that differ among governments. The South African government had chosen the policy objectives of apartheid or separate development (Leape, Baskin and Underhill, 1985; Sethi,

1987). From 1910 to 1948, blacks in South Africa had traditionally lived in different areas, undergone different training and encountered different work opportunities. However, in the general election of 1948, Daniel F. Malan officially included the policy of apartheid in the Afrikaner Nationalist Party's platform, bringing his party to power for the first time. Under the prime ministership of Hendrik Verwoerd, from 1958 to his assassination in 1966, apartheid mutated into the policy known as separate development, whereby each of the nine black African (Bantu) groups became a nation with its own homeland, or Bantustan. The government set aside an area totaling about 14 percent of the country's land for these homelands, and reserved the remainder, including the major mineral areas and the cities, for the whites. The separate development policy aimed to confine black African's rights and freedoms to their homelands, and to treat them as aliens in any other part of South Africa. Until 1991 to 1992 when President F.W. de Klerk repealed the laws bolstering apartheid, all South African governmental agencies embraced the policy and its objectives. Therefore, apartheid represented unified, South African policy objectives during the period under study.

Policy instruments include means that policy makers can command to determine if policy objectives are achievable (Katzenstein, 1978). Since 1948, the South African government had used extensive bureaucratic support to distinguish the races and to enhance white supremacy (Kaempfer, Lehman and Lowenberg, 1987; Seidman, 1986; Tatum, 1987). When Prime Minister Hendrik Verwoerd took office in 1958, and until the policy was repealed in 1991, the government used policy instruments to segregate physically the races. The government forced large segments of the Asian and colored populations to relocate out of so-called white areas. It also demolished African townships that had been overtaken by white urban sprawl and removed their occupants to new townships beyond city limits through regulations such as the Group Areas Acts. Between the passage of the Group Areas Acts of 1950 and 1986, the government forcibly removed about 1.5 million black and colored Africans from cities to rural reservations. All blacks living outside the Bantustans had to follow strict curfew regulations and passbook requirements, especially in the cities; if they could not produce passbooks when challenged, they were subject to arrest. In 1962, the government granted the police sweeping powers of preventive detention, initially for 30 days and later for indefinite periods. Regulations strictly controlled movements to and between the black homelands and other parts of the country. The location of blacks' residences or employment (if permitted to work) was restricted, and they were not allowed to vote or to own land by law. For black-African, urban workers, including third- or fourth-generation city dwellers, only the necessary labor permits granted according to the labor markets by the government, allowed residency within urban areas. Such permits often did not include the spouse or family of a permit holder, contributing to the breakup of family life among many black Africans. In this fashion, strong, policy instruments achieved the South African government's policy objectives regarding apartheid.

Finally, the ideal setting should involve an engaging and important issue concerning the relationship between multinationals and environments, one that, regardless of its outcome, would make a difference to the social and economic milieu surrounding multinationals and their stakeholders as well as inform on how they change and to what influences they may succumb. This study of multinationals operating in South Africa offered such an opportunity to analyze a historic situation when ethics, values and strategies clashed.

The Time Frame

This study analyzes headquarters' actions to maintain a subsidiary's presence in South Africa from 1984 to 1987, and the effects of environmental influences on the multinational from 1982. This section identifies the factors that affected the selection of the time frame. Figure 7.1 provides a time line to organize the discussion.

External protests over the ethics of apartheid began in the 1960s, and in 1961, South Africa withdrew from the Commonwealth of Nations rather than abandon apartheid. Also in 1961, the three South African denominations of the Dutch Reformed Church left the World Council of Churches for the same reason. However, US stakeholders began pressuring multinationals to modify their South African operations only from the early 1970s (Gladwin and Walter,

Figure 7.1 Time Line for US Multinational Corporations in South Africa.

1948	Afrikaner Nationalist Party officially adopts policy of apartheid in its platform, bringing it to power in South Africa
1982	UNO proclaims International Year for Mobilization of Sanctions against South Africa
1982	Starting point for data on company-level and environmental variables
1983 (Feb.)	South African government abolishes two-tier exchange rate for non-residents
1984	Starting point for data on subsidiaries' presence in South Africa
1985 (Sept.)	South African government reintroduces two-tier exchange rate for non-residents
1986 (Oct.)	US government bans new US investments in South Africa
1987	Ending point for data on all company-level and environmental variables
1988	US government eliminates credits for taxes paid in South Africa
1991	President de Klerk repeals apartheid laws and calls for drafting of a new South African constitution

1984-1985: In study, period of *No Regulation* affecting subsidiary's leaving and staying
1986-1987: In study, period of *Regulation* affecting subsidiary's leaving and staying

1980). The year 1982 marked a formal, public acknowledgement of these pressures because the United Nations General Assembly proclaimed it as the International Year of Mobilization for Sanctions against South Africa. In this study, 1982 was chosen to begin tracing stakeholders' voice and exit actions, and multinationals' strategies and performance. The United Nations General Assembly had historically provided strong, symbolic support for anti-apartheid movements and its founding at the end of World War II precipitated persistent and organized international anti-apartheid efforts (Love, 1985). A significant amount of the debates around governmental sanctioning of South Africa centered on the United Nations. The United Nations Center Against Apartheid also monitored and encouraged private companies and organizations to sanction South Africa through its publications, research, publicity and co-sponsorships of conferences and receptions (Love, 1985). Therefore, 1982 provided a suitable point in time to begin identifying social and economic influences questioning headquarters' actions on ethical grounds. The time frame and structure for this study also included four major legislative acts and one international event that affected multinationals' operations in South Africa.

First, in February 1983, the South African government abolished the system of exchange controls for nonresidents (Leape, Baskin and Underhill, 1985). Till 1983, the South African government had used exchange controls to restrict capital outflows from South Africa. In particular, the South African government had instituted dual-currency rates for nonresidents: the commercial-rand rate to repatriate dividends and profits and to conduct trade and the financial-rand rate to lend, to invest and to disinvest in South Africa. Because of the system of exchange controls, multinationals could leave South Africa only by selling operations and assets through the financial-rand market. As the financial rand traded at an exchange rate of about 40 percent lower than the commercial rand, multinationals that left South Africa had to sell their assets at much below market value. Consequently, prior to 1983, the exchange-control system discouraged multinationals that wanted to leave South Africa. Conversely, from 1984 to 1985, exchange controls did not deter multinationals from leaving South Africa, providing a window to observe leaving behaviors unfettered by direct regulation.

Second, in September 1985, the South African government reintroduced the two-tier exchange rate. In 1986 and 1987, the financial rand traded at an exchange rate of about 20 percent lower than the commercial rand (Kibbe and Hauck, 1988). In 1986, US multinationals that left South Africa had to contend with the implications of the reintroduced legislation.

Third, in October 1986, the US Congress passed the Comprehensive Anti-Apartheid Act. Among other sanctions, the act banned new US investments in South Africa. However, the act did not prohibit reinvesting profits earned from existing investments with majority US ownership or secondary-market sales of South African stocks and bonds that had been issued prior to the act's passage. Historically, about 80 percent of all foreign direct investment in South Africa came from reinvesting profits. Consequently, the significance of this act revolved around its prohibiting new US companies from entering South Africa.

Fourth, in 1988, the US Congress eliminated credits for corporate taxes paid in South Africa. US multinationals generally pay US taxes on their worldwide incomes. However, when multinationals earn part of their income in foreign countries, they also generally pay taxes in those countries. To prevent double taxation of the same income, US laws permit multinationals to claim tax credits, thereby allowing them to reduce their tax burden by the taxes paid in the foreign countries (Skelly and Hobbs, 1988). The elimination of tax credits for South Africa increased the effective tax rates for some multinationals and encouraged their leaving after 1988. For example, in April 1989, Mobil sold its $400 million refinery and service stations to a South African company, General Mining Union Corp., for a bargain price of $150 million. Mobil spokesmen said that the new tax laws had meant a 72 percent tax rate for Mobil and had cost the company five million dollars (*Newsweek*, 1989).

In this study, the period from 1984 to 1985 presents an unusual situation in that very little legislation directly affected US multinationals' leaving and staying in South Africa. Consequently, for the purposes of the study, 1984 to 1985 represents a period of *No Regulation*. In 1986, the South African government limited how multinationals left South Africa and in 1987, the US Government banned new investments in South Africa. Consequently, for the purposes of the study, 1986 to 1987 represents a period of intrusive *Regulation*. Separate analyses were conducted on the two sets of years for all the hypotheses.

To accommodate time lags between social and economic influences and headquarters' actions to maintain a subsidiary's presence in South Africa, the independent variables were lagged for one year in all the analyses. Idiosyncratic differences between subsidiaries' accounting and strategic practices also encouraged incorporating a one-year time lag. First, some of the independent variables (especially those dealing with the subsidiary's assets) and the dependent variable on leaving South Africa (that captured changes in assets) were expected to be spuriously correlated if measured contemporaneously. Second, the length of time between US multinationals' final decisions to leave South Africa and the implementation of this decision seemed to have been about six months (GAO/NSIAD 88-165:32). Finally, multinationals' fiscal year ends varied from one to six months, affecting their reporting of accounting data.

The Population

The population in the study consisted of all US multinationals in South Africa that owned ten percent or more of active South African subsidiaries or affiliates in 1984, as recorded by the Investor Responsibility Research Center (322 companies). Table 7.1 lists the population of companies. Table 7.2 identifies the companies that had to be excluded from the study. Generally,

Table 7.1   Population of US multinational corporations in South Africa.

Afia Worldwide Insurance	Amdahl Corp.
AM International Inc.	American Airlines Inc.
AMCA International Corp.	American Cyanamid Co.
AMR Inc.	American Express Co.
Abbott Laboratories	American Home Products Corp.
Accuray Corp.	American Hospital Supply Corp.
Air Express International Corp.	American International Group Inc.
Air Products & Chemicals Inc.	Applied Power Inc.
Albany International Corp.	Armco Inc.
Alexander & Alexander Services Inc.	Ashland Oil Inc.
Allegheny International Inc.	Associated Metals and Minerals Corp.
Louis A. Allen Associates Ltd.	Automatic Switch Co.
Allis-Chalmers Corp.	Avery International Corp.

Table 7.1   (*Continued*)

BBDO International Inc.	Champion Spark Plug Co.
The Badger Co. Inc.	The Chase Manhattan Corp.
Baker International Corp.	Chesebrough-Ponds Inc.
Bandag Inc.	Chicago Pneumatic Tool Co.
Ted Bates Worldwide Inc.	Citicorp
Bausch & Lomb Inc.	City Investing Co.
Baxter Travenol Laboratories Inc.	Coca-Cola Co.
Beatrice Companies Inc.	Colgate-Palmolive Co.
Bechtel Group Inc.	Columbus McKinnon Corp.
Beckman Instruments Inc.	Computer Sciences Corp.
Bell & Howell Co.	The Continental Corp.
Black & Decker Manufacturing Co.	Continental Grain Co.
Blue Bell Inc.	Control Data Corp.
Boeing Co.	Cooper Industries Inc.
Borden Inc.	Cooper Laboratories Inc.
Borg-Warner Corp.	Corning Glass Works
Born Inc.	Coulter Electronics Inc.
Bristol-Myers Co.	John Crane-Houdaille Inc.
Buckman Laboratories Inc.	Crown Cork & Seal Co. Inc.
Bucyrus-Erie Co.	Cummins Engine Co. Inc.
Bundy Corp.	D'Arcy-Macmanus & Masius Worldwide Inc.
Burroughs Corp.	Dames & Moore
Butterick Co. Inc.	Dart & Kraft Inc.
CBI Industries Inc.	Deere & Co.
CBS Inc.	Del Monte Corp.
Cigna Corp.	Deltak Corp
CPC International Inc.	Diamond Shamrock Corp.
Caltex Petroleum Corp.	Do-All Co.
Canada Dry Corp.	Donaldson Co. Inc.
Card KeySystems	Dow Chemical Co.
Carman Industries Inc.	Dow Corning Corp.
Carnation Co.	Dr Pepper Co.
Carrier Corp.	Dresser Industries Inc.
Cascade Corp.	E. I. Du Pont de Nemours & Co.
J. I. Case Co.	Dukane Corp.
Caterpillar Tractor Co.	The Dun & Bradstreet Corp.
Celanese Corp.	Eastman Kodak Co.

Table 7.1   (*Continued*)

Eaton Corp.	The Getz Corp.
Echlin Co.	Gilette Co.
Ecolaire	The Goodyear Tire & Rubber Co.
Emery Air Freight	W. R. Grace & Co.
Emhart Corp.	Grey Advertising Inc.
Engelhard Corp.	Grolier Inc.
Envirotech Corp.	Harnischfeger Corp.
Erico Products Inc.	The Harper Group
Eriez Magnetics	Hay Associates
Esmark Inc.	Hayes/Hill Inc.
Euclid. Inc.	Healthdyne Inc.
Exxon Corp.	Heinemann Electric Co.
FMC Corp.	Walter E. Heller Overseas Corp.
Federal-Mogul Corp.	Henkel Corp.
Ferro Corp.	Heublein Inc.
Firestone Tire & Rubber Co.	Hewlett-Packard Co.
Fisher Controls International Inc.	Honeywell Inc.
Flow General Inc.	Hoover Co.
John Fluke Manufacturing Co.	Houdaille Industries Inc.
Fluor Corp.	Huck Manufacturing Co.
Foote Cone & Belding Communications Inc.	Hughes Tool Co.
Ford Motor Co.	Hydro-Air Engineering Inc.
Foster Wheeler Corp.	ICS-International
Franklin Electric Co. Inc.	IMS International Inc.
Fruehauf Corp.	Illinois Tool Works Inc.
GAF Corp.	Ingersoll-Rand Co.
GATX Corp.	International Business Machines Corp.
GTE Corp.	International Flavors & Fragrances Inc.
Gang-Nail Systems Inc.	International Harvester Co.
The Gates Rubber Co.	International Minerals & Chemical Corp.
Gelco Corp.	International Playtex Inc.
General Electric Co.	International Staple & Machine Co.
General Foods Corp.	International Telephone & Telegraph Corp.
General Motors Corp.	The Interpublic Group of Companies Inc.
General Signal Corp.	JWT Group Inc.
A. J. Gerrard & Co.	Johnson & Johnson Co.

Table 7.1   (*Continued*)

S. C. Johnson & Son Inc.	Monsanto Co.
Johnson Controls Inc.	Motorola Inc.
Joy Manufacturing Co.	Muller & Phipps International Corp.
KFC Corp.	NCNB Corp.
Kellogg Co.	NCR Corp
Kendavis Industries International Inc.	Nabisco Brands Inc.
Kimberly-Clark Corp.	Nalco Chemical Co.
Koehring Cranes & Excavators	National Education Corp.
L&M Radiator Co.	National-Standard Co.
Estee Lauder Inc.	National Starch & Chemical Corp.
Leco Corp.	National Utility Service Inc.
Leeds & Northrup Co.	Newmont Mining Corp.
Libbey–Owens-Ford Co.	A. C. Nielsen Co.
Eli Lilly & Co.	Norton Co.
Loctite Corp.	Oak Industries Inc.
Longyear Co.	Ogilvy & Mather International Inc.
The Lubrizol Corp.	Olin Corp.
Lykes Bros. Steamship Co.	Opico Inc.
Macmillan Inc.	Otis Group
Maremont Corp.	Pan American World Airways Inc.
Marriott Corp.	Parker Hannifin Corp.
Marsh & McLennan Cos. Inc.	The Parker Pen Co.
Martin Marietta Corp.	Pennwalt Corp.
Masonite Corp.	Pepsico Inc.
McLean Industries	Perkin-Elmer Corp.
McCormack & Dodge	Pfizer Inc.
McGraw-Hill Inc.	Phelps Dodge Corp.
Measurex Corp.	Phibro-Salomon Inc.
Medtronic Inc.	Phillips Petroleum Co.
Memorex Corp.	Pizza Inn Inc.
Merck & Co. Inc.	Precision Valve Corp.
Metallurg Inc.	Preformed Line Products Co.
Midland-Ross Corp.	Quaker Chemical Corp.
Millipore Corp.	Ramsey Engineering
Mine Safety Appliances Co.	Raytheon Co.
Minnesota Mining & Manufacturing Co.	Reader's Digest Association Inc.
Mobil Corp.	Redland Braas Corp.
Mohawk Data Sciences Corp.	Reed Mining Tools Inc.

Table 7.1   (*Continued*)

Revlon Inc.	Tenneco Inc.
Rexnord Inc.	Texaco Inc.
R. J. Reynolds Industries Inc.	J. Walter Thompson Co.
Richardson-Vicks Inc.	Tidwell Industries Inc.
Riker Laboratories	The Timken Co
The Robbins Co	Titanium Industries
H. H. Robertson Co	Tokheim Corp.
A. H. Robins Co. Inc.	The Trane Co.
Rohm & Haas Co.	Trans World Corp.
SPS Technologies Inc.	Twentieth Century-Fox Film Corp.
Salsbury Laboratories Inc.	Twin Disk Inc.
Schnectady Chemicals Inc.	UAL Inc.
Schering- Plough Corp.	U.S. Industries Inc.
Scovill Inc.	Union Carbide Corp.
G. D. Searle & Co.	Uniroyal Inc.
The Sentry Corp.	Unit Rig & Equipment
Sigmaform Corp	United States Gypsum Co.
Simplicity Pattern Co. Inc.	United States Line SA
The Singer Co.	United States Steel Corp.
Skok Systems Inc.	United Technologies Corp.
Smith International Inc.	Upjohn Co.
SmithKline Beckman Corp.	VF Corp.
Sperry Corp.	The Valeron Corp.
Square D Co.	Valvoline Oil Co.
Squibb Corp.	Van Dusen Air Inc.
W. R. Stamler Corp.	Wang Laboratories Inc.
Standard Oil Co. (Ohio)	Warner Communications Inc.
Standard Oil Co. (California)	Warner Electric Brake & Clutch Co.
The Stanley Works	Warner-Lambert Co.
Stauffer Chemical Co.	Wean United Inc.
Steiner Corp.	West Point-Pepperell Inc.
Sterling Drug Inc.	Westin Hotel Co.
Stone & Webster Inc.	Westinghouse Electric Corp.
Sullair Corp.	Wilbur-Ellis Co.
Sun Chemical Corp.	John Wiley & Sons Inc.
Sybron Corp.	Wynn's International Inc.
Tambrands Inc.	Xerox Corp.
TOTAL = 322 multinationals	

Source: Newman and Bowers (1984)

Table 7.2   Multinational corporations excluded from study.[1]

	Excluded Multinational	Owner
1	American Airlines Inc.	AMR Inc.
2	The Badger Co. Inc.	Raytheon Co.
3	Beckman Instruments Inc.	SmithKline Beckman Corp.
4	Canada Dry Corp.	Dr. Pepper Co.
5	Carrier Corp.	United Technologies Corp.
6	J. I. Case Co.	Tenneco Inc.
7	Corning Glass Works	Dow Corning Corp.
8	John Crane-Houdaille Inc.	Houdaille Industries Inc.
9	Del Monte Corp.	R. J. Reynolds Industries
10	Envirotech Corp.	Baker International Corp.
11	Esmark Inc.	Beatrice Companies Inc.
12	Fisher Controls International Inc.	Monsanto Co.
13	Gang-Nail Systems Inc.	Redland Braas Corp.
14	Heublien Inc.	R. J. Reynolds Industries
15	Huck Manufacturing Co.	Federal-Mogul Corp.
16	ICS International	National Education Corp.
17	International Playtex Inc.	Beatrice Companies Inc.
18	KFC Corp.	R. J. Reynolds Industries
19	Leeds & Northrup Co.	General Signal Corp.
20	Masonite Corp.	United States Gypsum Co.
21	McCormack & Dodge	The Dun & Bradstreet Corp.
22	Memorex Corp.	Burroughs Corp.
23	Muller & Phipps International Corp.	Getz Group
24	Otis Group	United Technologies Corp.
25	Ramsey Engineering	Baker International Corp.
26	Reed Mining Tools Inc.	Baker International Corp.
27	Riker Laboratories	Minnesota Mining & Manufacturing Co.
28	Standard Oil Co. (California)	Caltex Petroleum Corp.
29	Texaco Inc.	Caltex Petroleum Corp.
30	J. Walter Thompson Co.	JWT Group Inc.
31	Unit Rig & Equipment	Kendavis Industries International
32	United States Line SA	McLean Industries
33	The Valeron Corp.	GTE Corp.
34	Valvoline Oil Co.	Ashland Oil Inc.
35	Westin Hotel Co.	UAL Inc.

[1] Table 7.1 listed 322 multinationals in the population under study. Thirty-five multinationals belonged to wholly-owned subsidiaries of multinationals already in the population, in effect accounting for their operations more than once. Consequently, they were excluded from further consideration in the study.

the US multinationals held over 50 percent of the equity of their subsidiaries and affiliates in South Africa. None of these subsidiaries or affiliates was listed on the Johannesburg Stock Exchange. This section outlines some of the advantages that the population offers researchers.

First, the population included meaningful similarities and differences across multinationals. Researchers sometimes control for the influence of some extraneous variables, such as market structure, by analyzing multinationals with similar characteristics such as membership in an industry (e.g. Miles and Cameron, 1982). The population of US multinationals in South Africa included numerous firms facing common industrial environments, and covered numerous industries, permitting comparisons within and across industries of headquarters' actions to maintain a subsidiaries' presence in South Africa. Table 7.3 indicates staying and leaving behaviors across industrial sectors.

Table 7.3   US multinational corporations in South Africa by industrial sector.

Industrial Sectors	1984		1985		1986		1987		Percent Leaving (%)
	Stayed	Left	Stayed	Left	Stayed	Left	Stayed	Left	
Services	42	2	37	5	30	7	20	10	54.5
Paper/Glass	8	0	8	0	7	1	7	0	12.5
Agr./Ind. Equipment	63	0	59	4	54	5	52	2	17.5
Pharm./Chemicals	42	0	38	4	33	5	30	3	28.6
Office/Electronics	39	0	30	9	21	9	16	5	59.0
Extractive	22	2	20	2	14	6	13	1	45.6
Food/Tobacco	11	0	8	3	4	4	3	1	72.7
Rubber/Plastics	9	0	9	0	8	1	6	2	33.3
Hardware/Household	8	0	7	1	5	2	4	1	50.0
Fabric	4	0	2	2	2	0	2	0	50.0
Printing/Publishing	6	0	5	1	4	1	2	2	66.7
Miscellaneous	22	3	14	8	5	9	2	3	92.0
TOTAL	276	7	237	39	187	50	157	30	44.5
Percent Leaving (%)	2.5		14.1		21.1		16		

Source: Investor Responsibility Research Center

Second, the environmental threats seem to have provoked a variety of actions from the multinationals ranging from relatively superficial to fundamental. For example, despite environmental threats, in 1987, 157 US multinationals stayed in South Africa with active subsidiaries (Investor Responsibility Research Center). Conversely, perhaps because of environmental threats, from 1984 to 1987, about 126 US multinationals left South Africa when most were meeting profit and volume goals (GAO/NSIAD-88-165:31).

Third, consistent and objective data for both subsidiaries and headquarters were available over an extended period of time. Most studies of organization-environment relations have relied primarily on perceptual data from key individuals and on cross-sectional data (Miles and Cameron, 1982:xvi–xvii). However, cross-sectional data do not offer an adequate basis to infer cause-effect relations and to answer what caused the multinationals to leave. The primary data for this study came from archival sources. For at least a decade, organizations such as the United Nations Organization, the Investor Responsibility Research Center, the Interfaith Center on Corporate Responsibility, the United Nations Center on Transnational Corporations and Arthur D. Little had routinely monitored multinationals in South Africa. The data they collected were expressed in objective and consistent units throughout the six-year period under study. Public sources, such as 10-K reports, provided other data on multinationals' operations for the study. Therefore, the data for the study comprised factual matters of public record and reflected real-time uncertainties as well as multinationals' reactions to events as they occurred, rather than retrospective reports of what managers now think occurred in the past. By paying attention to chronological events, the study could then present developments as they unfolded in real time. In addition, the study's longitudinal nature enhanced the probability that changes in multinationals' strategies, such as their adopting symbolic behaviors, were not chance aberrations.

Fourth, the population provided an avenue to distinguish managerial influences, ethics and values from those of other stakeholders. For example, some researchers have assumed that managers act as agents for stockholders who delegate their decision-making powers to these managers. Consequently, stockholders lose much of their ability to influence firms (Jensen and Meckling, 1976; Mitnick, 1987). Yet, stockholders of US multinationals in South Africa introduced resolutions that opposed managerial policies and that questioned corporate operations on ethical grounds. The US home government, and many state governments also opposed multinationals' operations in South Africa, through regulation, on ethical grounds. The South African host government espoused values and policies that opposed those of the US stakeholders and sometimes blocked their strategies. Therefore, the multinationals in South Africa provided opportunities to observe conditions under which stockholders, governments as well as managers, espoused diverse ethics, values and strategies and to gauge the extent of their influence on multinationals' operations.

The Variables

This section provides details on the concepts and the ways in which they have been made operational in the study and includes data sources, as well as potential problems and solutions associated with measuring variables. Table 7.4 lists the variables and primary data sources used in this study.

Headquarters' Actions on Subsidiary's Presence (PRESENCE)

PRESENCE consisted of ordered categories indicating how subsidiaries left and stayed in South Africa ranging from Low to High including (1) Total Liquidation & Piecemeal Sales of Assets; (2) Sale to South African or European Company; (3) Sale to another US Company; (4) Sale to Local Management; (5) Formation of Trust; (6) No Additional Investment by Headquarters; and, (7) Increased Investment by Headquarters. Because insufficient numbers existed across categories, for the purposes of analysis, PRESENCE was collapsed into a dichotomous variable measuring Left (categories one to five) and Stayed (categories six to seven). Figure 7.2 indicates the annual number of US multinationals that left or stayed in South Africa from 1984 to 1987. The proportion of multinationals that left South Africa increased

Table 7.4 Variables and data sources for multinational corporations in South Africa.

Variable	Source
Headquarters' Actions on Subsidiary's Presence in South Africa: PRESENCE *Dummy coding*	Subsidiary's leaving and staying in South Africa from 1984–1987 (*US and Canadian Investment in South Africa*, Investor Responsibility Research Center, May 1986, October–January 1989; *Company Profiles*, Investor Responsibility Research Center, 1984–1987).
Headquarters' Inducements to Stakeholders (banks and other providers of debt & suppliers of material and labor; stockholders & US government): INDUCE1 & INDUCE2 *Factor scores*	Interest expenses from 1982–1987 divided by total assets from 1982–1987 (*Compustat Annual Industrial File*, 1982–1987) & Cost of goods sold from 1982–1987 divided by total assets from 1982–1987 (*Compustat Annual Industrial File*, 1982–1987); Total dividends from 1982–1987 divided by total assets from 1982–1987 (*Compustat Annual Industrial File*, 1982–1987) & US federal taxes from 1982–1987 divided by total assets from 1982–1987 (*Compustat Annual Industrial File*, 1982–1987).
Voice and Exit Actions of Headquarters' Stakeholders (resolutions, divestment, legislation on purchasing, legislation on divestment): SR, SD, GP, GD *Dummy coding*	Dichotomous variable indicating presence of stockholders' resolutions against South African operations from 1982–1987 (*Church Proxy Resolutions*, Interfaith Center on Corporate Responsibility, 1981–1988; *How Institutions Voted on Shareholders' Resolutions*, Investor Responsibility Research Center, 1982–1987); Dichotomous variable indicating presence of stockholders' divestment to protest South African operations from 1982–1987 (*Response of Colleges and Universities to Calls for Divestment*, Investor Responsibility Research Center, March 1986; *Response of Colleges and Universities to Calls for Divestment*, South Africa Review Service, November 1986); Dichotomous variable indicating presence of state, county and city legislation against purchasing because of South African operations from 1982–1987 (*States, Counties*

Table 7.4   (Continued)

Variable	Source
	and Cities that Have Taken Economic Action against Apartheid, American Committee on Africa, 1989); Dichotomous variable indicating presence of state, county and city legislation on divestment because of South African operations from 1982–1987 (Public Investment and South Africa, American Committee on Africa, October 1986, November 1989).
Dominant Coalition's Stability: TMT Dummy coding	Dichotomous variable indicating if top three managers at headquarters and subsidiary's top manager stayed the same from previous year from 1982–1987 (Principal International Businesses, Dun and Bradstreet 1982–1987; Reference Book of Top Management, Dun and Bradstreet, 1982–1987).
Dominant Coalition's Benefits: BENEFITS Ratio scale	Directional content analysis of US press coverage of South African subsidiary from 1982–1987 (Dow Jones News, 1982–1987).
Multinational's Competitive Strategies (advertising, R&D, diversification, order backlogs, vertical integration): ADVERTISING, RESEARCH, DIVERSIFICATION, BACKLOGS, INTEGRATION Ratio scale or Dummy coding (for INTEGRATION)	Multinational's advertising expenses from 1982–1987 divided by net sales from 1982–1987 (Compustat Annual Industrial File, 1982–1987); Multinational's R&D expenses from 1982–1987 divided by net sales from 1982–1987 (Compustat Annual Industrial File, 1982–1987); Diversification index for multinational derived from net sales in subsidiary's 4-digit SIC codes from 1982–1987 (Compustat Business Segment File, 1982–1987; International Directory of Corporate Affiliates, 1982–1987); Multinational's order backlogs from 1982–1987 divided by net sales from 1982–1987 (Compustat Annual Industrial File, 1982–1987); Dichotomous variable indicating existence of forward or backward integration for multinational from 1982–1987 (Compustat Business Segment File, 1982–1987).

Table 7.4 (*Continued*)

Variable	Source
Subsidiary's Symbolic Actions: SYMBOL *Ordinal scale*	Subsidiary's adherence to the Sullivan Principles from 1982–1987 (*US and Canadian Investment in South Africa*, Investor Responsibility Research Center, May 1982, December 1984, May 1986, October 1987, January 1989).
Subsidiary's Profits in South Africa: ROA *Ratio scale*	Subsidiary's operating profits in South Africa from 1982–1987 divided by identifiable assets in South Africa from 1982–1987 (*Compustat Geographic Segment File*, 1982–1987; *US and Canadian Investment in South Africa*, Investor Responsibility Research Center, May 1982, December 1984, May 1986, October 1987, January 1989).
Subsidiary's Importance in Global Operations (assets, sales, employees): ASSETS, SALES, EMPLOYEES *Ratio scale*	Subsidiary's identifiable assets in South Africa from 1982–1987 divided by global assets from 1982–1987 (*US and Canadian Investment in South Africa*, Investor Responsibility Research Center, May 1982, December 1984, May 1986, October 1987, January 1989; *Compustat Annual Industrial File*, 1982–1987); Subsidiary's net sales in South Africa from 1982–1987 divided by net global sales from 1982–1987 (*US and Canadian Investment in South Africa*, Investor Responsibility Research Center, May 1982, December 1984, May 1986, October 1987, January 1989; *Compustat Annual Industrial File*, 1982–1987); Subsidiary's full-time employees in South Africa from 1982–1987 divided by total employees from 1982–1987 (*US and Canadian Investment in South Africa*, Investor Responsibility Research Center, May 1982, December 1984, May 1986, October 1987, January 1989; *Compustat Annual Industrial File*, 1982–1987).

Table 7.4   (Continued)

Variable	Source
Subsidiary's Noncompetitive Strategies (contracting, co-opting): CONTRACT, COOPT *Ratio scale*	Proportion of subsidiary's sales to South African government agencies from 1982–1987 (*Summary of US Sales to the South African Public Sector*, South Africa Review Service, November 1986, May 1988); Number of government agencies on which subsidiary was represented (*McGregor's Who Owns Whom*, 1983–1987; *Johannesburg Stock Exchange Handbook*, 1984–1987).
Suppression of Exit and Voice Actions by Host State: SUPPRESS *Dummy coding*	Dichotomous variable indicating presence of South African legislation which suppressed protest or exit as it applied to the South African subsidiary from 1982–1987 (*US Companies and Support for the South African Government: The Legal Requirements*, South Africa Review Service, 1985, 1987).
Subsidiary's Inducements to Host State: INDUCE3 *Ratio scale*	Dollar amount of taxes paid to the South African government by the subsidiary from 1982–1987 (*Doing Business in South Africa*, Price Waterhouse, 1982–1987; *Compustat Geographic Segment File*, 1982–1987).

Figure 7.2   US multinational corporations' staying in and leaving South Africa.

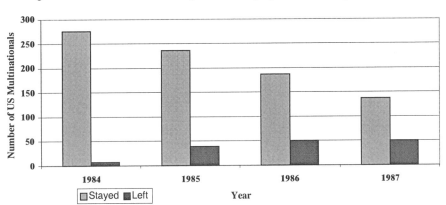

Figure 7.3   How US multinational corporations left South Africa.

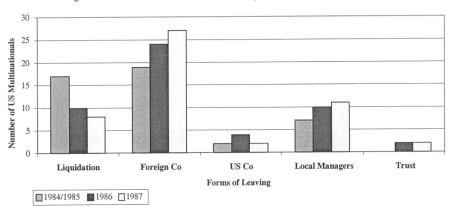

over the years. Figure 7.3 shows how the multinationals in the study left South Africa from 1984 to 1987. The greatest number of multinationals left by selling their subsidiaries to foreign (South African or European) companies.

Measurement:

Headquarters' actions on the subsidiary's presence indicated headquarters' negation, maintenance or endorsement of the subsidiary's assets, personnel and business practices (including the subsidiary's name, technology, product and managerial style), and therefore its identity, through forms of leaving and staying from 1984 to 1987. This variable was measured at the level of each subsidiary in South Africa.

The study relied on several detailed accounts of how US multinationals left South Africa to generate the categories for this dependent variable (Kibbe and Hauck, 1988; GAO/NSIAD-88-165). As discussed in Chapter 4, *Total Liquidation* dissolved the subsidiary's assets, personnel and business practices, and therefore, the subsidiary's identity. Operations were shut down and assets were sold piecemeal. A *Sale to a South African or European Company* partially dissolved the subsidiary's identity. The subsidiary's assets, business practices and personnel were modified or pared as they were integrated into the buyer's existing operations. A *Sale to another US Company* also partially dissolved the subsidiary's identity. The subsidiary's assets, business practices and personnel were modified or pared as they were integrated into the buyer's existing operations. However, as the buyer remained another US company, fewer major changes in business practices and personnel may have been necessary than in the previous category (Franko, 1976; Jedel and Kujawa, 1976). A *Sale to Local Management* maintained the subsidiary's identity to a large extent. Assets were often left intact and local managers often retained the majority of earlier business practices and personnel through detailed licensing and contractual arrangements with the parent company. The *Formation of a Trust* constituted a leaving facade as existing assets, business practices and personnel essentially remained unaltered. The parent company created an onshore (in South Africa) or offshore (outside South Africa) trust fund that bought and administered the subsidiary. The parent company chose the trustees, and wrote the trust deed that governed the overseeing of the South African operations. The South African operations made streams of payments to the trust, and consequently to the parent. Although the parent generally decided on how to dispense the payments, the trust often involved a reduction of the parent company's control over its South African operations as sabotage, blocked capital outflows or fluctuating foreign-exchange rates could reduce the South African operation's payments to the trust, and therefore to the parent. The parent company also could not invest or lend money to the subsidiary as it used to do. *No Additional Investment by Headquarters* tacitly endorsed the status quo of assets, business practices and personnel, forming another category of headquarters' actions on subsidiary's presence. The subsidiary's managers used retained earnings and borrowings from local sources to finance any changes in the subsidiary's assets, business practices and personnel. *Additional Investment by Headquarters* actively endorsed the subsidiary's assets, business practices and personnel and therefore the subsidiary's identity.

As Figures 7.2 and 7.3 indicated, the number of multinationals varied across the categories of PRESENCE. Insufficient numbers existed in each category to test the hypotheses or to confirm an ordinal scale. Consequently, for the purposes of analysis, PRESENCE was reduced to a dichotomous variable encompassing leaving and staying behaviors. *Left* comprised the categories Total Liquidation, Sale to a South African or European Company, Sale to another US Company, Sale to Local Management and the Formation of a Trust and was coded as 0. *Stayed* comprised the categories No Additional Investment by Headquarters and Additional Investment by Headquarters and was coded as 1.

Primary Sources of Data and Checks:

The Investor Responsibility Research Center issued detailed annual reports on how US subsidiaries left South Africa including Hauck's reports (1987) on multinationals from 1984 to 1987 and Kibbe and Hauck's (1988) from 1986 to 1988. The Investor Responsibility Research Center also issued reports on how individual subsidiaries grew in South Africa and how they financed this growth.

As a secondary check, the study used data from the United Nations Center for Transnational Corporations, including the *CTC Reporter*, on how US multinationals left and stayed in South Africa. When the primary and secondary data sources disagreed, the study relied on newspaper reports (particularly in the *Wall Street Journal* and the *New York Times*) to resolve discrepancies.

Headquarters' Inducements to Stakeholders (INDUCE1 and INDUCE2)

INDUCE1, measuring inducements to banks and other providers of debt as well as suppliers of materials and labor, was a factor score comprising interest expenses divided by total assets and cost of goods sold divided by total assets, from 1982 to 1987 or to the subsidiary's leaving. For the same time period, INDUCE2, measuring inducements to stockholders and the US government, was a factor score comprising total dividends divided by total assets and US federal taxes divided by total assets.

Measurement:

These two variables dealt with headquarters' distributions of benefits from the multinationals' operations to banks, suppliers, the US government and stockholders from 1982 to 1987. This variable was measured at the level of headquarters. Because of its exploratory nature, and the high degree of interdependence between the various indicators of inducement, factor analysis (principal components and varimax rotation) was used to reduce the indicators to the two sets of factors, INDUCE1 and INDUCE2.

Bartlett's test of sphericity tested the assumption that the sample came from a multivariate normal population: a large statistic (111.347) and small significance ($p < .000$) indicated the appropriateness of the data for factor analyses. Of the two factors, INDUCE1 had an eigenvalue of 1.380 and INDUCE2 an eigenvalue of 1.033. For INDUCE1, inducements to suppliers yielded a high factor loading of .792, and inducements to banks another high factor loading of .763. For INDUCE2, inducements to the US government yielded a high factor loading of .792, and inducements to stockholders another high factor loading of .748. Indicators loading on one factor had very low (under .1) and negative loadings on the other factor.

Primary Sources of Data and Checks:

The *Compustat Annual Industrial File* provided data on headquarters' dividends, interest expenses, federal taxes, cost of goods sold and total assets from 1982 to 1987.

As a secondary check, the study used *Moody's Industrials* for data on headquarters' dividends, interest expenses, federal taxes, cost of goods sold and total assets. When the two sources of data disagreed, multinationals' 10-K reports filed with the Securities and Exchange Commission provided additional information to resolve the discrepancies.

Voice and Exit Actions of Headquarters' Stakeholders (SR, SD, GP and GD)

SR, SD, GP and GD measured Voice and Exit actions of headquarters' stakeholders and were dichotomous variables. As Voice actions, SR measured the presence of stockholders' resolutions against South African operations, and GP of state, county and city legislation against purchasing because of South African operations, from 1982 to 1987 or to the subsidiary's leaving. Simultaneously, Exit actions, SD measured the presence of stockholders' divestment to protest South African operations, and GD of state, county and city legislation on divestment because of South African operations.

Measurement:

These variables measured stakeholders' actions to change the status quo through legitimate channels (Voice) or by leaving the multinational system (Exit). The variables were measured at the level of headquarters. Stakeholders' actions were sometimes directed against specific multinationals and at other times against entire industries or against all multinationals with headquarters in certain geographical regions and these were coded for each multinational as 1 for actions and 0 for no actions.

Primary Sources of Data and Checks:

From 1982 to 1987, for Voice actions, the Interfaith Center on Corporate Responsibility provided annual reports on *Church Proxy Resolutions* against multinationals and the Investor Responsibility Research Center on *How Institutions Voted on Shareholders' Resolutions*. The American Committee on Africa's *States, Counties and Cities that have taken Economic Actions against Apartheid* provided information on legislation affecting selective contracting and purchasing from 1982 to 1987. For Exit actions, the Investor Responsibility Research Center detailed stockholders' divestments from 1982 to 1987 in their publication, *Responses of Colleges and Universities to Calls for Divestment* and the South Africa Review Service published another version of this report. Governmental actions including legislation on divestment from 1982 to 1987 were listed in the American Committee on Africa's *States, Counties and Cities that have taken Economic Actions against Apartheid.*

As a secondary check, for stockholders' Voice and Exit actions, the Investor Responsibility Research Center's *Divestment Action Roundup* provided some information on stockholders' resolutions; a cross-section of the multinationals were checked against the statistics that publication provided. The United Nations Center for Transnational Corporations listed all state and some municipal legislation against multinationals and these data were used to check governments' Voice and Exit actions. In particular, United Nations' public hearings regarding multinationals in South Africa (UNCTC, *Transnational Corporations in South Africa and Namibia: Policy Instruments and Statement*, Vol. IV 1987; and UNCTC, *Activities of Transnational Corporations in South Africa and the Responsibilities of Home Countries with Respect to their Operations in this Area*, 1986) proved very useful in isolating governments' investment regulations regarding purchasing and divestment. When sources of data disagreed, the *Business Periodicals Index* was consulted for news items to resolve the discrepancies.

Dominant Coalition's Stability (TMT)

TMT was a dichotomous variable that measured if the top three managers at US headquarters and the South African subsidiary's general manager had changed or remained the same from the previous year. In this study, the top three managers at headquarters consisted of the Chief Executive Officer (CEO) and two senior directors. Data were gathered from 1982 to 1987 or to the subsidiary's leaving.

Measurement:

This variable to gauge the composition and stability of the dominant coalition was measured at the levels of headquarters and the South African subsidiary. Individual rather than aggregate data, for the four managers, were collected. The data were coded separately for each of the four managers and then collapsed into one dummy variable (1, the dominant coalition remained the same, or 0, the dominant coalition changed).

Primary Sources of Data and Checks:

Several annual directories provided data on corporate managers from 1982 to 1987 including the National Register Publishing Co.'s *International Directory Of Corporate Affiliates*, Dun and Bradstreet's *Reference Book of Top Management* and Dun and Bradstreet's (1984) *Handbook of Corporate Leaders.*

As a secondary check, Standard and Poor's *Register of Corporations, Directors and Executives* (three volumes) gave information on managers and their job histories. When sources of data disagreed, Dun and Bradstreet's *Principal International Businesses* and Dun Marketing's *America's Corporate Families and International Affiliat*es were used to resolve discrepancies.

Dominant Coalition's Benefits (BENEFITS)

BENEFITS captured some prestige and other benefits that accrued to the dominant coalition of managers (headquarters' top three managers and the subsidiary's general manager) through directional content analysis of press coverage of the South African subsidiary or the multinational's South African operations and decisions from 1982 to 1987 or to the subsidiary's leaving.

Measurement:

This variable to ascertain benefits to the dominant coalition was measured at the level of the subsidiary. A count of all items that mentioned the South African subsidiary in the American press was done. A simple, directional analysis of *Unfavorable* (items reporting social conflict and disorganization), *Neutral* (items reporting balanced content or noncontroversial material), and *Favorable* (items reporting social cohesion and cooperation) was then conducted (Budd, Thorpe and Donahue, 1967: 53). Janis and Fadner's Coefficient of Imbalance was used to judge directional biases in news coverage (Lasswell, Leites and Associates, 1949). The Coefficient provides a single figure to show the relationship between favorable and unfavorable materials:

$$C_f = \frac{f^2 - fu}{rt}$$

where,

f = favorable number of news items that deal with subsidiary
u = unfavorable number of news items that deal with subsidiary
t = total number of news items
r = total number of news items that deal with subsidiary

Primary Sources of Data and Checks:

Dow Jones News provided news items of US press coverage in journals and newspapers of the South African subsidiaries and operations of multinationals. News items from 1982 to 1987 were checked and tabulated.

As a secondary check, the *Business Periodicals Index* indicated US press coverage of the subsidiary. A sub-sample of the press-coverage assessments were checked with another coder with a formula for Inter-coder Reliability (North *et al.*, 1963):

$$R = \frac{2(C_{1,2})}{C_1 + C_2}$$

where, R = reliability

$C_{1,2}$ = number of categories both coders agreed upon
$C_1 + C_2$ = total category assessments made by both coders

When inter-coder reliability was less than .7, the news items were rediagnosed till a higher reliability level was reached (Krippendorff, 1980: 148). Some news items proved more difficult to code than others; those news items that seemed difficult to code were examined more carefully to find ways of adjusting the recorded instructions to their properties. Krippendorff's (1980:149) detailed instructions were used to break down the news items and to locate the source of the low reliability.

Multinational's Competitive Strategies (ADVERTISING, RESEARCH, DIVERSIFY, BACKLOGS and INTEGRATION)

ADVERTISING, RESEARCH, DIVERSIFY, BACKLOGS and INTEGRATION captured the multinational's annual market-conduct activities from 1982 to 1987 or to the subsidiary's leaving. ADVERTISING was advertising expenses divided by net sales, RESEARCH was research and development expenses divided by net sales, DIVERSIFY was a diversification index derived from net sales in a subsidiary's four-digit SIC codes from 1982 to 1987, BACKLOGS was order backlogs divided by net sales and INTEGRATION was a dichotomous variable indicating the existence of forward or backward integration.

Measurement:

As market-conduct and diversification strategies are decided at headquarters for the multinational, these variables were all measured at that level and included data for the whole multinational. For INTEGRATION, a dummy code of 1 (Vertically integrated) or 0 (Not vertically integrated) was assigned if the multinational's SIC codes belonged to more than one of the categories raw materials (SIC 0100-1999), manufacturing (SIC 2000-3999) or services (SIC 4000-9999). The formula used to calculate DIVERSIFY relied on sales figures by SIC codes as extrapolated by Montgomery (1982). Montgomery (1982) showed that the results derived from this formula did not differ significantly from Rumelt's (1974) more labor-intensive classification.

Consequently, DIVERSIFY was calculated as

$$\text{four-digit total diversification} = \frac{1 - \sum_j \text{mij2}}{\left(\sum_j \text{mij}\right)^2}$$

where, mij = percentage of firm i's total sales in market j (in this study, the subsidiary's SIC codes).

Primary Sources of Data and Checks:

The Compustat data bases (*Industrial* and *Business Information Segments*) provided information on advertising and R&D expenses, net sales, up to ten primary SIC codes per multinational, the multinational's sales by SIC codes and order backlogs.

As a secondary check, Standard & Poor's *Register of Corporations, Directors and Executives* gave four-digit SIC codes for headquarters and the National Register's *International Directory of Corporate Affiliates* did so for subsidiaries. R&D and advertising expenses, sales and order backlogs were checked for a sub-sample of the multinationals against annual reports obtained through the United Nations Center for Transnational Corporations. Also for a secondary check, estimates of vertical integration were made through Stopford's (1984) *World Directory of Multinational Enterprises*, which provided case by case information on several multinationals and their subsidiaries. When the sources of data disagreed, Dun Marketing's *America's Corporate Families and International Affiliates* gave additional information on SIC codes in which the multinationals operated. Additionally, some multinationals' Public Relations offices (such as Coca Cola's) often issued reports on foreign operations that were used to resolve discrepancies.

Subsidiary's Symbolic Actions (SYMBOL)

SYMBOL measured the subsidiaries adherence to the Sullivan Principles from 1982 to 1987, or to the subsidiary's leaving, and was an ordinal scale ranging from Low to High including (1) Not a Sullivan Signatory; (2) New Signatory for Less than a Year (did not have time to implement); (3) Signatory that

Did Not Report on Implementation; (4) Signatory with No or Few Employees in South Africa (Principles could not be implemented); (5) Signatory that Did Not Pass Basic Requirements (after implementation); (6) Signatory that Passed Basic Requirements but Received Low Point Ratings; (7) Signatory that Made Progress Based on Short-Form Reporting; (8) Signatory that Made Progress Based on Full Reporting; (9) Signatory that Made Good Progress. In 1987, about 161 subsidiaries had signed the Principles accounting for 90 percent of the labor employed by US multinationals in South Africa (Paul, 1987; Weedon, 1987).

Measurement:

The subsidiary itself completed the forms covering the implementation of the Sullivan Principles and all data were collected at the level of the South African subsidiary. The subsidiary also paid an annual fee to auditors to review the forms before submitting them. Arthur D. Little then rated the forms on the type of reporting (short or long) and the detail of information that the subsidiary provided. Arthur D. Little also publicly announced these ratings in annual reports on the progress of the signatory companies in implementing the Principles.

At a minimum, a subsidiary met nine basic requirements in order to get ratings of I or II. Failure to meet any of the requirements automatically consigned a subsidiary to a rating of III. The basic requirements covered issues like equal pay for equal work, desegregation, minimum wages, trade unions' rights and elimination of racial discrimination in pay or benefits. If a subsidiary met all the basic requirements, it was then evaluated and assigned points in four major areas including efforts on behalf of black education, training and advancement of black employees, community development and active efforts against apartheid laws.

The rating scheme follows with the figures in brackets representing the ratings assigned by Arthur D. Little. A revised scale, derived from the original Sullivan ratings, was used in this study. The revised scale reversed the subsidiary's Sullivan ratings (that is High became Low). Also, ratings of IV and V were reconstructed in the scale. This reconstruction corresponded to perceived increases in the subsidiary's symbolic behaviors as revealed in its implementation of the Principles. For example, a rating of V reflected low symbolic value as the subsidiary accepted the basic tenets of the Principles but did not have time to implement them. A rating of VI represented a higher degree of symbolic value as the subsidiary remained a signatory for over a year but did not report on its implementation of the Principles. A rating of IV represented a still higher degree of symbolic value as the subsidiary remained a signatory for over a year; however, as it had very few or no employees, it could not implement all the Sullivan Principles. The other ratings reflected the subsidiary's level of commitment as revealed in its implementations of all the Principles: 1 Not a Sullivan Signatory; 2 (V) New Signatory For Less Than a Year (did not have time to implement Principles); 3 (VI) Signatory that Did Not Report on Implementation; 4 (IV) Signatory With No or Few Employees in South Africa (Principles could not be implemented); 5 (III-B) Signatory that Did Not Pass Basic Requirements (after implementation); 6 (III-A) Signatory that Passed Basic Requirements but Received Low Point Ratings; 7 (II-B) Signatory that Made Progress Based on Short-Form Reporting; 8 (II-A) Signatory that Made Progress Based on Full Reporting; 9 (I) Signatory that Made Good Progress.

As previously stated in Chapter 6, the Sullivan signatory went through periodic, public justifications and interpretations of its stances vis-à-vis the South African government, informing employees that it remained a signatory and of its Sullivan ratings, reviewing its progress with representative groups of employees several times a year and subjecting its progress to independent audits from outside accounting firms.

Primary Sources of Data and Checks:

Arthur D. Little had annually rated subsidiaries' adherence to the six Sullivan Principles from 1976. The Investor Responsibility Research Center listed these ratings, by subsidiary, in their annuals on *US and Canadian Investment in South Africa*.

The Interfaith Center on Corporate Responsibility also kept lists of Arthur D. Little's Sullivan ratings. Errors could have arisen because the data had to be recoded to include multinational nonsignatories in South Africa, to make ratings of II and IIIA and IIIB into discrete categories, to reverse the scaling order by turning High into Low, and vice versa. A random sub-sample of the multinationals was therefore checked for coding errors.

Subsidiary's Profits (ROA)

ROA measured the subsidiary's profits in South Africa from 1982 to 1987, or to the subsidiary's leaving, and included the subsidiary's operating profits in South Africa divided by its identifiable assets in South Africa.

Measurement:

Data on operating profits and assets were gathered at the level of the South African subsidiary.

Primary Sources of Data and Checks:

Annual directories on *US and Canadian Investment in South Africa* from the Investor Responsibility Research Center provided information on the subsidiary's identifiable assets and Compustat's *Geographic Segment File* had information on the multinational's operating profits in South Africa.

A cross-section of the sample was checked against data from multinationals' annual reports available at the United Nations Center for Transnational Corporations. When two data sources disagreed on the subsidiary's profits, data for selective years were obtained from investment houses including Trinity (1981 to 1982), Wilshire (1981 to 1984), Capital Management Sciences (1981) and Daniels and Bells (1981).

Subsidiary's Importance in Global Operations (ASSETS, SALES and EMPLOYEES)

ASSETS, SALES and EMPLOYEES gauged the South African subsidiary's relative importance in the multinational's global operations from 1982 to 1987 or to the multinational's leaving. ASSETS included the subsidiary's identifiable assets in South Africa divided by the multinational's global assets; SALES included the subsidiary's net sales in South Africa divided by the multinational's net global sales; and, EMPLOYEES included the subsidiary's full-time employees in South Africa divided by the multinational's global employees.

Measurement:

Data for the measures of relative importance in global operations were gathered at the levels of the South African subsidiary and also across all the multinational's global operations.

Primary Sources of Data and Checks:

Annual directories on *US and Canadian Investment in South Africa* from the Investor Responsibility Research Center provided information on the subsidiary's sales, assets and employees; *Compustat Annual Industrial File* had information on the multinational's global sales, assets and employees.

A cross-section of the sample was checked against data from multinationals' annual reports available at the United Nations Center for Transnational Corporations. When two data sources disagreed, data for selective years were obtained from investment houses including Trinity (1981 to 1982), Wilshire (1981 to 1984), Capital Management Sciences (1981) and Daniels and Bells (1981).

Subsidiary's Noncompetitive Strategies with Host State (CONTRACT and COOPT)

CONTRACT and COOPT measured the subsidiary's explicit or tacit agreements with South African governmental agencies made annually from 1982 to 1987, or to the subsidiary's leaving. CONTRACT gauged contracting and was measured by the proportion of the subsidiary's sales to South African governmental agencies. COOPT gauged co-opting and was measured by the number of South African governmental agencies on which the subsidiary was represented.

Measurement:

These variables were measured at the level of the South African subsidiary. The variables measured the subsidiary's contracting and co-opting strategies with all 11 apartheid-enforcing agencies and all 13 parastatal institutions (businesses established with public funds and controlled either wholly or partly by the South African government) as identified by the Investor Responsibility Research Center. Data were collected from the South African Departments of Community Development, Constitutional Development and Planning, Development Aid, Education and Training, Foreign Affairs and Information, Home Affairs, Justice, Law and Order and National Security; the South African Defence Force and Railways Police; the Atomic Energy Corporation; the Development Bank of South Africa; the Council for Scientific and Industrial Research; the Electricity Supply Commission; the Industrial Development Corporation; the Iron and Steel Corporation; the Small Business Development Corporation; the South African Armaments Corporation; the South African Broadcasting Corporation; the South African Coal, Oil and Gas Corporation; the South African Land Bank; the South African Transport Services; and the Southern Oil Exploration Corporation.

Subsidiaries rarely released information on their boards of directors. Additionally, most subsidiaries of US multinationals were not listed on the Johannesburg Stock Exchange and, information on their boards of directors proved difficult to obtain from public sources. However, the South African governmental agencies were listed on the Johannesburg Stock Exchange. To establish interlocking directorates between subsidiaries and South African governmental agencies, a round-about method was followed. First, the governmental agencies' boards of directors were identified. Second, the directors' job affiliations were traced to reveal the number of subsidiary boards on which the directors sat.

Primary Sources of Data and Checks:

Sales and purchase statistics were obtained through the Investor Responsibility Research Center's *Summary of US Sales to the South African Public Sector.* Boards of directors of South African state organizations were identified in

McGregor's *Who owns Whom* (Johannesburg, South Africa). Multinationals' sales to South African governmental agencies were also provided in Compustat's *Business Information Segments*. Some multinationals' boards of directors could also be identified through the *Johannesburg Stock Exchange's Handbook*.

As a secondary check, the directors' professional affiliations were also verified in Argus' *Who's Who of Southern Africa*. Additionally, a sub-sample of the multinationals were cross-checked against annual reports held at the United Nations Center for Transnational Corporations. When two sources of data disagreed, the South African Economic Counsel provided arbitrating information.

Suppression of Voice and Exit Actions by Host State (SUPPRESS)

SUPPRESS was a dichotomous variable measuring legislation initiated by the South African government to suppress political and social protests (Voice) and withdrawals (Exit) by the subsidiary from 1982 to 1987, or to the subsidiary's leaving. It included legislation demanding the subsidiary's financial support for the South African state; legislation restricting the information that the subsidiary could release to its stakeholders; legislation forcing the subsidiary to sell to the South African government; and the National Key Points Act.

Measurement:

The variable was measured at the level of the South African subsidiary. Some legislation applied to specific multinationals (such as Mobil); other legislation applied to entire industries or to all US multinationals. The coding scheme used binary indicators to reveal if the legislative acts applied to the subsidiary (yes: 1; no: 0).

Host State's Suppression of Voice and Exit Actions included a range of legislation. First, some South African legislation demanded the subsidiary's financial commitment to the South African state and institutions through restrictions on foreign banks' liquid assets; legislation which stipulated that banks invested in South African debt instruments and other prescribed investments in governmental agencies; and the South African Insurance Act which specified that 53 percent of foreign insurance companies' net liabilities remained in South African prescribed investments. Second, some South African legislation restricted the amounts of information that a subsidiary could release to stakeholders through the Petroleum Products Act and the Protection of Business Act. Third, some South African legislation suppressed the subsidiary's leaving and these actions varied across and within industries. For example, South African legislation could force a subsidiary into sustained contractual agreements with the South African government in cases of national emergency through legislation such as the Nuclear Energy Act; the Defense Act; the National Supplies Procurement Act; the Armament Development and Production Act; and the Price Control Act. The South African government could also take possession of the subsidiary if it perceived a threat to national security, and the National Key Points Act granted the government permission to occupy the premises of a subsidiary in a strategic industry or area.

Primary Sources of Data and Checks:

South African legislation as it applied to US multinationals and their subsidiaries was listed in the Investor Responsibility Research Center's, *US Companies and Support for the South African Government: The Legal Requirements.*

For a secondary check, governmental actions were listed in United Nation's public hearings regarding multinationals in South Africa (UNCTC, *Transnational Corporations in South Africa and Namibia: Policy Instruments and Statement*, Vol. IV, 1987.) When the two sources disagreed, the South African Economic Consulate provided arbitrating information.

Subsidiary's Inducements to Host State (INDUCE3)

INDUCE3 gauged inducements that the subsidiary offered the South African government from 1982 to 1987, or to the subsidiary's leaving, through taxes paid to the South African government.

Measurement:

The variable measured dollar amounts of taxes paid in South Africa at the subsidiary level.

Primary Sources of Data and Checks:

Price Waterhouse's *Doing Business in South Africa* provided tax rates and tax formulae for multinationals in South Africa, which were used to derive taxes paid by the subsidiary. Compustat's *Geographic Segments* provided data on taxes paid by multinationals in South Africa across all subsidiaries.

A subsection of the multinationals' taxes were checked against annual reports from the United Nations Center for Transnational Corporations. When two sources of data disagreed greatly, multinationals' 10-K reports filed with the Securities and Exchange Commission provided some arbitrating information with subsidiary-level data.

Summary

This chapter has defined the main variables in the study on multinationals, indicated how they were measured as well as how problems were resolved and the sources for the data. Table 7.4 has defined the variables and identified the sources of data. The next chapter covers the analyses and results that indicate how multinationals left South Africa.

8. Analyses and Results

This chapter presents tests and results of the hypotheses covered in Chapter 6. The first section outlines the analytical techniques. The next section covers the results that were generated. The final section discusses the generalizability of the results.

The Analyses

The analyses mainly examined headquarters' actions to maintain the subsidiary's presence in South Africa (PRESENCE) for four years from 1984 to 1987. As explained in Chapter 7, the independent variables were lagged for one year in all the analyses. For each multinational, data were collected at the level of the individual subsidiary in South Africa and at headquarters for the multinational across global operations. As most of the data were at the level of the individual subsidiary in South Africa, the analyses were conducted at that level.

Analyses of Variance were conducted across all seven levels of PRESENCE. Correlations, *t*-tests and logistic regression analyses were conducted at the binary level of PRESENCE (*Left* or *Stayed* in South Africa as described in Chapter 7). The *t*-tests used all the available observations for the two variables involved; correlations and logistic regression analyses used smaller sets of observations, with no missing observations for any of the variables involved. Separate variance estimates were used for the *t*-tests when the F-test emerged significant; when the F-test proved nonsignificant, pooled variance estimates were used.

The study used logistic regression as the primary analytical technique to assess the effects of the independent variables on the binary dependent variable, headquarters' actions to maintain the subsidiary's presence in South Africa. When dependent variables can have only two values (as in PRESENCE which included Left or Stayed in South Africa), the assumptions necessary for hypotheses testing in regression analysis are necessarily violated. For example, one cannot assume normal distribution of errors. Also, in linear regression, predicted values need not fall in the interval between 0 and 1 and therefore, cannot be interpreted as probabilities. However, in logistic regression, one can directly estimate the probability of an event occurring.

For the case of a single independent variable, one can use the logistic regression model to argue:

$$\text{Probability (event)} = \frac{1}{1+e^{-(B_0+B_1X)}}$$

where B_0 and B_1 represent coefficients estimated from the data, X represents the independent variable, and e constitutes the base of the natural logarithm, approximately 2.718.

For more than one independent variable, one can use the model to argue:

$$\text{Probability (event)} = \frac{1}{1+e^{-z}}$$

where Z consists of the linear combination, $Z = B_0 + B_1X_1 + B_2X_2 + \cdots + B_pX_p$.

While the coefficients of a linear regression model are estimated using the least-squares method, the parameters of the logistic regression model are estimated using the maximum-likelihood method, i.e., the coefficients making the observed results "most likely" are selected. The logistic coefficients can be interpreted as changes in the log odds associated with one-unit changes in the independent variables. Since the logistic regression model is nonlinear, an iterative algorithm is used for parameter estimation.

The Analytical Models

Sets of independent variables were analyzed together to guard against high multicolinearity and the correlation matrices revealed none for the variables in the models. The sets of variables were chosen to capture natural linkages in the theory of multinationals as chameleons. The residuals revealed no blatant violations of the regression assumptions. The adequacy of the resulting models was tested through a variety of diagnostic methods. The deviances were small indicating that the models did fit the cases well and the deviances were also approximately normally distributed. Cook's Distance and DFBETA identified the influence of individual cases and located outliers. Leverage scores were generated to detect observations that had large impact on the predicted values. No cases were deleted from the analyses.

For reasons provided in Chapter 7, analyses in the period of *No regulation* examined changes in PRESENCE in either 1984 or 1985 as a single, combined, cross-section. Pooled, cross-section analyses were used to analyze the multinationals under *Regulation* in 1986 and 1987 because although regulation distinguished the two cross-sections from each other, no formal hypotheses distinguished the two. The number of observations for the analyses also increased through pooling.

The data for the period under regulation neatly fit the assumptions underlying neither time-series nor panel analyses (Markus, 1986; Sayrs, 1989). In time-series analyses, one observes single entities (such as corporations) at relatively large numbers of time points; conversely, in panel analyses, one observes many entities at relatively few time points, almost always four or less (Markus, 1986). In this study, the period under regulation comprised two cross-sections of one year each. Also, in time-series analyses, time forms the unit of analysis (Ostrom, 1978), while in panel analyses, individual units (such as corporations) form the basis of analysis. This study's methodology bestowed importance both on time as an indicator of regulation, and on the individual subsidiaries. Appropriately, the analyses used the rich conventions of event-history analyses that draw on both time-series and panel analyses (Allison, 1984).

In pooled cross-section analyses, several opportunities arise for violating linear and logistic regression assumptions such as equality of variance and independence of error. The pools create opportunities for error to be contaminated from correlations between time points within one cross-section, from correlations in the errors from different cross-sections and different time points, or from correlations in the errors from different cross-sections and the same time points (Sayrs, 1989). A natural way to proceed then is to characterize the relationship between the right-hand side variables and the errors in pooled cross-sections. Generally, four types of models are used: Constant-coefficient models, least-square dummy-variable (LSDV) models, error-component models (like GLS), and structural-equation models. LSDV models recognize nonconstant, heteroscedastic variation by fixing the errors in dummy variables. The models capture variations unique to the cross sections in intercepts that vary from cross-section to cross-section. Judge *et al.* (1985) recommended fixed-effect approaches, such as LSDV, when the dummies and the explanatory variables might be correlated. LSDV is also widely used in event-history analyses (e.g., Allison, 1984:20). Consequently, it was earmarked as a preferred method to deal with detected heteroscedasticity.

The residuals in the period of regulation were examined to discriminate between the effects of the cross-sections, the effects of time and the effects of other random factors. The Studentized residuals were plotted against the predicted values. The variances in the residuals were not constant and revealed graphic evidence of heteroscedasticity. The residuals were also plotted against sequence numbers, revealing no discernible pattern. The LSDV model in this study used intercepts to capture the effects unique to the cross-sections and those that might be unique to time. Some time periods can systematically influence the error terms, just as some cross-sections can. The intercepts characterized the variances that attempted to minimize the biases in the true explanations. The intercepts thus embodied what Maddala (1977) called "specific ignorance" in contrast to our general ignorance that the error terms captured.

A new categorical variable called *Time* was created to distinguish the regulatory environments facing the multinationals in 1986 and in 1987. With this coding scheme, the logistic regression coefficients indicated how much better or worse each category was compared to the average effect of all the categories. The coefficients for the new categorical variables represented the differences from the average effect of all categories. For the analyses, the coefficients for the new variable, *Time*, represented the effects of the regulatory environment in 1986 to the average effect of the regulatory environments in both 1986 and 1987. Deviation coefficients were used to code Time and 1986 = 1. The value of the coefficient for 1987 was not displayed but it is the negative of the coefficient for 1986, i.e., 1987 = −1. Consequently, the pool permitted treating the unique effects of time as if time were a surrogate for systematic effects observed in time.

Some terms in the model represented multiplicative products of single terms. For example, the relationship between headquarters' inducements to stakeholders with Voice and Exit actions of headquarters' stakeholders was depicted as an interaction term. The next section highlights this study's main results.

The Results

Table 8.1 summarizes the hypotheses regarding multinationals as chameleons that were tested and indicates whether they were accepted. Figure 8.1 specifically indicates which variables significantly affected whether subsidiaries left or stayed in South Africa. Generally, studies do not reveal the analyses behind hypotheses that were not accepted. Yet, theoretically interesting relationships almost always emerge from rejecting previous theories and hypotheses (Davis, 1971). The exploratory nature of this study justified the reporting of some significant, though unexpected results. In this book, in the interests of cogency and relevance, only the analyses associated with statistically significant relationships are discussed. To aid readability, results discussing why multinationals left or stayed in South Africa lead in each sub-section, followed by highlights of other significant relationships in the theory of multinationals as chameleons. Interested readers may consult Haley (1990b) for earlier analyses of the data, including non-significant relationships. This section covers the significant findings in this study.

Table 8.1 Relationships tested in study on multinational corporations in South Africa.

Independent Variable (Lagged)	Direction of Relationship	Dependent Variable	Hypothesized Relationship	
			No Reg	Reg
HQ's Inducements to Stakeholders				
H1: Induce 1 & Induce 2	+	Presence		
Voice & Exit Actions of HQ's Stakeholders				
H2: Voice & Exit Actions	−	Presence	No^	
H3: Interaction of Induce 2 & Voice, Exit Actions	+	Presence		No**
H4: Voice Actions	+	Exit Actions	Yes**	Yes**
Dominant Coalition's Stability				
H5: Voice & Exit Actions	−	Dominant Coalition's Stability	Yes^/No^	No*
H6: Dominant Coalition's Stability	+	Presence		
H7: Dominant Coalition's Stability	+	Managerial Benefits		
Multinational's Competitive Strategies				
H8a: Advertising	+	Managerial Benefits		
H8b: R&D	+	Managerial Benefits		
H8c: Order Backlogs	−	Managerial Benefits		Yes^
H8d: Vertical Integration	+	Managerial Benefits	No**	
H8e: Product Diversification	−	Managerial Benefits		
H9a: Advertising	+	Presence		Yes*
H9b: R&D	+	Presence		
H9c: Order Backlogs	−	Presence	Yes^	
H9d: Vertical Integration	+	Presence		
H9e: Product Diversification	−	Presence		Yes^

Table 8.1 *(Continued)*

Independent Variable (Lagged)	Direction of Relationship	Dependent Variable	Hypothesized Relationship	
			No Reg	Reg
Subsidiary's Symbolic Actions				
H10: Symbolic Actions	+	Presence	Yes**	
H11: Interactions of Induce 1, Induce 2 & Symbolic Actions	+	Presence		
Subsidiary's Profits & Importance in Global Operations				
H12a: Subsidiary's Profits	+	Presence	Yes**	
H12b: Subsidiary's Assets, Sales, Employees	+	Presence		No^
Subsidiary's Noncompetitive Strategies with Host State				
H13: Contracting & Co-opting	–	Symbolic Actions	No**	
H14: Contracting & Co-opting	+	Subsidiary's ROA		No**
H15: Contracting & Co-opting	+	Presence		
Suppression of Subsidiary's Voice & Exit Actions by Host State				
H16: Suppression of Voice & Exit Actions	–	Symbolic Actions	No*	
H17: Suppression of Voice & Exit Actions	–	Subsidiary's ROA		No*
H18: Contracting & Co-opting	–	Suppression of Voice & Exit Actions	No^	
H19: Suppression of Voice & Exit Actions	–	Presence		No**
Subsidiary's Inducements to Host State				
H20: Induce3	+	Symbolic Actions		
H21: Induce3	–	Suppression of Voice & Exit Actions		

** = Sig. at ≤ .05 level   * = Sig. at ≤ .10 level   ^ = Sig. at ≤ .15 level

Figure 8.1   Main effects on subsidiary's presence in South Africa.

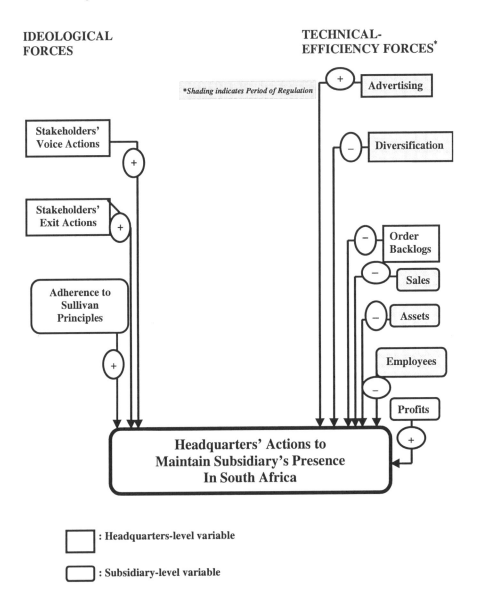

Voice and Exit Actions of Headquarters' Stakeholders

Links to Headquarters' Actions on Subsidiary's Presence:

Analysis of Variance, as indicated in Table 8.2, showed that in the period of no regulation, SD (stockholders' divestitures), differed significantly across the seven levels of PRESENCE. Descriptive statistics revealed that in the period of no regulation the multinationals that sold their subsidiaries to other US companies (Mean = 1.00, N = 1) and to local managers (Mean = .43, Standard Deviation = .53, N = 7), encountered the most number of stockholders' divestitures; the multinationals that invested more in South Africa (N = 2), encountered no stockholders' divestitures.

PRESENCE was collapsed into two categories, Left or Stayed in South Africa, for subsequent *t*-test, correlation and logistic regression analyses. *T*-tests in Table 8.3 showed that in the period of no regulation, multinationals that stayed in South Africa encountered more stockholders' resolutions, less stockholders' divestitures and less legislation on divestitures than those that left.

Correlation matrices showed that GP (legislation on purchasing and an indicator of Voice actions) and GD (legislation on divestitures and an indicator of Exit actions) correlated positively in both periods of regulation (Correlation = .26, 1-tailed Significance = −.001, N = 177) and no regulation

Table 8.2   Analysis of Variance for SD (stockholders' divestitures) by levels of PRESENCE.[1]

SD in period of NO REGULATION (1984 & 1985)					
Source	Sum of Squares	D.F.	Mean Square	F	Sig.
Between Groups	1.46	5	.29	2.50	.03
Within Groups	32.15	276	.12		
Eta = .21 Eta Squared = .04					

[1] Criterion variables in this model included SYMBOL, INDUCE1, INDUCE2, SR, SD, GD and GP. In the interests of cogency, only significant relationships are reported in this book; please consult Haley (1990b) for reports of nonsignificant results as well.

Table 8.3   *T*-tests for SR (stockholders' resolutions), SD (stockholders' divestitures) and GD (legislation on divestitures) by Left or Stayed in South Africa.

SR in period of NO REGULATION (1984 & 1985)				
	N	Mean	S.D.	S.E.
Left	44	.02	.15	.02
Stayed	238	.08	.28	.02

$F = 3.40$ 2-Tail Probability = .00
$t = -2.11$ D.F. = 106.44   2-Tail Probability = .04 (separate variance)

SD in period of NO REGULATION (1984 & 1985)				
	N	Mean	S.D.	S.E.
Left	44	.23	.42	.06
Stayed	238	.12	.33	.02

$F = 1.67$ 2-Tail Probability = .02
$t = -1.57$ D.F. = 52.91   2-Tail Probability = .12 (separate variance)

GD in period of NO REGULATION (1984 & 1985)				
	N	Mean	S.D.	S.E.
Left	44	.59	.50	.08
Stayed	238	.45	.50	.03

$F = 1.01$ 2-Tail Probability = 1.00
$t = -1.68$ D.F. = 280   2-Tail Probability = .10 (pooled variance)

(Correlation = .52, 1-tailed Significance = .001, N = 200) providing some support for hypothesis 4. Stockholders' Voice and Exit actions did not correlate significantly in either period.

As explained in the previous section, a set of independent variables was analyzed together to guard against high multicolinearity. Table 8.4 indicates the results of a logistic regression model in the period of no regulation through which hypothesis 2 was weakly disconfirmed. The greater the stockholders' resolutions, the more likely the subsidiary was to stay in South Africa.

Table 8.4 Logistic regression model for HQ's inducements to stakeholders, actions of HQ's stakeholders and subsidiary's symbolic actions on Left or Stayed in South Africa in period of no regulation.

Function:	Logistic
Dependent Variable:	Left or Stayed in 1984 & 1985
Number of cases:	177

Dependent Variable Encoding:

Original Value	*Label*
0	Left South Africa
1	Stayed in South Africa

−2 Log Likelihood   151.19

Estimation terminated at iteration number 5

	Chi-Square	df	Significance
Model Chi-Square	24.96	13	.02

	Variables in the Equation							
	Variable	B	*S.E.*	*Wald*	*df*	*Sig*	R	*Exp(B)*
H1:	INDUCEI	−0.03	0.18	0.03	1	0.86	0.00	0.97
	INDUCE2	−0.19	0.38	0.24	1	0.62	0.00	0.83
H2:	**SR**	**1.77**	**1.19**	**2.22**	**1**	**0.14**	**0.04**	**5.86**
	SD	−0.74	0.56	1.70	1	0.19	0.00	0.48
	GP	−1.01	0.85	1.39	1	0.24	0.00	0.37
	GD	−0.63	0.50	1.58	1	0.21	0.00	0.53
H3:	INDUCE2 by SR	0.16	1.26	0.02	1	0.90	0.00	1.18
	INDUCE2 by SD	0.02	0.71	0.00	1	0.97	0.00	1.02
	INDUCE2 by GP	−1.43	1.35	1.12	1	0.29	0.00	0.24
	INDUCE2 by GD	0.36	0.50	0.52	1	0.47	0.00	1.43
H10:	**SYMBOL**	**0.29**	**0.12**	**6.23**	**1**	**0.01**	**0.17**	**1.33**
H11:	INDUCEl by SYMBOL	0.01	0.12	0.01	1	0.90	0.00	1.01
	INDUCE2 by SYMBOL	0.18	0.13	1.81	1	0.18	0.00	1.20
	Constant	1.45	0.44	11.04	1	0.00		

Table 8.5   Logistic regression model for HQ's inducements to stakeholders, actions of HQ's stakeholders and subsidiary's symbolic actions on Left or Stayed in South Africa in period of regulation.

Function:	Logistic
Dependent Variable:	Left or Stayed in 1986 & 1987
Number of cases:	200

Dependent Variable Encoding:

Original Value	*Label*
0	Left South Africa
1	Stayed in South Africa

	Year	*Freq*	*Deviation Coefficients*
TIME			(1)
SA Regulation	1986	88	1.000
US Regulation	1987	112	−1.000

−2 Log Likelihood   213.27
Estimation terminated at iteration number 4

	Chi-Square	df	Significance
Model Chi-Square	16.00	14	.31

							Variables in the Equation		
	Variable	B	*S.E.*	*Wald*	*df*	*Sig*	R	*Exp(B)*
H1:	INDUCEI	0.61	0.43	2.02	1	0.16	0.01	1.85
	INDUCE2	0.74	0.57	1.66	1	0.20	0.00	2.10
H2:	SR	−0.37	0.41	0.82	1	0.37	0.00	0.69
	SD	0.57	0.83	0.48	1	0.49	0.00	1.77
	GP	−0.10	0.50	0.04	1	0.84	0.00	0.90
	GD	0.31	0.52	0.36	1	0.55	0.00	1.37
H3:	INDUCE2 by SR	0.20	0.32	0.42	1	0.52	0.00	1.23
	INDUCE2 by SD	1.15	1.05	1.21	1	0.27	0.00	3.17
	INDUCE2 by GP	0.25	0.24	1.10	1	0.30	0.00	1.29
	INDUCE2 by GD	**−1.19**	**0.50**	**5.69**	**1**	**0.02**	**−0.13**	**0.30**
H10:	SYMBOL	−0.02	0.06	0.10	1	0.75	0.00	0.98
H11:	INDUCEl by SYMBOL	−0.06	0.08	0.46	1	0.50	0.00	0.95
	INDUCE2 by SYMBOL	0.01	0.04	0.05	1	0.83	0.00	1.01
	TIME (1986)	0.38	0.22	3.04	1	0.08	0.07	1.46
	Constant	1.53	0.51	9.02	1	0.00		

Table 8.5 indicates the results of a logistic regression model in the period of regulation. Again, no evidence of multicolinearity existed among the independent variables. The overall model was not significant, however, hypothesis 3 was disconfirmed. In the period of regulation, the greater the multinational's inducements to the US government, the more likely that the government's exit actions appeared to influence the multinational's leaving South Africa. Significant differences existed across time and overall, multinationals seemed more likely to stay in South Africa in 1986 than in 1987.

Dominant Coalition's Stability

Links to Headquarters' Actions on Subsidiary's Presence:

Analysis of Variance, as indicated in Table 8.6, showed that in the period of regulation, TMT (the dominant coalition's stability) varied significantly across all seven levels of PRESENCE. Descriptive statistics showed no clear pattern as multinationals that invested more (Mean = 0.00, Standard Deviation = 0.00, N = 2), formed trusts (Mean = 0.00, Standard Deviation = 0.00, N = 2) or sold to local managers (Mean = 0.00, Standard Deviation = 0.00, N = 100) experienced the greatest change in dominant coalitions, whereas multinationals that sold their South African subsidiaries to other US

Table 8.6   Analysis of Variance for TMT by levels of PRESENCE.[1]

TMT in period of REGULATION (1986 & 1987)					
Source	Sum of Squares	D.F.	Mean Square	F	Sig.
Between Groups	2.75	6	.46	2.49	.02
Within Groups	35.11	191	.18		
Eta = .27 Eta Squared = .07					

[1] Criterion variables in this model included TMT, SUPPRESS, CONTRACT and COOPT. In the interests of cogency, only significant relationships are reported in this book; please consult Haley (1990b) for reports of nonsignificant results as well.

Table 8.7 *T*-test for TMT by Left or Stayed in South Africa.

TMT in period of NO REGULATION (1984 & 1985)				
	N	Mean	S.D.	S.E.
Left	21	.52	.51	.11
Stayed	139	.68	.47	.04
$F = 1.20$ 2-Tail Probability = .52				
$t = -1.44$ D.F. = 158 2-Tail Probability = .15 (pooled variance)				

companies (Mean = 1.00, Standard Deviation = 0.00, N = 3) had the most stable dominant coalitions.

PRESENCE was collapsed into two categories, Left or Stayed in South Africa, for subsequent *t*-test, correlation and logistic regression analyses. Table 8.7 shows the results of a *t*-test in the period of no regulation, providing some support for hypothesis 6. In the period of no regulation, multinationals that stayed in South Africa had more stable dominant coalitions than those that left. However, this hypothesis was not supported by subsequent logistic regression analyses.

Links to Voice and Exit Actions of Headquarters' Stakeholders:

The correlation matrices for the period of regulation showed that SD (stockholders' divestitures) correlated positively with TMT (Correlation = .18, 1-tailed Significance = .01, N = 195), contrary to hypothesis 5. Table 8.8 indicates the results of a logistic regression model used to test hypothesis 5 in the period of no regulation. The weakly significant model provided mixed results for hypothesis 5. As hypothesized, GP (legislation on purchasing) had a negative effect on the dominant coalition's stability, but SR (stockholders' resolutions) and GD (legislation on divestitures) had small positive effects. In the period of no regulation, the greater the stockholders' resolutions and the greater the legislation on divestitures, the more likely that the dominant coalition remained the same. However, the greater the legislation

Table 8.8   Logistic regression model for stakeholders' Voice and Exit actions on the dominant coalition's stability in period of no regulation.

Function:	Logistic							
Dependent Variable:	TMT in 1984 & 1985							
Number of cases:	158							

Dependent Variable Encoding:

Original Value	*Label*
0	Change in Dominant Coalition
1	Stability in Dominant Coalition

−2 Log Likelihood   219.01
Estimation terminated at iteration number 2

	Chi-Square	df	Significance
Model Chi-Square	6.73	4	.15

	Variables in the Equation							
	Variable	B	*S.E.*	*Wald*	*df*	*Sig*	R	*Exp(B)*
H5:	**SR**	**0.84**	**0.54**	**2.43**	**1**	**0.12**	**0.04**	**2.32**
	SD	0.11	0.43	0.07	1	0.80	0.00	1.12
	GD	**0.55**	**0.34**	**2.56**	**1**	**0.11**	**0.05**	**1.73**
	GP	**−1.13**	**0.77**	**2.14**	**1**	**0.14**	**−0.03**	**0.32**
	Constant	−0.33	0.23	2.05	1	0.15		

on government purchasing, the more likely that the dominant coalition changed.

Table 8.9 indicates the results of a logistic regression model used to test hypothesis 5 in the period of regulation. The overall model is significant but hypothesis 5 is again partially disconfirmed as SD (stockholders' divestitures) had a positive effect on TMT. In the period of regulation, the greater the stockholders' divestitures, the more likely that the dominant coalition remained the same. Significant differences existed across time and the dominant coalition appeared more stable in 1987 with increased US legislation aimed at multinationals' South African operations.

Table 8.9 Logistic regression model for stakeholders' Voice and Exit actions on dominant coalition's stability in period of regulation.

Function:	Logistic
Dependent Variable:	TMT in 1986 & 1987
Number of cases:	195

Dependent Variable Encoding:

Original Value	Label
0	Change in Dominant Coalition
1	Stability in Dominant Coalition

	Year	Freq	Deviation Coefficients
TIME			(1)
SA Regulation	1986	89	1.000
US Regulation	1987	106	−1.000

−2 Log Likelihood 235.64
Estimation terminated at iteration number 3

	Chi-Square	df	Significance
Model Chi-Square	11.69	5	.04

Variables in the Equation							
Variable	B	S.E.	Wald	df	Sig	R	Exp(B)
H5: SR	−0.03	0.35	0.01	1	0.93	0.00	0.97
SD	**1.05**	**0.59**	**3.20**	**1**	**0.07**	**0.07**	**2.86**
GD	−0.36	0.45	0.64	1	0.43	0.00	0.70
GP	0.26	0.43	0.36	1	0.55	0.00	1.30
TIME (1986)	−0.44	0.19	5.51	1	0.02	−0.12	0.64
Constant	−0.90	0.30	8.84	1	0.00		

Multinational's Competitive Strategies

Links to Headquarters' Actions on Subsidiary's Presence:

Analyses of Variance highlighted in Table 8.10 showed that in the period of regulation, INTEGRATION (vertical integration), and DIVERSIFICATION

Table 8.10   Analyses of Variance for INTEGRATION and DIVERSIFICATION by levels of PRESENCE.[1]

INTEGRATION in period of REGULATION (1986 & 1987)					
Source	Sum of Squares	D.F.	Mean Square	F	Sig.
Between Groups	3.58	6	.60	4.00	.00
Within Groups	33.18	222	.15		
Eta = .31 Eta Squared = .10					
DIVERSIFICATION in period of REGULATION (1986 & 1987)					
Source	Sum of Squares	D.F.	Mean Square	F	Sig.
Between Groups	33.89	6	5.65	1.84	.09
Within Groups	680.52	222	3.07		
Eta = .22 Eta Squared = .05					

[1] Criterion variables in this model included ADVERTISING, RESEARCH, BACKLOGS, INTEGRATION and DIVERSIFICATION. In the interests of cogency, only significant relationships are reported in this book; please consult Haley (1990b) for reports of nonsignificant results as well.

(product diversification) differed significantly across the seven levels of PRESENCE. Descriptive statistics revealed that in the period of regulation, multinationals that sold their South African subsidiaries to their local managers were the most vertically integrated (Mean = .57, Standard Deviation = .51, N = 14) and those that grew through retained earnings were the least vertically integrated (Mean = .14, Standard Deviation = .35, N = 170). Descriptive statistics also showed that in the period of regulation, multinationals that invested more in their South African subsidiaries were the most diversified (Mean = 5.00, Standard Deviation = 4.24, N = 2) and those that sold their subsidiaries to other US companies were the least diversified (Mean = 1.67, Standard Deviation = .58, N = 3). No significant differences emerged across the seven levels of PRESENCE in the period of no regulation.

PRESENCE was collapsed into two categories, Left or Stayed in South Africa, for subsequent *t*-test, correlation and logistic regression analyses. *T*-tests in Table 8.11 revealed that multinationals that stayed in South Africa

Table 8.11 *T*-tests for ADVERTISING, RESEARCH, INTEGRATION and DIVERSIFICATION by Left or Stayed in South Africa.

ADVERTISING in period of NO REGULATION (1984 & 1985)				
	N	Mean	S.D.	S.E.
Left	15	.02	.02	.00
Stayed	89	.06	.13	.01

$F = 52.85$ 2-Tail Probability = .00
$t = -2.51$ D.F.=100.88 2-Tail Probability = .01 (separate variance)

ADVERTISING in period of REGULATION (1986 & 1987)				
	N	Mean	S.D.	S.E.
Left	31	.04	.04	.01
Stayed	97	.07	.10	.01

$F = 6.55$ 2-Tail Probability = .00
$t = -1.64$ D.F. = 121.15 2-Tail Probability = .11 (separate variance)

RESEARCH in period of REGULATION (1986 & 1987)				
	N	Mean	S.D.	S.E.
Left	41	.03	.03	.00
Stayed	134	.05	.03	.00

$F = 1.80$ 2-Tail Probability = .03
$t = -3.04$ D.F. = 88.18 2-Tail Probability = .00 (separate variance)

INTEGRATION in period of REGULATION (1986 & 1987)				
	N	Mean	S.D.	S.E.
Left	57	.37	.49	.06
Stayed	172	.15	.35	.03

$F = 1.90$ 2-Tail Probability = .00
$t = -3.19$ D.F. = 76.53 2-Tail Probability = .00 (separate variance)

DIVERSIFICATION in period of REGULATION (1986 & 1987)				
	N	Mean	S.D.	S.E.
Left	57	2.96	1.83	.24
Stayed	172	2.49	1.74	.13

$F = 1.11$ 2-Tail Probability = .60
$t = -1.75$ D.F. = 227 2-Tail Probability = .08 (pooled variance)

engaged in significantly more advertising than those that left in the periods of no regulation and regulation. In the period of regulation, multinationals that stayed also did more R&D, were less vertically integrated and less diversified than those that left.

The correlation matrix revealed some support for the hypotheses. BACKLOGS (order backlogs) correlated negatively with PRESENCE (Correlation = −.51, 1-tailed Significance = .001, N = 36) in the period of no regulation as hypothesis 9c proposed. Generally, the greater the order backlogs, the more likely that the multinational maintained a lower presence

Table 8.12 Logistic regression model for multinational's competitive strategies on Left or Stayed in South Africa in period of no regulation.

Function:	Logistic
Dependent Variable:	Left or Stayed in 1984 &1985
Number of cases:	36

Dependent Variable Encoding:

Original Value	*Label*
0	Left South Africa
1	Stayed in South Africa

−2 Log Likelihood 32.44
Estimation terminated at iteration number 6

	Chi-Square	df	Significance
Model Chi-Square	8.01	5	.16

	Variables in the Equation							
	Variable	B	*S.E.*	*Wald*	*df*	*Sig*	R	*Exp(B)*
H9a:	ADVERTISING	3.74	16.78	0.05	1	0.82	0.00	41.93
H9b:	RESEARCH	−15.66	18.59	0.71	1	0.40	0.00	0.00
H9c:	**BACKLOGS**	**−4.32**	**2.92**	**2.20**	**1**	**0.14**	**−0.08**	**0.01**
H9d:	INTEGRATION	1.40	1.82	0.59	1	0.44	0.00	4.04
H9e:	DIVERSIFICATION	−0.10	0.33	0.10	1	0.75	0.00	0.90
	Constant	3.42	1.43	5.72	1	0.02		

in South Africa. In the period of regulation, as hypothesis 9e proposed, DIVERSIFICATION correlated negatively with PRESENCE (Correlation = −.57, 1-tailed Significance = .001, N = 35); yet, contrary to hypothesis 9d, INTEGRATION also did (Correlation = −.40, 1-tailed Significance = .01, N = 35). Generally, in the period of regulation, less vertically integrated and less diversified multinationals seemed more likely to stay in South Africa. Other researchers have noticed the high correlation between vertical integration and product diversity (e.g., Khandwalla, 1981) and in this study, INTEGRATION and DIVERSIFICATION were highly correlated in the period of no regulation (Correlation = .60, 1-tailed Significance = .001, N = 36) as well as regulation (Correlation = .73, 1-tailed Significance = .001, N = 35). However, as the correlations were less than .8 it was assumed that high multicolinearity did not exist (Lewis-Beck, 1980) and all the variables dealing with the multinational's competitive strategies were introduced into the two logistic equations.

Table 8.12 indicates the results of a logistic regression model used to test the hypotheses in the period of no regulation. The overall model was not significant but hypothesis 9c was weakly supported. In the period of no regulation, the greater the order backlogs, the less likely that the multinational stayed in South Africa. Table 8.13 indicates the results of the logistic regression model in the period of regulation. The overall model was significant and hypotheses 9a and 9e were supported, the latter weakly. In the period of regulation, the greater the multinational's advertising and the less its product diversification, the more likely that the multinational stayed in South Africa.

Links to Dominant Coalition's Benefits:

A correlation matrix for the period of no regulation revealed that contrary to hypothesis 8a, ADVERTISING (advertising expenditures) correlated negatively with BENEFITS or managerial benefits (Correlation = −.82, 1-tailed Significance = .01, N = 8). As DIVERSIFICATION correlated very highly with BACKLOGS in the period of no regulation (Correlation = .83, 1-tailed Significance = .01, N = 8) and with INTEGRATION in the period of regulation (Correlation = .80. 1-tailed Significance = .001, N = 15), it was dropped from the linear regression models.

Table 8.13 Logistic regression model for multinational's competitive strategies on Left or Stayed in South Africa in period of regulation.

Function:	Logistic
Dependent Variable:	Left or Stayed in 1986 & 1987
Number of cases:	35

Dependent Variable Encoding:

Original Value	*Label*
0	Left South Africa
1	Stayed in South Africa

	Year	*Freq*	*Deviation Coefficients*
TIME			(1)
SA Regulation	1986	15	1.000
US Regulation	1987	20	−1.000

−2 Log Likelihood 45.00
Estimation terminated at iteration number 5

	Chi-Square	df	Significance
Model Chi-Square	14.91	6	.02

		Variables in the Equation						
	Variable	B	*S.E.*	*Wald*	*df*	*Sig*	R	*Exp(B)*
H9a:	**ADVERTISING**	**48.17**	**26.52**	**3.30**	**1**	**0.07**	**0.17**	**8.28E+20**
H9b:	RESEARCH	7.60	18.56	0.17	1	0.68	0.00	2003.53
H9c:	BACKLOGS	3.75	3.64	1.06	1	0.30	0.00	42.35
H9d:	INTEGRATION	−0.91	1.61	0.32	1	0.57	0.00	0.40
H9e:	**DIVERSIFICATION**	**−0.87**	**0.58**	**2.27**	**1**	**0.13**	**−0.08**	**0.42**
	TIME (1986)	0.46	0.51	0.80	1	0.37	0.00	1.58
	Constant	0.56	1.64	0.12	1	0.73		

Table 8.14 indicates the results of a linear regression model used to test the hypotheses in the period of no regulation. The overall model was not significant, however hypothesis 8d was disconfirmed. In the period of no regulation, the greater the vertical integration, the less the managerial benefits.

Table 8.14   Linear regression model for multinational's competitive strategies on managerial benefits in period of no regulation.

Dependent Variable: BENEFITS in 1984 & 1985
Number of cases: 8
DIVERSIFICATION dropped because of high multicollinearity

Multiple R	.18
R Square	.03
Adjusted R Square	.01
Standard Error	.20

Analysis of Variance

	DF	Sum of Squares	Mean Square
Regression	5	0.26	0.05
Residual	180	7.43	0.04

F = 1.25   Significance F = .29

			Variables in the Equation			
	Variable	*B*	*S.E. B*	*Beta*	*T*	*Sig T*
H7:	TMT	0.02	0.03	0.05	0.74	0.46
H8a:	ADVERTISING	−0.30	0.25	−0.09	−1.22	0.22
H8b:	RESEARCH	0.20	0.55	0.03	0.36	0.72
H8c:	BACKLOGS	−0.01	0.06	−0.01	−0.18	0.86
H8d:	**INTEGRATION**	**−0.07**	**0.04**	**−0.15**	**−1.90**	**0.05**
	Constant	0.84	0.04		22.41	0.00

Table 8.15 indicates the results of a linear regression model in the period of regulation. The overall model was not significant, however hypothesis 8c was weakly supported. In the period of regulation, the greater the order backlogs, the less the managerial benefits.

Table 8.15 Linear regression model for multinational's competitive strategies on managerial benefits in period of regulation.

Dependent Variable: BENEFITS in 1986 & 1987					
Number of cases: 15					
DIVERSIFICATION dropped because of high multicollinearity					

Multiple R	.16	
R Square	.02	
Adjusted R Square	.00	
Standard Error	.48	

Analysis of Variance

	DF	Sum of Squares	Mean Square
Regression	6	1.63	0.27
Residual	282	64.38	0.23

F = 1.19   Significance F = .31

		Variables in the Equation				
	Variable	*B*	*S.E. B*	*Beta*	*T*	*Sig T*
H7:	TMT	0.03	0.07	0.02	0.36	0.72
H8a:	ADVERTISING	−0.42	0.46	−0.05	−0.92	0.36
H8b:	RESEARCH	0.87	1.02	0.05	0.85	0.40
H8c:	**BACKLOGS**	**−0.22**	**0.15**	**−0.09**	**−1.52**	**0.13**
H8d:	INTEGRATION	−0.04	0.07	−0.04	−0.60	0.55
	TIME	−0.08	0.06	−0.08	−1.31	0.19
	Constant	1.22	0.11		11.34	0.00

Subsidiary's Symbolic Actions

Links to Headquarters' Actions on Subsidiary's Presence:

Analyses of Variance as indicated in Table 8.16 revealed that SYMBOL, (subsidiary's symbolic actions), differed significantly across the seven levels of PRESENCE in the two periods of no regulation and regulation. Subsidiaries

Table 8.16   Analyses of Variance for SYMBOL by levels of PRESENCE.[1]

SYMBOL in period of NO REGULATION (1984 & 1985)					
Source	Sum of Squares	D.F.	Mean Square	F	Sig.
Between Groups	93.96	5	18.79	1.95	.09
Within Groups	2666.11	276	9.66		
Eta = .18 Eta Squared = .03					
SYMBOL in period of REGULATION (1986 & 1987)					
Source	Sum of Squares	D.F.	Mean Square	F	Sig.
Between Groups	204.79	6	34.13	3.04	.01
Within Groups	3724.75	332	11.22		
Eta = .23 Eta Squared = .05					

[1] Criterion variables in this model included SYMBOL, INDUCE1, INDUCE2, SR, SD, GP and GD. In the interests of cogency, only significant relationships are reported in this book; please consult Haley (1990b) for reports of nonsignificant results as well.

that maintained higher levels of PRESENCE in South Africa also seemed to engage in greater symbolic actions for headquarters' stakeholders. Descriptive statistics showed that in the period of no regulation, multinationals that invested more in South Africa (Mean = 5.0, Standard Deviation = 4.24, N = 2) or grew threw retained earnings (Mean = 3.69, Standard Deviation = 3.23, N = 236) engaged in the greatest symbolic actions, whereas multinationals that sold their subsidiaries to other US companies (Mean = 1.00, Standard Deviation = 0, N = 1) or to foreign companies (Mean = 2.05, Standard Deviation = 1.99, N = 19), engaged in the least. Similarly, in the period of regulation, multinationals that invested more in South Africa (Mean = 8.00, Standard Deviation = 1.00, N = 3) engaged in the most symbolic actions, and those that liquidated their South African subsidiaries (Mean = 2.71, Standard Deviation = 3.07, N = 14) engaged in the least.

PRESENCE was collapsed into two categories, Left or Stayed in South Africa, for subsequent t-test, correlation and logistic-regression analyses. T-tests in Table 8.17 also showed that in the periods of no regulation and

Table 8.17 *T*-tests for SYMBOL by Left or Stayed in South Africa.

SYMBOL in period of NO REGULATION (1984 & 1985)				
	N	Mean	S.D.	S.E.
Left	44	2.16	2.11	.32
Stayed	238	3.70	3.24	.21
F = 2.34 2-Tail Probability = .00				
t = −4.05 D.F. = 85.45 2-Tail Probability = .00 (separate variance)				
SYMBOL in period of REGULATION (1986 & 1987)				
	N	Mean	S.D.	S.E.
Left	80	3.31	3.37	.38
Stayed	259	4.05	3.41	.21
F = 1.02 2-Tail Probability = .92				
t = −1.69 D.F. = 337 2-Tail Probability = .09 (pooled variance)				

regulation, subsidiaries that left or stayed in South Africa differed significantly in their symbolic actions. Multinationals that stayed, in both periods, engaged in significantly more symbolic actions.

As explained in the previous section, a set of independent variables was analyzed together to guard against high multicolinearity and the correlation matrix revealed none. Table 8.4 indicated the results of a logistic regression model used to test hypotheses 10 in the period of no regulation. The overall model was significant and hypothesis 10 was supported. In the period of no regulation, the greater the subsidiary's symbolic actions, the more likely that the subsidiary stayed in South Africa.

Subsidiary's Profits and Importance in Global Operations

Links to Headquarters' Actions on Subsidiary's Presence:

Analyses of Variance in Table 8.18 showed that in the period of no regulation, ROA (subsidiary's profits) differed significantly across the seven levels of PRESENCE. Descriptive statistics showed that subsidiaries that grew through

Table 8.18   Analyses of Variance for ROA, SALES and ASSETS by levels of PRESENCE.[1]

ROA in period of NO REGULATION (1984 & 1985)					
Source	Sum of Squares	D.F.	Mean Square	F	Sig.
Between Groups	1.48	4	.37	7.59	.00
Within Groups	2.00	41	.05		
Eta = .65 Eta Squared = .43					
SALES in period of NO REGULATION (1984 & 1985)					
Source	Sum of Squares	D.F.	Mean Square	F	Sig.
Between Groups	.03	4	.01	1.74	.14
Within Groups	.74	149	.01		
Eta = .21 Eta Squared = .04					
ASSETS in period of REGULATION (1986 & 1987)					
Source	Sum of Squares	D.F.	Mean Square	F	Sig.
Between Groups	.05	6	.01	1.72	.12
Within Groups	1.12	220	.01		
Eta = .21 Eta Squared = .04					

[1] Criterion variables in this model included ROA, ASSETS, SALES and EMPLOYEES. In the interests of cogency, only significant relationships are reported in this book; please consult Haley (1990b) for reports of nonsignificant results as well.

retained earnings had the highest ROA (Mean = .20, Standard Deviation = .21, N = 39) and subsidiaries that were sold to foreign companies were making losses (Mean = −.53, Standard Deviation = .43, N = 3). No significant differences existed for ROA across the seven levels of PRESENCE in the period of regulation.

Analyses of Variance in Table 8.18 also showed that in the period of no regulation SALES (South African sales as a proportion of global sales) differed significantly across the seven levels of PRESENCE. Multinationals that invested more (Mean = .20, N = 1) or sold to local managers (Mean = .08, Standard Deviation = .10, N = 5) had the highest sales, and those that liquidated (Mean = .02, Standard Deviation = .02, N = 6) had the lowest. Table 8.18 additionally showed that in the period of regulation, ASSETS (South African assets as a proportion of global assets) varied significantly across the seven levels of PRESENCE. Descriptive statistics identified that multinationals that formed trusts (Mean = .20, N = 1) or liquidated their assets (Mean = .11, Standard Deviation = .14, N = 4) had the largest proportion of global assets in South Africa, while those that that sold their subsidiaries to foreign companies (Mean = .04, Standard Deviation = .07, N =28), or grew through retained earnings (Mean = .04, Standard Deviation = .07, N = 175), had the smallest.

PRESENCE was collapsed into two categories, Left or Stayed in South Africa, for subsequent *t*-test, correlation and logistic regression analyses. A *t*-test, as described in Table 8.19, revealed that in the period of no regulation, multinationals that stayed in South Africa enjoyed significantly higher ROA than those that left which were experiencing losses. No significant difference existed in the period of regulation. The correlation matrix indicated that ROA correlated positively with PRESENCE in the period of no regulation

Table 8.19   *T*-tests for ROA and EMPLOYEES by Left or Stayed in South Africa.

ROA in period of NO REGULATION (1984 & 1985)				
	N	Mean	S.D.	S.E.
Left	6	−.20	.45	.19
Stayed	40	.19	.21	.03
$F = 4.90$ 2-Tail Probability = .00				
$t = -2.08$ D.F. = 5.31 2-Tail Probability = .09 (separate variance)				
EMPLOYEES in period of NO REGULATION (1984 & 1985)				
	N	Mean	S.D.	S.E.
Left	13	.01	.02	.00
Stayed	100	.02	.03	.00
$F = 3.56$ 2-Tail Probability = .02				
$t = -1.51$ D.F. = 25.01 2-Tail Probability = .14 (separate variance)				

(Correlation = .51, 1-tailed Significance = .01, N = 46) providing some support for hypothesis 12a.

A *t*-test also showed, as indicated in Table 8.19, that in the period of no regulation, multinationals that stayed in South Africa had more EMPLOYEES in South Africa (employees in South Africa as a percent of global operations) than those that left, providing some support for hypothesis 12b.

Table 8.20 indicates the results of a logistic regression model used to test hypotheses 12a in the period of no regulation. The overall model with ROA is significant and hypothesis 12a is supported. In the period of no regulation, the higher the subsidiary's ROA, the more likely it was to stay in South Africa. In the period of no regulation, a subsidiary's profits did not affect whether it stayed in or left South Africa.

Table 8.20   Logistic regression model for subsidiary's profits on Left or Stayed in South Africa in period of no regulation.

Function:	Logistic
Dependent Variable:	Left or Stayed 1984 & 1985
Number of cases:	46

Dependent Variable Encoding:

Original Value	*Label*
0	Left South Africa
1	Stayed in South Africa

−2 Log Likelihood   35.62
Estimation terminated at iteration number 5

	Chi-Square	df	Significance
Model Chi-Square	10.98	1	.00

	Variables in the Equation						
Variable	B	*S.E.*	*Wald*	*df*	*Sig*	R	*Exp(B)*
H12a: **ROA**	**7.44**	**3.45**	**4.64**	**1**	**0.03**	**0.27**	**1702.17**
Constant	1.41	0.57	6.09	1	0.01		

No significant correlations existed between the variables ASSETS, SALES and EMPLOYEES and the variable PRESENCE in either the period of no regulation or regulation. However, ASSETS and SALES were highly correlated in both periods (Correlation = .93, 1-tailed significance = .01, N = 98 in no regulation, 152 in regulation). To avoid high multicolinearity,

Table 8.21   Logistic regression model for subsidiary's importance in global operations on Left or Stayed in South Africa in period of regulation.

Function:	Logistic
Dependent Variable:	Left or Stayed in 1986 & 1987
Number of cases:	152

SALES dropped because of high multicollinearity

Dependent Variable Encoding:

Original Value	*Label*
0	Left South Africa
1	Stayed in South Africa

	Year	*Freq*	*Deviation Coefficients*
TIME			(1)
SA Regulation	1986	85	1.000
US Regulation	1987	67	−1.000

−2 Log Likelihood   145.23
Estimation terminated at iteration number 3

	Chi-Square	df	Significance
Model Chi-Square	2.06	3	.56

Variables in the Equation							
Variable	B	*S.E.*	*Wald*	*df*	*Sig*	R	*Exp(B)*
H12b: **ASSETS**	**−3.70**	**2.51**	**2.18**	**1**	**0.14**	**−0.03**	**0.02**
EMPLOYEES	0.00	.01	.00	1	0.97	0.00	1.00
TIME (1986)	−0.03	.21	.02	1	0.89	0.00	0.97
Constant	1.67	.28	34.30	1	0.00		

SALES was dropped from the two equations dealing with importance in global operations.

Table 8.21 indicates the results of the logistic regression model used to test hypothesis 12b in the period of regulation. Although the model was not significant, hypothesis 12b was weakly disconfirmed. In the period of regulation, the greater the proportion of the multinational's global assets in South Africa, the more likely that it left.

Subsidiary's Noncompetitive Strategies with Host State

Links to Headquarters' Actions on Subsidiary's Presence:

Table 8.22 indicates *t*-tests for CONTRACT (the subsidiary's contracting with South African governmental agencies) and COOPT (the subsidiary's co-opting South African governmental agencies) when PRESENCE was collapsed into two categories, Left or Stayed in South Africa. In the period of no regulation, multinationals that stayed in South Africa engaged in more

Table 8.22 *T*-tests for CONTRACT and COOPT by Left or Stayed in South Africa.

CONTRACT in period of NO REGULATION (1984 & 1985)				
	N	Mean	S.D.	S.E.
Left	38	.00	.00	.00
Stayed	169	.03	.12	.01

$F = 1380.45$ 2-Tail Probability = .00
$t = -3.54$ D.F. = 169.08   2-Tail Probability = .00 (separate variance)

COOPT in period of NO REGULATION (1984 & 1985)				
	N	Mean	S.D.	S.E.
Left	42	.12	.40	.06
Stayed	222	.89	2.06	.14

$F = 27.12$ 2-Tail Probability = .00
$t = -5.09$ D.F. = 261.91   2-Tail Probability = .00 (separate variance)

contracting and co-opting with South African governmental agencies than those that left, providing some support for hypothesis 15. However, the hypothesis was not confirmed by subsequent logistic regression analysis.

Links to Subsidiary's Symbolic Actions:

A correlation matrix for the period of no regulation showed that contrary to hypothesis 13, COOPT correlated positively with SYMBOL or the subsidiary's symbolic behaviors for headquarters' stakeholders (Correlation = .42,

Table 8.23 Linear regression model for subsidiary's noncompetitive strategies and suppression of subsidiary's Voice and Exit actions by host state on subsidiary's symbolic actions in period of no regulation.

Dependent Variable:	SYMBOL in 1984 & 1985
Number of cases:	36

Multiple R	.40
R Square	.16
Adjusted R Square	.15
Standard Error	2.97

Analysis of Variance

	DF	Sum of Squares	Mean Square
Regression	4	479.99	120.00
Residual	278	2448.26	8.81

F = 13.63   Significance F = .00

	Variables in the Equation				
Variable	*B*	*S.E. B*	*Beta*	*T*	*Sig T*
H13:	**COOPT**	**0.48**	**0.12**	**0.28**	**3.97**	**0.00**
	CONTRACT	**5.05**	**2.09**	**0.15**	**2.41**	**0.02**
H16:	**SUPPRESS**	**0.83**	**0.47**	**0.10**	**1.75**	**0.08**
H20:	INDUCE3	8.814749E-03	9.93454E-03	0.06	0.89	0.37
	Constant	2.80	0.32		8.80	0.00

1-tailed Significance = .01, N = 36). Generally, in the period of no regulation, the higher the subsidiary's co-optation of South African governmental agencies, the greater the subsidiary's symbolic actions for headquarters' stakeholders.

Tables 8.23 and 8.24 indicate the results of linear regression models used to test hypotheses 13 in the periods of no regulation and regulation. The overall models were significant however, hypothesis 13 was not supported. In

Table 8.24 Linear regression model for subsidiary's noncompetitive strategies and suppression of subsidiary's Voice and Exit actions by host state on subsidiary's symbolic actions in period of regulation.

Dependent Variable:	SYMBOL in 1986 & 1987					
Number of cases:	64					

Multiple R	.31
R Square	.10
Adjusted R Square	.09
Standard Error	3.20

Analysis of Variance

	DF	Sum of Squares	Mean Square
Regression	5	469.40	93.88
Residual	419	4280.28	10.22

F = 9.19   Significance F = .00

	Variables in the Equation					
	Variable	*B*	*S.E. B*	*Beta*	*T*	*Sig T*
H13:	CONTRACT	4.44	1.63	0.14	2.72	0.01
	COOPT	0.30	0.08	0.20	3.75	0.00
H16:	SUPPRESS	0.71	0.42	0.08	1.68	0.09
H20:	INDUCE3	4.328250E-03	6.96496E-03	0.03	0.62	0.53
	TIME	0.34	0.31	0.05	1.10	0.27
	Constant	2.33	0.53		4.39	0.00

both time periods, COOPT and CONTRACT had positive effect on SYMBOL. The more the subsidiary co-opted and contracted with South African government agencies, the greater the subsidiary's symbolic actions for headquarters' stakeholders.

Suppression of Voice and Exit Actions by Host State

Links to Headquarters' Actions on Subsidiary's Presence:

Analysis of Variance, as indicated in Table 8.25, revealed that in the period of regulation, SUPPRESS (the South African government's suppression of the subsidiary's Voice and Exit actions) varied significantly across all seven levels of PRESENCE. Descriptive statistics showed no clear pattern as multinationals that formed trusts experienced the greatest SUPPRESS (Mean = .75, Standard Deviation = .50, N = 4), and those that invested more (Mean = 0.00, Standard Deviation = 0.00, N = 4) or sold their subsidiaries to local managers (Mean = .11, Standard Deviation = .32, N = 19) experienced the least. Hypothesis 19 was not supported by subsequent regression analysis.

Links to Subsidiary's Symbolic Actions:

Tables 8.23 and 8.24 also indicated the results of linear regression models used to test hypotheses 16 in the periods of no regulation and regulation.

Table 8.25 Analysis of Variance for SUPPRESS by levels of PRESENCE.[1]

SUPPRESS in period of REGULATION (1986 & 1987)					
Source	Sum of Squares	D.F.	Mean Square	F	Sig.
Between Groups	1.58	6	.26	1.77	.10
Within Groups	57.96	389	.15		
Eta = .16 Eta Squared = .03					

[1] Criterion variables in this model included SUPPRESS, TMT, CONTRACT and COOPT. In the interests of cogency, only significant relationships are reported in this book; please consult Haley (1990b) for reports of nonsignificant results as well.

The overall models were significant but hypotheses 16 was not supported. In both time periods, SUPPRESS had positive effect on SYMBOL (the subsidiary's symbolic actions for headquarters' stakeholders). The greater the suppression of the subsidiary's Voice and Exit by the host state, the greater the subsidiary's symbolic actions for headquarters' stakeholders.

Links to Subsidiary's Noncompetitive Strategies:

Contrary to hypothesis 18, a correlation matrix for the period of regulation showed that CONTRACT (the subsidiary's contracting with South African governmental agencies) correlated positively with SUPPRESS (Correlation = .15, 1-tailed Significance = .01, N = 295). Tables 8.26 and 8.27

Table 8.26 Logistic regression model for subsidiary's noncompetitive strategies on suppression of subsidiary's Voice and Exit actions by host state in period of no regulation.

Function:	Logistic
Dependent Variable:	SUPPRESS in 1984 & 1985
Number of cases:	208

Dependent Variable Encoding:

Original Value	*Label*
0	No suppression of Voice and Exit actions by South African government
1	Suppression of Voice and Exit actions by South African government

−2 Log Likelihood 191.66
Estimation terminated at iteration number 4

	Chi-Square	df	Significance
Model Chi-Square	2.73	2	.26

	Variables in the Equation						
Variable	B	*S.E.*	*Wald*	*df*	*Sig*	R	*Exp(B)*
H18: **CONTRACT**	**2.80**	**1.80**	**2.40**	**1**	**0.12**	**0.05**	**16.40**
COOPT	−0.09	0.17	0.26	1	0.61	0.00	0.92
Constant	−1.62	0.19	69.79	1	0.00		

Table 8.27 Logistic regression model for subsidiary's noncompetitive strategies on suppression of subsidiary's Voice and Exit actions by host state in period of regulation.

Function:	Logistic	
Dependent Variable:	SUPPRESS in 1986 & 1987	
Number of cases:	295	

Dependent Variable Encoding:

Original Value	*Label*
0	No suppression of Voice and Exit actions by South African government
1	Suppression of Voice and Exit actions by South African government

	Year	*Freq*	*Deviation Coefficients*
TIME			(1)
SA Regulation	1986	167	1.000
US Regulation	1987	128	−1.000

−2 Log Likelihood 262.04232
Estimation terminated at iteration number 4

	Chi-Square	df	Significance
Model Chi-Square	5.69	3	.13

		Variables in the Equation						
	Variable	B	*S.E.*	*Wald*	*df*	*Sig*	R	*Exp(B)*
H18:	**CONTRACT**	**2.72**	**1.31**	**4.32**	**1**	**0.04**	**0.09**	**15.25**
	EMPLOYEES	−0.04	0.12	0.11	1	0.74	0.00	0.96
	TIME (1986)	0.05	0.16	0.09	1	0.77	0.00	1.05
	Constant	−1.75	0.17	101.47	1	0.00		

indicate logistic regression models used to test hypothesis 18 in the periods of no regulation and regulation. The overall model in the first period was not significant, and in the second was weakly significant. However, hypothesis 18 was partially unsupported in both instances. Although COOPT (the subsidiary's co-opting South African governmental agencies) had no significant effect, CONTRACT had a positive effect on SUPPRESS. The more the subsidiary contracted with South African governmental agencies, the more the South African government suppressed the subsidiary's voice and exit actions.

Subsidiary's Inducements to Host State

Links to Subsidiary's Symbolic Actions:

A correlation matrix revealed that as predicted in hypothesis 20, in the period of no regulation, INDUCE3 (subsidiary's inducements to the host state) correlated significantly with SYMBOL or the subsidiary's symbolic actions for headquarters' stakeholders (Correlation = .47, 1-tailed Significance = .01, $N = 36$). Generally, in the period of no regulation, the higher the subsidiary's inducement's to the host state, the greater the subsidiary's symbolic behaviors for headquarters' stakeholders. However the hypothesis was not supported through subsequent linear regression analyses as Tables 8.23 and 8.24 showed.

Summary

This section has presented the results of the tests of hypotheses dealing with the theory of multinationals as chameleons. Table 8.1 has summarized the results and Figure 8.2 has honed in on the significant results dealing with why multinationals left or stayed in South Africa. The next section discusses the generalizability of this study and its limitations.

Generalizability of the Results

This study comprised a theory-building exercise and most of the analyses explored the relevance and applicability of hypotheses across disciplines. Consequently, the results raised at least as many questions as they answered. The analyses attempted to answer the central question of why multinationals left or stayed in South Africa. Yet, three major considerations potentially limit the generalizability of this study: (1) missing data (2) attrition in the sample and, (3) varying *n*'s across the sets of analyses.

First, much missing data characterized some sets of analyses. Researchers use several techniques to circumvent graphic missing data. For example, some researchers would have used averages for the variables that had missing data rather than the values for the individual subsidiaries. Yet, problems attend these problem-solving techniques too and none have universal acceptability. In the case of multinationals in South Africa, these problems were compounded by the characteristics of the population. For example, the multinationals in the sample ranged in size from one employee to thousands, consequently one could not justify using average measures for independent variables, such as ROA, across the population.

Second, the study's design included attrition of the population as the multinationals left South Africa over time. Yet, systematically different characteristics may have distinguished the multinationals that left in the period of no regulation from those that stayed for the period of regulation. As the multinationals that stayed over time may have had different characteristics, one should interpret the results in the period of regulation cautiously

Finally, the *n*'s, or number of multinationals, varied in the sets of analyses. Consequently, one can argue that multinationals with different characteristics emerged in each set of analysis.

One way to argue that the results have generalizability across the multinationals in the population, would be to run one equation with the supported results for hypotheses that dealt with why multinationals left or stayed. In the period of regulation, the equation dealing with competitive strategies (Table 8.13) provided the only results that supported the hypotheses on PRESENCE, thereby providing an equation with generalizability. Table 8.28 displays a separate logistic regression equation for the period under no regulation with the three variables that the analyses supported as explaining PRESENCE. The results should be interpreted cautiously, yet, the overall equation is significant, the classification table predicts perfectly and the coefficients have the expected signs. One can argue that despite the varying *n*'s, the results of the analyses generalize across all the multinationals in the population. One can say with some confidence that this study provides reasons for why multinationals left or stayed in South Africa and why they may do so in other countries and situations. The next chapter discusses the implications of these results for international business, strategic management and public policy.

Table 8.28   Logistic regression model for significant influences on Left or Stayed in South Africa in period of no regulation.

Function:	Logistic
Dependent Variable:	Left or Stayed in 1984 & 1985
Number of cases:	24

Dependent Variable Encoding:

Original Value	Label
0	Left South Africa
1	Stayed in South Africa

−2 Log Likelihood   18.08
Estimation terminated at iteration number 22 because a perfect fit is detected.
This solution is not unique.

	Chi-Square	df	Significance
Model Chi-Square	18.09	3	.00

Classifcation Table for Left and Stayed in South Africa

	Predicted Left	Predicted Stayed	Percent Correct
Observed Left	3	0	100%
Observed Stayed	0	21	100%
Overall			100%

Variables in the Equation

	Variable	B	S.E.	Wald	df	Sig	R	Exp(B)
H9c:	BACKLOGS	−7.35	–	–	1	–	–	0.00
H10:	SYMBOL	0.12	–	–	1	–	–	1.13
H12a:	ROA	225.87	–	–	1	–	–	1.24E+98
	Constant	12.92	–	–	1	–		

PART V

THEORETICAL AND
STRATEGIC IMPLICATIONS

9. Understanding and Influencing Multinational Corporations

Viewing them as complex organizations in changing environments, this book has explored why multinationals stay in or leave host states. The answers have reframed and tested aspects of staying and leaving as snapshots in the development of multinationals over time. This book has argued that multinationals act as chameleons that respond to environmental demands while constrained by some general forces. To test this theory, the arguments traversed fundamental debates in economics, strategic management and organization theory over the significance of environmental forces and managerial actions, of organizational dependence and autonomy.

The final chapter discusses the import of this study and its findings. It highlights the circumstances under which multinationals left and stayed in South Africa, discusses the theoretical significance of the results and offers some avenues for future research. It also explores the strategic implications of the results through reinterpreting stakeholders' activism against Nike and Myanmar.

Understanding Multinationals

The book has used a political-action framework to explore how technical-efficiency, ideological and political forces may influence why multinationals stay in or leave host states. Structural changes in multinationals maintain equilibrium between these competing general forces. To maintain homeostatic equilibrium, multinationals alter their structures, sometimes in unanticipated ways and sometimes to deceive stakeholders.

The theory of multinationals as chameleons augments other theories of strategic management and organization theory: it couples the behavioral theory of the firm to a holistic, long-term view of organizations that incorporates top managers' strategic decisions in organizational development. The theory also supplements other theories of international business: it makes different assumptions about and provides alternate explanations for multinationals' strategic actions including their incremental investments in host states and reasons for leaving.

Decoding the Results

This study confirmed the important effects of social legitimacy, profits and some competitive strategies for multinationals' strategic behaviors. In the period of no regulation, as hypothesized, more symbolic actions, higher profits and lower order backlogs influenced whether multinationals stayed in South Africa. In the period of regulation, as hypothesized, greater advertising and less product diversification influenced whether multinationals stayed in South Africa.

The results also generated some resounding nonfindings, especially dealing with stakeholders' Voice and Exit actions, casting doubts on the efficacy and utility of certain sanctions, legislations and resolutions to affect multinationals' behaviors. However, significant differences distinguished the variables that explained leaving and staying actions in periods of no regulation and regulation, indicating that broad-based governmental regulation that affected multinationals' profits such as policies impacting repatriation of funds and taxation, greatly influenced multinationals' behaviors including the criteria that managers used to make strategic decisions.

Other than its effectiveness in symbolically placating headquarters' stakeholders, maintaining high profits, and contributing directly and indirectly to the multinational's competitive strategies, a subsidiary's strategic behaviors and its top management appeared to have had little direct effect on whether a multinational stayed in or left South Africa. Subsidiaries that stayed in South Africa engaged in significantly more co-opting and contracting with South African governmental agencies; the multinationals that stayed also enjoyed more stable dominant coalitions including fewer changes in the subsidiaries' top management. Yet, contrary to theoretical rationales and populist fears, co-opting and contracting South African governmental agencies, changes in top management, and the South African government's suppression of the subsidiary's Voice and Exit actions in South Africa, did not affect whether a multinational left or stayed in South Africa. Decisions to leave or to stay are often made at the headquarters' levels and subsidiaries' managers probably had less to say in these decisions than headquarters' managers.

Voice and Exit Actions of Headquarters' Stakeholders:

The results strongly suggest that stockholders' resolutions and governmental legislation on divestitures, aimed as sanctions, may not influence multi-nationals to leave host states. Indeed, some stakeholders' Voice actions may have unintended effects. In the period of no regulation, the greater the number of stockholders' resolutions directed against operations in South Africa, the more likely the subsidiary was to stay in South Africa. Escalating commitment (Haley, 1997; Haley and Stumpf, 1989) and perseverance cognitive biases may cause stakeholders to increase commitment to these courses of action even when multinationals continue to maintain operations.

A multinational's inducements to the US government affected whether it stayed in or left South Africa, but not as predicted. In the period of regulation, contrary to the hypothesis, the greater a multinational's inducements to the US government as taxes collected on operations, the more likely that legislation on divestitures caused the multinational to leave South Africa. This could indicate clashes between various stakeholders that use multinationals and governments to advance conflicting goals (see Haley, 2000b for another discussion of this phenomenon).

Dominant Coalition's Stability:

Stakeholders' Voice and Exit actions generally did not have the expected effects on the stability of the dominant coalition of top managers. In the period of no regulation, the greater the stockholders' resolutions and legislation on divestitures, the more likely that the dominant coalition remained the same. In the period of regulation, the effects became more significant and stockholders' divestitures exercised a strong positive influence on managerial tenure, intensifying with US regulation. The unusual results of divestitures may have stemmed from their relatively small amounts. For example, in 1985, the Investor Responsibility Research Center estimated that $450 million dollars had been divested by multinationals in response to stakeholders' actions. By comparison, three days trading in IBM, a major company in South Africa at that time, totaled around $570 million. However, in the period of no regulation, the greater the legislation on governmental purchasing, the less likely that the dominant coalition remained the same: Large portions of multinationals' sales came through governmental contracts. Governmental abilities to influence multinationals and managers may have heightened as governments assumed prominent roles as suppliers, consumers and partners (Levine and White, 1961; Litwak and Hylton, 1966; Pfeffer and Salancik, 1978).

Analyses of the composition and stability of the dominant coalition on whether the multinational left or stayed in South Africa yielded resounding "nonfindings" as prophesized by West and Schwenk (1996).

Multinational's Competitive Strategies:

The results regarding the effects of competitive strategies on managerial benefits were confusing as prophesized by West and Schwenk (1996). Managerial benefits, as captured by favorable press coverage, increased with vertical integration in the period of no regulation. In the period of regulation, contrary to the hypothesis, the greater the order backlogs, the less the managerial benefits.

Managers often justified their actions to remain in South Africa on the bases of global, competitive strategies. The results did indicate that in the period of no regulation, the greater the order backlogs, the less likely the multinational was to stay in South Africa. This result may signify that the multinational was reducing inventories in anticipation of leaving South Africa. As hypothesized, in the period of regulation, diversification seemed to lower some exit barriers and the more diversified the multinational, the less likely it was to stay in South Africa. Also as hypothesized, in the period of regulation, the greater the advertising expenditures, the more likely the multinational was to stay in South Africa.

Subsidiary's Symbolic Actions:

Social legitimacy played an important role in whether a multinational left or stayed in South Africa. In both periods of no regulation and regulation, subsidiaries that stayed in South Africa engaged in significantly greater symbolic actions, captured by adherence to the Sullivan Principles, than those that left. In the period of no regulation, subsidiaries' symbolic actions increased their probability of staying in South Africa. Yet, symbolic actions had no effect on staying or leaving in the period of regulation, which seemed to override some of the benefits of social legitimacy. Some descriptive statistics suggest that even in the period of regulation, symbolic actions may have provided multinationals with goodwill and legitimacy at home influencing how they left or stayed. Multinationals that engaged in greater symbolic actions also seemed to maintain stronger national ties during this period. For example, in the period of regulation, multinationals with the strongest adherence to the Sullivan Principles sold their subsidiaries to other US companies, formed trusts, or invested more; they did not liquidate their subsidiaries or sell them to local managers.

Subsidiary's Profits and Importance in Global Operations:

Managers generally touted slacking or booming performance as reasons for leaving or staying in South Africa. Indeed, in the period of no regulation, the higher the subsidiary's ROA, the more likely it was to stay in South Africa. Subsidiaries that grew through retained earnings enjoyed the highest ROAs;

those that were sold to South African or European companies had the lowest. However, ROA had no significant influence on actions to leave or to stay in regulation. This finding may support Hout, Porter and Rudden's (1982) observation that when economic, financial and social changes occur, as they did in the period of regulation, multinationals have to re-establish profit-maximizing criteria.

In the period of regulation, the greater the proportion of global assets in South Africa, the more likely the multinational was to leave South Africa. The finding though contradicting some international-business theories, probably demonstrated a cautionary long-term view of regulation and evidence of contingency planning by multinationals. Governmental regulation extracts control of the environment from multinationals to governments, thereby decreasing the flexibility of multinationals, decreasing their ability to respond to market forces and increasing their business risk. Rational multinationals would incorporate this environmental change into their long-term plans and strive to re-establish their flexibility and control as well as to reduce their risk.

Subsidiary's Noncompetitive Strategies with Host State:

In both no regulation and regulation, co-opting and contracting South African governmental agencies had positive effects on a subsidiary's symbolic actions. This result could indicate that the South African government was aware that the Sullivan principles had primarily symbolic and ritualistic, rather than substantive, value. It could also indicate a compensatory mechanism on the part of the subsidiaries. Subsidiaries could have incurred ethical and moral costs, including losses of legitimacy, by linking with the South African governmental agencies. By accepting positions in South African governmental agencies, the subsidiaries also could have become associated with governmental actions, reducing their ideological purity in the eyes of headquarters' stakeholders. These circumstances could have demanded increased symbolic behaviors from subsidiaries and the greater the co-opting and contracting with South African governmental agencies, the more important ritual conformity with social norms at headquarters probably became.

Suppression of Subsidiary's Voice and Exit Actions by Host State:

The South African government's suppression of the subsidiary's Voice and Exit actions also had positive effects on its symbolic actions. Further analyses of the results could indicate which multinationals engaged in more symbolic actions under these circumstances; however, the results do seem to confirm that adherence to the Sullivan Principles by the subsidiaries were aimed as a gesture towards headquarters' stakeholders rather than as a substantive policy stance towards the South African government.

Contrary to theoretical rationales, in no regulation and regulation, the subsidiaries' co-opting of South African governmental agencies had no significant effects on this host state's suppression of the subsidiaries' Voice and Exit actions; however, contracting had positive effects on suppression of Voice and Exit. The greater the economic benefits that the South African government could extract from the subsidiaries, the more important control of the subsidiaries probably became to the host state. March (1982) argued that harassment and difficulties might serve as strategies to induce future partnerships. If the South African government utilized suppression of a subsidiary's Voice and Exit to increase the likelihood of economic partnerships with it, increased contracting could have increased suppression.

Future Research

In this study, stakeholders' resolutions, sanctions and divestitures either did not have any effect on whether multinationals stayed in or left South Africa, or had undesired effects. For example, logistic regression analyses revealed that stockholders' resolutions might have weakly influenced multinationals to stay in South Africa. Future research needs to enquire into the circumstances under which stakeholders' Voice and Exit actions influence multinationals and the sorts of behaviors they extract.

Some exploratory data analysis suggests that Voice and Exit actions may indeed affect forms of leaving. For example, the stepwise discriminant

Table 9.1   Stakeholders' Voice and Exit actions on how multinational corporations left South Africa in period of no regulation.

Discriminating Variables: Stakeholders' Actions (2-year lag)
Dependent Variable: Forms of Leaving in 1984 & 1985

Canonical Discriminant Functions

Fcn	Eigen	Pct of Variance	Cum Pct	Can Corr on	After Fcn	Wilks' Lambda	Chi sq	DF	Sig
					: 0	.62	18.78	12	.09
1*	.46	80.84	80.84	.56	: 1	.90	4.10	6	.66
2	.07	12.54	93.38	.26	: 2	.96	1.43	2	.49
3	.04	6.62	100.00	.19	:				

* canonical discriminant functions remaining in the analysis

Standardized Canonical Discriminant Function Coefficients
                                          FUNC 1
SR (Stockholders' Resolutions)   .74
SD (Stockholders' Divestitures)   −.63
GP (Legislation on Purchasing)   −.66
GD (Legislation on Divestitures)   .99

Structure Matrix: pooled-within-groups correlations
                         FUNC 1
GD   .43
SD   −.39
SR   .34
GP   −.11

Canonical Discriminant Functions evaluated at Group Means (Group Centroids)

Group	FUNC 1
1	−.72
2	.66
3	−1.00
4	.10

Table 9.1   (*Continued*)

Actual Group	No. of Cases	Predicted Group Membership			
		1	2	3	4
Liquidation 1	7	6	1	8	2
		35.3%	5.9%	47.1%	11.8%
Foreign Co 2	19	2	7	1	9
		10.5%	36.8%	5.3%	47.4%
American Co 3	1	0	0	1	0
		.0%	.0%	100.0%	.0%
Local Mgrs 4	7	2	1	1	3
		28.6%	14.3%	14.3%	42.9%
Ungrouped Cases	229	34	59	43	93
(Stayed in South Africa)		14.8%	25.8%	18.8%	40.6%

Classification Results –

Percent of "grouped" cases correctly classified: 38.64%

analyses of stakeholders' Voice and Exit actions in Table 9.1 indicates that a function composed of stakeholders' actions, correctly classified over 38 percent of the cases that left during the period of no regulation, considerably more than chance. Stockholders' resolutions and governmental legislation on divestitures formed major components of this function, yet appeared to influence favorably whether a multinational maintained operations through sale of its South African subsidiary to local managers, the category of leaving with the highest percentage of cases correctly classified. This would indicate that to obviate the effects on legitimacy (of stockholders' resolutions) and on performance (of governmental legislation on divestitures), multinationals sold their operations to local managers and thereby left South Africa. As indicated in Chapter 4, elaborate contracts often maintained old operations and personnel, but the influence of the values and ethics of headquarters' stakeholders was eliminated. The stockholders, local and state governments that strived to change the behaviors of multinationals in South Africa most probably did not intend for these effects and the ensuing loss of their Voice and ethical influence.

Influencing Multinationals

Stakeholders, including governments, consumers and stockholders continue to use sanctions against multinationals to influence their behaviors in host states and to align these behaviors with stakeholders' values and ethics. Two interesting recent cases of stakeholders using sanctions against multinationals include Myanmar (Burma) and Nike.

Sanctioning Myanmar

Myanmar has been hailed as the new South Africa (see the Free Burma Coalition's WWW site at http://www.freeburmacoalition.org; Noble, 2000). The USA and Europe have shunned Myanmar's ruling military regime for its harsh treatment of the pro-democracy opposition (which won elections under Aung San Suu Kyi in 1990 but that the military regime never let govern), and its poor human-rights record. However, Myanmar constitutes a major trading partner for Japan, China, Singapore and Malaysia and a member of the Association of South-East Asian Nations (ASEAN) that opposes sanctions. Aung San Suu Kyi has advocated forcing multinationals to leave Myanmar as a way of breaking the military regime's hold.

In July 1991, due to the lack of political reform, President Bush refused to renew the bilateral textile agreement that lapsed in December 1990 between Myanmar and the USA. However, as Table 9.2 shows, the percent of textile and apparel exports to the USA, as a percent of Myanmar's total exports to the USA, continued to increase.

In May 1997, the USA imposed sanctions on all new foreign investment in Myanmar, leaving existing commitments as well as trade and service contracts untouched. Some European Union (EU) countries objected to US sanctions, particularly France in protecting the interests of Total, while others (the Scandinavian countries, the UK, the Netherlands, Germany and Italy) threatened to impose their own to force the ruling military regime to compromise with the opposition. On July 18, 1996, the European Parliament passed a nonbinding resolution, urging the EU's members to end all trade, tourism and investment ties with Myanmar. The EU has resisted sanctions

Table 9.2   Myanmar's textile apparel exports to the USA, 1989 to 1999.

	1989	1990	1991	1992	1993	1994	1995	1996	1997	1998	1999
Textiles/ Apparel (US$m)	7.1	9.2	11.5	27.3	30.1	47.0	65.0	83.8	85.6	128.2	185.8
Total (US$m)	17.1	22.7	26.8	38.4	46.3	67.2	80.9	107.7	115.3	163.7	232.1
Texitiles/ Apparel as % of Total (%)	41.3	40.3	42.8	71.2	64.9	69.9	80.4	77.8	74.2	78.3	80.0

Source: United States International Trade Commision

before, with some countries arguing that they would have no effect without similar sanctions from the Asian countries, including China. Asian multinationals have engaged in a wide range of projects in Myanmar and have shown a willingness to fill a vacancy should a Western multinational pull out — e.g., Tiger Beer took Carlsberg and Heineken's niches and market shares when the latter pulled out (McCarthy, 2000).

As previously in South Africa, the 1997 US ban on new investments in Myanmar appears to have deterred further investments. The US government claimed that the cumulative total of actual US investments from 1989/1990 to 1997/1998 comprised only 28 percent of the total approved investments for the same period (McCarthy, 2000). In South Africa, 80 percent of the growth of US multinationals came from reinvesting subsidiaries' profits rather than from new investments by headquarters; yet, the results in the study showed that US legislation that restricted new investments also enormously affected multinationals' actions to leave or to stay in South Africa and legislation may similarly have affected Myanmar. Most of the US multinationals that left also maintained economic ties with South Africa. Therefore, one can still question the merit of sanctions that force US multinationals to leave Myanmar.

The move for sanctioning Myanmar has recently picked up additional force. Trade unions called in November 2000 for governments, companies and international organizations to re-examine their relations with Myanmar's junta or to face strong sanctions. The warning followed a recommendation, the first in 81 years, by the International Labor Organization (ILO) to its members, which include employers and trade unions as well as countries, to reconsider their relations with Myanmar because of its continued use of forced labor. An unprecedented move that opens the way to sanctions, the recommendation, adopted on November 16 by the ILO in Geneva, came into affect on November 30 (Fujii, 2000).

The ILO also asked governments and international organizations to report on their relevant measures taken. Each member organization will decide on specific measures. Some diplomats speculated that the sanctions would have no effect. Others voiced concern that the sanctions could get out of hand when more than 200 governments and international organizations started to make decisions based on the mandate given by the ILO. Asian countries, including Japan and Malaysia, asked for a delay in implementing the sanctions since the military junta was making some progress in complying with the ILO's demands; but, Western countries, led by the USA and Britain, pushed for sanctions. Clearly, the results in the South Africa study revealed that some sanctions, such as stockholders' resolutions, may have unintended effects on multinationals, while most have none. Measures directly affecting multi-nationals' profitability though, did have an effect, and the ILO should look into such measures. Though the ILO's sanctions will probably not affect commerce and business immediately in Myanmar, they do provide the opportunity to present a cohesive, global front opposing the ruling, military junta's ethics and values. For example, despite ASEAN's objections, trade unions as members of the ILO are not necessarily bound by their governments' stands. Consequently, although Malaysia has tried to shield Myanmar, the Malaysian workers' delegate at the ILO in June expressed criticism of Yangon's apparent foot-dragging and declared that the government could resolve the issue "tomorrow", if it sincerely wished to do so (Wain, 2000). The ILO's sanctions provide a real opportunity for concerted action against Myanmar if effectively implemented. Consequently, choice of sanctions assumes great importance as noted in this study.

In an official statement in December 2000, the International Confederation of Free Trade Unions (ICFTU), based in Brussels and which groups 221 national trade unions from 148 countries, confirmed that it planned to obtain the "rapid withdrawal of foreign investors whose presence has the direct or indirect effect of aiding or abetting forced labor". The ICFTU will initially target for trade unions' pressure multinationals involved in oil and gas, timber, rice, textiles, tobacco and tourism, about 300 multinationals from 30 countries. According to the ICFTU, nearly one million people currently are subject to forced labor in Myanmar, particularly in building roads, railways and military installations. The ICFTU has singled out Myanmar's army as a main offender, due to its practice of using villagers as porters. Bill Jordan, the ICFTU's general secretary, said in the statement: "In the past, governments and companies were hiding behind the absence of a global and binding decision on Burma (Myanmar) to justify their inaction, now there is a global decision by a UN body which gives them legitimate grounds to take action". In November 2000, the ICFTU had requested that travel agencies and Western multinationals in Myanmar adopt the ILO's recommendations. Several Western multinationals investing in Myanmar have maintained that they do not use forced labor (Agence France-Press, 2000).

Meanwhile, in December 2000, the Massachusetts Legislature, undaunted by the US Supreme Court's rebuff of its 1996 law boycotting multinationals from doing business in Myanmar, filed a new bill to put pressure on the country's military rulers. The bill requires the state's $36 billion pension fund to divest itself over the next three years of multinationals that do business in Myanmar, said state representative Byron Rushing, the bill's chief sponsor. Rushing said the three-year timetable would give the pension fund time to sell stocks without hurting returns and would allow the fund's managers to pressure multinationals to stop operating in Myanmar. The divestment law would apply only to the $24.8 billion of the fund that belongs to the state, not the $11.2 billion from municipal-pension reserves, Rushing said. The new bill represents a shift in tactics after the US high court ruled unanimously in June that the use of trade sanctions by states to protest human-rights abuses abroad infringed on the US president's power to set foreign policy (*Economist*, 2000a; Noble, 2000). Twenty-three US cities, including San Francisco, have adopted the Massachusetts law, modeled on anti-apartheid laws aimed at South Africa (Prasso, 2000).

Rushing said efforts to foster democracy and to improve human rights in Myanmar mirror efforts from the early 1980's when Massachusetts used sanctions to target South Africa. "It's the next South Africa", Rushing said (Noble, 2000). With the law, Massachusetts would join Los Angeles and Minneapolis that recently passed measures urging their pension funds to divest from Myanmar. The new bill's backers, many of them veterans of the divestment drives in the 1980s aimed at South Africa's racist apartheid regime, said they believed they were on firmer legal ground with divestment, but conceded the new law would not have the same impact as the overturned 1996 "Burma Law". That measure effectively barred multinationals that did business with Myanmar from contracts in the state by adding ten percent to any bids received from those multinationals. Several multinationals pulled out of Myanmar after Massachusetts passed the law, including Apple Computer Inc., Kodak, Motorola and Hewlett-Packard, specifically citing the law as the basis for their decisions. Massachusetts' schools and agencies served as major consumers for computers and related sales from these multinationals. "Divestment doesn't have the same impact on companies as procurement restrictions do. It's more of a symbolic impact than economic," said Simon Billenness, an analyst with socially responsible asset investment firm, Trillium Asset Management, and a supporter of the bill (Noble, 2000). The results in the study on South Africa tend to support Billenness' conclusions: Divestment measures against multinationals in South Africa had no effect on whether they stayed or left, although measures that hurt their profits directly did. Although the efficacy of governmental sanctions is being debated, clearly regulation affects multinationals' behaviors, including the variables they see as influencing their operations. Sanctions on purchasing may also assume importance, especially if the government is an important consumer as was Massachusetts with semi-conductor and computer manufacturers.

The indirect approach of organized consumer and shareholder boycotts has had mixed effects on multinationals investing in Myanmar. Militant and politicized unions and even professional groups and employers have organized damaging boycotts. Despite the statistics displayed in Table 9.2, Myanmar's apparel industry, the biggest employer after the bureaucracy, and providing work for about 300,000 locals, has shown some vulnerability. An estimated 60 percent of the mostly cheap clothes produced by 400 factories goes to the USA, if indirectly, through regional traders. Anti-Myanmar activists in the USA long ago deterred high-profile multinationals from sourcing in Myanmar. Several multinationals in the US apparel industry decided not to renew contracts with Myanmar suppliers because of rights abuses, the suppression of the democracy movement in Myanmar, and not incidentally, stakeholders' activism, the US-based Free Burma coalition said in a statement in late May 2000. These multinationals included Oshkosh B'Gosh Inc., Liz Claiborne, Eddie Bauer, Levi Strauss and Macy's. However, activists are unsure if economic ties between these multinationals and Myanmar have been completely severed.

Some US, European and Asian multinationals have buckled to pressure groups, sold their investments or cancelled future investment plans in Myanmar. These include US and European multinationals Carlsberg, Heineken, Eddie Bauer, Liz Claiborne, Levi Strauss and Hong Kong multinational Victoria Garment Manufacturing. Total and Unocal have also come under increasing pressure from shareholders' resolutions and consumers' boycotts. For a complete list of multinationals that have responded to stakeholders' voice and exit actions, including stockholders' resolutions, divestitures and governmental legislations, see the Free Burma Coalition site at http://www.freeburmacoalition.org/frames/victories.htm.

One vivid recent case confirmed that multinationals in Myanmar have attempted to deceive headquarters' stakeholders and to reduce their strategic influence as they did in South Africa. In April 1996, PepsiCo pulled out halfway in an attempt to look responsive to pressure from activists in the USA about a week before the shareholder meeting. PepsiCo planned to sell its 40 percent equity stake in Pepsi-Cola Products, Myanmar (PPM), but also to maintain elaborate franchising and distribution agreements with PPM. For example, PepsiCo continued to sell syrup concentrate to PPM as well as to license PPM to use PepsiCo's soft-drink trademarks in Myanmar. Indeed, PepsiCo's withdrawal synchronized with leaving category *Sale to Local Managers* in South Africa, as all licensing and economic arrangements remained intact. Because of continued stakeholders' pressure, on January 27, 1997, PepsiCo severed all ties with its former franchise bottler, Thien Tun, who had publicly called for the democracy movement headed by Aung San Suu Kyi to be "ostracized and crushed" (for more details, see the Free Burma Coalition's WWW site at http://www.freeburmacoalition.org). Similarly, Philips, the Dutch electronics company, said it stopped limited direct sales in Burma in 1998 (*El Pais*, 1998), but continued to deal with importers serving the country. And, ABN Amro that the Free Burma Coalition labeled as leaving Myanmar in May 2000, did not sever ties completely, as indicated by observers. The US pro-democracy activists hope to replicate in Myanmar the same effects they thought they achieved during the anti-apartheid movement in the 1980s. However, this study has highlighted the mixed effects of stakeholders' actions on US multinationals in South Africa, which also probably exist in Myanmar.

Additionally, whereas South Africa's neighboring states supported the boycotts, Myanmar's neighbors continue to do business with the military regime, and Myanmar's admission into ASEAN weakens efforts to isolate economically the country. With the continual involvement of China, Singapore, Malaysia and Japan, forcing US multinationals officially to leave Myanmar, but to maintain economic ties, may result in the suffocation of US ethical influence and the inability of US stakeholders to shape Myanmar's economic development. Unlike South Africa, Myanmar lacks strong internal forces that give support to liberalizing movements. The US multinationals, controlled by US stakeholders, could provide these forces.

Unfortunately, sanctions do not have to succeed in order to influence developments in Myanmar. An unintended consequence of failed sanctions may involve strengthening those elements in the ruling military regime that have an interest in keeping the country isolated. Many reasons exist for imposing sanctions: a wish to punish, a wish to set an example or simply a wish to do something. But if stakeholders wish to play a positive role in fostering a more open and prosperous Myanmar, then they must develop a coherent strategy that allows different actors, both inside and outside the country, to work together, or at least towards the same goal. In many significant respects, despite activists' rhetoric, Myanmar is not South Africa.

The apartheid regime in South Africa had an economy connected to the global economy, its existence relied strongly on outside support and powerful internal forces, all conditions lacking in Myanmar today.

Monitoring Nike

Since 1988, stakeholders in the Western countries, notably the USA and Australia, have attempted to influence multinationals to incorporate the values and ethics of headquarters' stakeholders especially regarding child labor, safe working conditions, living wages as well as compliance with other international labor standards. In these avenues, Nike Inc., the world's largest retailer of athletic shoes with headquarters in Beaverton, Oregon, has come under increasing criticism over working conditions in its factories in Asia. Labor and human-rights groups have reported physical and verbal abuse of workers, hazardous working conditions, pennies per hour wages and anti-union efforts throughout Indonesia, China, Cambodia and Vietnam, where Nike and its subcontractors employ over 400,000 workers.

Stakeholders have used lawsuits, resolutions, boycotts and divestitures with mixed success as in South Africa. Despite controversy, Nike continues to make virtually all its shoes in the factories it subcontracts in Asia (Larimer and McCarthy, 1998). The following WWW sites provide a comprehensive overview including current stakeholders' activism against Nike:

Academics Studying Nike (http://cbae.nmsu.edu/~dboje/nike.html)
Boycott Action (http://www.coopamerica.org/boycotts/boycott_grid.htm)
Boycott Nike (http://www.saigon.com/nike/update.htm)
Clean Clothes Campaign (http://www.cleanclothes.org/)
Corporate Watch — Sweatshops (http://www.corpwatch.org/trac/nike/)
NikeWatch Campaign (http://www.caa.org.au/campaigns/nike/news.html)
Unite! (http://www.uniteunion.org/pressbox/nike-report.html)

Policymakers and corporations increasingly perceive stakeholders' activism as an accepted part of business environments (see *Economist*, 2000b). Many view corporate codes of conduct and espoused principles (especially those employing external auditors) as begun in South Africa, and embraced by Nike in the late 1990s, as responsible and effective corporate responses to stakeholders' activism (see *Economist*, 1999). Little systematic research exists at the corporate level of how multinationals use codes and principles to deceive stakeholders and as primarily symbolic activities.

This book has argued that multinationals in South Africa engaged in symbolic activities (such as adherence to the Sullivan Principles) and deception (such as trusts and other leaving facades) to stave off stakeholders' influence. Similarly, Nike initially responded to public criticisms by claiming it had no control over conditions inside factories making its shoes and clothing. The multinational argued that as it did not own any of the factories producing its products, it could not influence working conditions or wages (O'Rourke, 1997). Labor-rights groups challenged this claim, demanding that Nike take responsibility for its subcontractors' actions and as ensuing bad publicity built up, Nike changed its strategy (for an excellent overview, see O'Rourke, 1997). First, like the US multinationals in South Africa, Nike hired two public accounting firms, Ernst & Young and PriceWaterhouse Coopers, to perform internal audits of the labor and environmental practices inside its subcontractors for external audiences. Nike described the Ernst & Young audits as "systematic, unannounced evaluations by independent auditors" of current working conditions inside their factories. Second, it hired former United Nation's Ambassador Andrew Young's consulting firm, GoodWorks International LLC, to review the company's Code of Conduct and subcontractors' compliance. Nike made public Andrew Young's report that largely exonerated Nike, and followed this with a publicity campaign. The much more in-depth internal audits however, which Andrew Young claimed to have accessed, remained confidential (O'Rourke, 1997). Finally, Nike subsidized its own research, such as the now infamous Dartmouth Study, indicating that Nike paid living wages in Asia. The Transnational Resource and Action Center later revealed that MBA students at the Tuck School of Business (not business professors as suggested by Nike) conducted and authored the study as a class assignment, with all expenses paid by Nike (see activist group, Boycott Nike's WWW site at http://www.saigon.com/ nike/update.htm for more details).

Notwithstanding these revelations, Nike and other apparel manufacturers have argued that multinationals should employ their own accounting firms to perform audits for external stakeholders. Labor, religious and human-rights groups have disagreed with this notion and questioned the independence of Nike's and other multinationals' audits (O'Rourke, 1997). In his investigation of Ernst & Young's audit of Nike's Vietnam factory, O'Rourke (1997) revealed that while the accounting firm did not explicitly present its methodology, it stated that "the procedures we have performed were those that you [Nike] specifically instructed us to perform. Accordingly, we make no comment as to the sufficiency of these procedures for your purposes". Consequently, Ernst & Young did not perform an independent audit, but rather simply followed Nike's instructions. Ernst & Young's auditors spent approximately one week in the Tae Kwang Vina factory in Vietnam. O'Rourke's (1997) scathing investigation concluded that Ernst & Young's auditors relied largely on management information about working conditions, organizational practices and wages to write their report. The auditors performed no independent environmental monitoring or air sampling. Occupational health and safety information came entirely from secondary sources (largely Vietnamese government agencies). Information on workers' perceptions and attitudes came from a survey of 50 employees "randomly selected...from the payroll register". The auditing methodology and reporting failed to adhere to the conventions of occupational health and safety or environmental auditing (O'Rourke, 1997).

Nike has dedicated a significant portion of its business WWW site (http://nikebiz.com/labor) to disseminating its defense. "The reality is that our contract factories are among the best in China", stated Nike in its WWW site's news release chastising US critics who have not visited the Asian factories. "The workers in those factories received fair compensation and are treated with respect and dignity" (Hetter, 2000). Nike has repeatedly claimed that regular monitoring ensures that its factories break free of unethical working practices.

Despite its seeming efforts, Nike's factories have continually violated international labor standards and its own Code of Conduct in Indonesia, Malaysia, Australia, Vietnam and China. These violations span paying illegal training-level wages in Indonesia; physical assaults by managers on factory workers in Indonesia, China and Vietnam; serious violations of health regulations in Vietnam and China; extremely large worker/manager wage disparities in Vietnam; and the use of child labor in Vietnam (see Clean Clothes Campaign, 2000, and Nike Watch Campaign, 2000, for more complete lists of violations). The latest report on violations took place in October 2000 when a BBC program, *Panorama*, exposed that Nike was again using a factory in Cambodia that broke its own Code of Conduct and anti-sweatshop rules. *Panorama*'s team uncovered sweatshop-like working conditions and child labor at the June Textiles factory within days of arriving in Cambodia (BBC, 2000). After attempting to label the child labor in the Cambodian factory as an isolated case, Nike said it would no longer work with the Cambodian clothing manufacturer. The Singaporean-managed factory in Phnom Penh employed about 3,800 people making clothes for Nike, the Gap and other brands (Dworkin, 2000).

Meanwhile, in response to protests in the USA, efforts to construct industry-wide inspection systems are also taking place. Furthest along appears the Fair Labor Association (FLA), a monitoring group made up of industry and human-rights representatives that a Presidential task force created in mid-1999. In September 1999, former White House Counsel Charles Ruff signed on as the FLA's first chairman and in recent months, Adidas, Salomon AG and Levi Strauss & Co. joined the eight founding multinationals, including Nike, Reebok, Liz Claiborne and Phillips-Van Heusen, as members (Bernstein, 1999; Finley, 2000). According to news reports, the FLA's leaders were discussing how to ensure independence and integrity in their external audits of these multinationals. However, if the FLA follows founding-member Nike's auditing methodologies, it will reinforce primarily symbolic monitoring for multinationals, keeping their actual operations away from some stakeholders' values, ethics, scrutiny and influence.

Questions for the Future

We need new theories to influence multinationals' complex behaviors in host countries. Anti-apartheid activities in South Africa highlighted some of the issues that activists and policy makers need to address when sanctioning large groups of multinationals. One key set of questions concerns modes of leaving and include: How have the multinationals sold their assets? Who has purchased these assets? What parties have benefited from the sales?

Another set of questions revolves around the economic ties such as licensing, franchising and distribution that continue between many multinationals and their former subsidiaries. As indicated in Chapters 4 and 8, roughly half the US multinationals that left South Africa in the 1980s maintained such economic ties with the country. Although researchers have analyzed the effects of sanctions on countries (e.g., Elliott, Schott and Hufbauer, 2001) they have ignored effects on multinationals and the economic ties that continue between multinationals and former host countries. This book has attempted to show how sanctions may have affected multinationals as well as these economic ties. Similar concerns as existed in South Africa face Myanmar activists, university trustees, government officials and company shareholders. Should they continue to demand an end to direct investments when economic ties remain intact? Has the exodus of US multinationals from Myanmar reduced the US government's powers over that country? Most importantly, has the activists' success (in getting multinationals to leave Myanmar) been the movement's failure (in its ensuing loss of control over multinationals in Myanmar and over the future of that country)?

Like chameleons, multinationals adapt to their external environments. US multinationals may bolster existing social structures in Myanmar or other parts of the developing world. However, some evidence indicates that US multinationals also provide better jobs and better working conditions for many more than indigenous companies do. Like chameleons, multinationals may adapt to a very small range of environments. Needs to preserve integrity and consistency may force US multinationals to maintain many of their American social and work practices, thereby perpetuating some ethical influences from home. Activists should question the effectiveness of indiscriminately sanctioning all multinationals with operations in Myanmar. Rather, activists and policy makers should study the social environments to which multinationals may adapt and the ones that they may help change. Societies need symbols of social justice. One question, and one opportunity, may concern encouraging the more socially responsible multinationals to stay in Myanmar.

Influencing specific multinationals' behaviors, such as Nike's, exposes stakeholders and activists to other sets of problems. When accused by activists of manufacturing in sweatshops, brand-name marketers, such as Nike, have tended to dismiss the claims. But, generally, activists have been proven right (Bernstein, 2000). A year-long study by labor experts from Harvard and four other universities found that 13 factories making collegiate-logo clothing for US multinationals in seven developing countries engaged in nonpayment of wages, lax safety and excessive overtime (Bernstein, 2000). What strategies should activists implement to affect multinationals' operations? This book has identified that stockholders' resolutions and boycotts may not work. However, governmental regulation specifically designed to reduce the profits of multinationals manufacturing in sweatshops, detrimentally affecting repatriation of profits or increasing taxes, may prove effective. Should activists continue to expend time and money on strategies that fail to affect corporate profits? This book clearly indicates — no. Indeed, despite a decade of activism directed against Nike, and much bad publicity, almost no evidence exists that activists have affected Nike's profits, and therefore Nike's substantive behaviors. Perhaps the activists should turn their attention to influencing US legislation against Nike and similar multinationals, which this book reveals could greatly influence their operations in host countries.

When dealing with Nike, Reebok and other multinationals in the apparel industry, stockholders and activists should realize the limits of their ability to influence foreign operations. The multinationals have deceived stakeholders by playing a giant shell game, moving sweatshop-like manufacturing operations from one developing country to another while using authoritative sources and external audits to grant legitimacy and to provide reassurances. In the decades since Nike has responded to and acknowledged activists' demands, it has amended few of its work practices. Nike is not alone. Indeed, investigators for US labor and human-rights groups estimate that thousands of sweatshops making products for US and European companies in Asia and Latin America do everything from force employees to work 16-hour days to cheat them out of already meager wages. "It would be extremely generous to say that even ten percent of [Western multinationals charged with abuses] have done anything meaningful about labor conditions", said S. Prakash

Sethi, a Baruch College business professor who helped to set up a monitoring system for Mattel at its dozen factories in China, Indonesia, Mexico and elsewhere (Bernstein, 2000). Abuses may actually be proliferating. Price hikes in US retail garments have lagged inflation since 1982, and Asian factory owners complain about intense pressure from headquarters to find new ways to squeeze out costs and to maintain high profit margins for multinationals (Bernstein, 2000).

What kind of monitoring will prevent multinationals' responses from revolving around the purely symbolic? Can stockholders surmount principal-agency problems and obtain the information necessary to control multinationals' operations? The experience with South Africa indicates that unless their profits get directly affected, the multinationals will probably not respond substantively to stakeholders' demands. A more complex understanding of the power of multinationals, including possible reasons for why they enter host states, why they may leave, and the relative power of stakeholders over time, should better inform strategies on how to influence multinationals and when strategies may prove most effective.

References

Abernathy, W. J. (1978) *The Productivity Dilemma: Roadblock to Innovation in the Automobile Industry*. Baltimore: Johns Hopkins University Press.

Agence France-Presse (2000) "International Trade Unions Threaten Action against Myanmar Investors", December 1.

Agmon, T. B. and Lessard, D. R. (1977) "Investor Recognition of Corporate International Diversification", *Journal of Finance*, September, 1049–1055.

Aharoni, Y. (1968) *The Foreign Investment Decision Process*. Boston: Graduate School of Business Administration, Harvard University.

Alchian, A. A. (1950) "Uncertainty, Evolution, and Economic Theory", *Journal of Political Economy*, **58**, 211–221.

Aldrich, H. E. (1971) "Organizational Boundaries and Inter-Organizational Conflict", *Human Relations*, **24**, 279–293.

Aldrich, H. E. and Mindlin, S. E. (1978) "Uncertainty and Dependence: Two Perspectives on Environment". In L. Karpik (Ed.), *Organization and Environment*, 149–170. Beverly Hills, CA: Sage Publications.

Aldrich, H. E. and Pfeffer, J. (1976) "Environments of Organizations", *Annual Review of Sociology*, **2**, 79–105.

Aliber, R. Z. (1970) "A Theory of Direct Foreign Investment". In C. P. Kindleberger (Ed.), *The International Corporation*, Cambridge, MA: MIT Press.

Allen, M. P. and Panian, S. K. (1982) "Power, Performance and Succession in the Large Corporation", *Administrative Science Quarterly*, **27**, 538–547.

Allison, G. T. (1971) *Essence of Decision*. Boston: Little, Brown.

Allison, P. D. (1984) *Event History Analysis*, Sage University Paper 46. Newbury Park, CA: Sage Publications.

Ansoff, I. H. (1965) "The Firm of the Future", *Harvard Business Review*, **43**, 162–178.

Ansoff, H. I., Declerck, R. P. and Hayes, R. L. (1976) *From Strategic Planning to Strategic Management*. New York: Wiley.

Asch, S. E. (1958) "Effects of Group Pressure upon the Modification and Distortion of Judgments". In E. E. Maccoby, T. M. Newcomb and E. L. Hartley (Eds.), *Readings in Social Psychology*. New York: Holt, Rinehart and Winston.

Ashby, W. R. (1956) *Introduction to Cybernetics*. London: Chapman and Hall.

Astley, W. G. and Van de Ven, A. H. (1983) "Central Perspectives and Debates in Organization Theory", *Administrative Science Quarterly*, **28**, 245–273.

Bacharach, S. B. and Lawler, E. J. (1980) *Power and Politics in Organizations*. San Francisco: Jossey-Bass.

Barnard, C. (1948) *Organization and Management*. Cambridge, MA: Harvard University Press.

Bartlett, C. A. (1986) "Building and Managing the Transnational: The New Organizational Challenge". In M. E. Porter (Ed.), *Competition in Global Industries*, 367–401, Boston, MA: Harvard Business School Press.

Bartlett, C. A. and Ghoshal, S. (2000) *Transnational Management*. New York: McGraw-Hill Higher Education.

Bartlett, C. A. and Ghoshal, S. (1987) "Managing across Borders: New Organizational Responses", *Sloan Management Review*, Fall, 43–53.

Baumol, W. J. (1962) "The Theory of the Expansion of the Firm", *American Economic Review*, December, 1078–1087.

Baumol, W. J. (1967) *Business Behavior. Values and Growth*. New York: Harcourt, Brace and World.

Baysinger, B. D. (1984) "Domain Maintenance as an Objective of Business Political Activity", *Academy of Management Review*, **9**, 248–258.

Baysinger, B. D., Keim, G. D. and Zeithaml, C. P. (1985) "An Empirical Evaluation of the Potential for Including Shareholders in Corporate Constituency Programs", *Academy of Management Journal*, **28**, 1, 180–200.

Baysinger, B. D., Meiners, R. and Zeithaml, C. P. (1981) *Barriers to Corporate Growth*. Lexington, MA: Heath Co.

BBC (2000) "Gap and Nike: No Sweat"?, *Panorama*, October 15.

Bennett, D. C. and Sharpe, K. E. (1985) *Transnational Corporations versus the State: The Political Economy of the Mexican Auto Industry*. Princeton, NJ: Princeton University Press.

Benson, J. K. (1975) "The Interorganizational Network as a Political Economy", *Administrative Science Quarterly*, **20**, 229–249.

Berg, N. A. (1969) "What's Different about Conglomerate Management"?, *Harvard Business Review*, 47, **6**, 112–120.

Berg, N. A. (1973) "Corporate Role in Diversified Companies". In B. Taylor and K. MacMillen (Eds.), *Business Policy: Teaching and Research*, New York: Halstead Press.

Berle, A., Jr. and Means, G. C. (1932) *The Modern Corporation and Private Property*. New York: Macmillan.

Bernstein, A. (1999) "Sweatshop Reform; How to Solve the Standoff", *Business Week*, May 3.

Bernstein, A. (2000) "A World of Sweatshops", *Business Week*, November 6.

Beyer, J. M. (1981) "Ideologies, Values, and Decision Making in Organizations". In P. C. Nystrom and W. H. Starbuck (Eds.), *Handbook of Organizational Design*, **2**, 166–202. New York: Oxford University Press.

Biersteker, T. (1978) *Distortion or Development? Contending Perspectives on the Multinational Corporation*. Cambridge, MA: MIT Press.

Biggart, N. (1977) "The Creative-destructive Process of Organizational Change", *Administrative Science Quarterly*, **22**, 410–424.

Birnbaum, P. H. (1985) "Political Strategies of Regulated Organizations as Functions of Context and Fear", *Strategic Management Journal*, **6**, 135–150.

Blankenship, L. V. and Elling, R. H. (1962) "Organizational Support and Community Power Structure: The Hospital", *Journal of Health and Human Behavior*, **3**, 257–269.

Boddewyn, J. J. (1983) "Foreign and Domestic Divestment and Investment Decisions: Like or Unlike?", *Journal of International Business Studies*, Winter, 23–35.

Boland, R. J. (1982) "Myth and Technology in the American Accounting Profession", *Journal of Management Studies*, **19**, 1, 109–127.

Bornschier, V. and Ballmer-Cao, T. H. (1979) "Income Inequality: A Cross-National Study of the Relationships between MNC Penetration, Dimensions of the Power

Structure and Income Distribution", *American Sociological Review*, **44**, 487–506.

Bornschier, V., Chase-Dunn, C. and Rubinson, R. (1978) "Cross-National Evidence of the Effects of Foreign Investment and Aid on Economic Growth and Inequality: A Survey of Findings and Reanalysis", *American Journal of Sociology*, **84**, 651–683.

Boswell, J. (1973) *The Rise and Fall of Small Firms*. London: Allen and Unwin.

Boulding, K. E. (1975) "The Management of Decline", *Change*, **64**, 8–9.

Bower, J. L. (1970) *Managing the Resource Allocation Process*. Boston: Graduate School of Business Administration, Harvard University.

Breton, A. (1964) "The Economics of Nationalism", *Journal of Political Economy*, **72**, 4.

Brooke, M. Z. and Remmers, H. L. (1970) *The Strategy of Multinational Enterprise*. London: Longman.

Buckley, P. J. (1985) "A Critical View of Theories of the Multinational Enterprise". In P. J. Buckley and M. C. Casson (1985) *The Economic Theory of the Multinational Enterprise*, 1–19. London: Macmillan.

Buckley, P. J. and Casson, M. C (1976) *The Future of the Multinational Enterprise*. London: Macmillan.

Buckley, P. J. and Casson, M. C. (1985) *The Economic Theory of the Multinational Enterprise*. London: Macmillan.

Buckley, P. J. and Davies, H. (1980) "Foreign Licensing in Overseas Operations: Theory and Evidence from the U.K.". In R. G. Hawkins and A. J. Prasad (Eds.), *Technology Transfer and Economic Development*, Greenwich, CT: JAI Press.

Buckley, P. J. and Ghauri, P. N. (1999) *The Internationalization of the Firm*. New York: International Thompson Business Press.

Budd, R. W., Thorpe, R. K. and Donohew, L. (1967) *Content Analysis of Communications*. New York: Macmillan.

Burt, R. S. (1980a) "Cooptive Corporate Actor Networks: A Reconsideration of Interlocking Directorates Involving American Manufacturing", *Administrative Science Quarterly*, **25**, 557–582.

Burt, R. S. (1980b) "Autonomy in a Social Typology", *American Journal of Sociology*, **85**, 892–925.

Burt, R. S. (1982) *Toward a Structural Theory of Action: Network Models of Social Structure, Perception and Action*. New York: Academic Press.

Burt, R. S. (1983) *Corporate Profits and Co-optation: Networks of Market Constraints and Directorate Ties in the American Economy*. New York: Academic Press.

Calleo, D. and Rowland, B. (1973) *America and the World Political Economy*. Bloomington, IN: Indiana University Press.

Cameron, K. (1983) "Strategic Responses to Conditions of Decline: Higher Education and the Private Sector", *Journal of Higher Education*, **54**, 359–380.

Cameron, K., Whetten, D. A. and Kim, M. (1986) "Organizational Dysfunctions of Decline", *Academy of Management Journal*, **30**, 1, 126–138.

Carroll, J. S. (1978) "The Effect of Imagining an Effect on Expectations for the Event: An Interpretation in Terms of the Availability Heuristic", *Journal of Experimental and Social Psychology*, **14**, 88–96.

Carter, B. E. (1988) *International Economic Sanctions*. Cambridge, England: University of Cambridge Press.

Carter, E. E. (1981) "Resource Allocation". In P. C. Nystrom and W. H. Starbuck (Eds.), *Handbook of Organizational Design*, **2**, 152–165. New York: Oxford University Press.

Caves, R. E. (1971) "International Corporations: The Industrial Economics of Foreign Investment", *Economica*, **38**, 1–27.

Caves, R. E. (1982) *Multinational Enterprise and Economic Analysis*. New York: Cambridge University Press.

Caves, R. E. and Porter, M. E. (1976) "Barriers to Exit". In R. T. Masson and P. D. Quails (Eds.), *Essays on Industrial Organization in Honor of Joe Bain*, Cambridge, MA: Ballinger.

Chandler, A. D. (1977) *The Visible Hand: The Managerial Revolution in American Business*. Cambridge, MA: Harvard University Press.

Channon, D. F. (1974) "Prediction and Practice in Multinational Strategic Planning", Working Paper, Manchester Business School.

Chase-Dunn, C. (1975) "The Effects of International Economic Dependence on Development and Inequality", *American Sociological Review*, **40**, 720–739.

Child, J. (1972) "Organization Structure, Environment, and Performance: The Role of Strategic Choice", *Sociology*, **6**, 2–21.

Child, J., Francis, A., Keiser, A., Nyman, S. and Silberston, A. (1975) "The Growth of Firms as a Field of Research", Working Paper 30, University of Aston, Management Centre.

Child, J. and Keiser, A. (1981) "Development of Organizations over Time". In P. C. Nystrom and W. H. Starbuck (Eds.), *Handbook of Organizational Design*, 1, 28–64. New York: Oxford University Press.

Ciscel, D. H. (1974) "Determinants of Executive Compensation", *Southern Economic Journal*, **40**, 613–617.

Clean Clothes Campaign (2000) "Nike's Track Record 1988–2000", http://www.cleanclothes.org/companies/niketrack.htm

Cohen, M. D. and March, J. G. (1974) *Leadership and Ambiguity*. New York: McGraw-Hill.

Condry, J. (1977) "Enemies of Exploration: Self-initiated versus Other-Initiated Learning", *Journal of Personality and Social Psychology*, **35**, 459–477.

Connolly, T., Conlon, E. J. and Deutsch, S. J. (1980) "Organizational Effectiveness: A Multi-Constituency Approach", *Academy of Management Review*, **5**, 2, 211–217.

Crozier, M. (1964) *The Bureaucratic Phenomenon*. Chicago: University of Chicago Press.

Crozier, M. (1974) *The Stalled Society*. New York: Viking Press.

Cummings, T. G. and Worley, C. G. (1997) *Organization Development and Change*. Cincinnati, OH: South-Western College Publishing.

Cyert, R. M. (1978) "The Management of Universities of Constant or Decreasing Size", *Public Administration Review*, **38**, 344–349.

Cyert, R. M. and March, J. G. (1963) *A Behavioral Theory of the Firm*. Englewood Cliffs, NJ: Prentice-Hall.

Czechowicz, I. J., Choi, F. D. S. and Baveshi, V. B. (1982) *Assessing Foreign Subsidiary Performance: Systems and Practices of Large Multinational Companies*. New York: Business International Corporation.

Daft, R. L., Sormunen, J. and Parks, D. (1988) "Chief Executive Scanning, Environmental Characteristics, and Company Performance: An Empirical Study", *Strategic Management Journal*, **9**, 123–139.

Dahl, R. A. (1957) "The Concept of Power", *Behavioral Science*, **2**, 201–215.

Dahl, R. A. (1963) *Modern Political Analysis.* Englewood Cliffs, NJ: Prentice-Hall.

Dahrendorf, R. (1959) *Class and Class Conflict in Industrial Society.* Palo Alto, CA: Stanford University Press.

Dalton, M. (1959) *Men who Manage.* New York: John Wiley.

Davidson, W. H. (1982) *Global Strategic Management.* New York: John Wiley.

Davis, M. S. (1971) "That's Interesting!", *Philosophy of Social Science*, **1**, 309–344.

Dewar, R. and Hage, J. (1978) "Size, Technology, Complexity and Structural Differentiation: Toward a Theoretical Synthesis", *Administrative Science Quarterly*, **23**, 111–136.

Di Maggio, P. J. and Powell, W. W. (1983) "The Iron Cage Revisited: Institutional Isomorphism and Collective Rationality in Organizational Fields", *American Sociological Review*, **48**, 147–160.

Dowling, J. and Pfeffer, J. (1975) "Organizational Legitimacy: Social Values and Organizational Behavior", *Pacific Sociological Review*, **18**, 122–136.

Downs, A. (1967) *Inside Bureaucracy.* Boston: Little, Brown.

Doz, Y. L. (1980) "Strategic Management in Multinational Companies", *Sloan Management Review*, Fall, 15–29.

Doz, Y. L. (1986) "Government Policies and Global Industries". In M. E. Porter (Ed.), *Competition in Global Industries,* 225–266. Boston: Harvard Business School Press.

Doz, Y. L. and Prahalad, C. K. (1981) "Headquarters Influence and Strategic Control in MNCs", *Sloan Management Review*, Fall, 15–29.

Duhaime, I. M. and Grant, J. H. (1984) "Factors Influencing Divestment Decision-making: Evidence from a Field Study", *Strategic Management Journal*, **5**, 301–318.

Dunbar, R. L. M. and Wasilewski, N. (1985) "Regulating External Threats in the Cigarette Industry", *Administrative Science Quarterly*, **30**, 540–559.

Dunning J. H. (1973) "The Determinants of International Production", *Oxford Economic Papers*, November, 289–336.

Dunning, J. H. (1974) *Economic Analysis and the Multinational Enterprise.* London: Allen and Unwin.

Dunning, J. H. (1981) *International Production and the Multinational Enterprise.* London: Allen and Unwin.

Dunning, J. H. (1983) "Market Power of the Firm and International Transfer of Technology", *International Journal of Industrial Organization*, **1**, 333–351.

Dworkin, A. (2000) "Nike Parts Ways with Factory in Cambodia", *Portland Oregonian*, October 5.

Eaton, B. C. and Lipsey, R. G. (1980) "Exit Barriers are Entry Barriers: The Durability of Capital as a Barrier to Entry", *Bell Journal of Economics*, **11**, 721–730.

Eaton, B. C., and Lipsey, R. G. (1981) "Capital, Commitment and Entry Equilibrium", *Bell Journal of Economics*, **12**, 593–605.

Eccles, R. (1981) "The Quasifirm in the Construction Industry", *Journal of Economic Behavior and Organization*, **2**, 335–357.

Eccles, R. (1982) *A Synopsis of Transfer Pricing: An Analysis and Action Plan.* Mimeograph, Harvard Business School, Cambridge, MA.

Eccles, R. (1983) "Transfer Pricing, Fairness and Control", Working Paper 83–167, Harvard Business School.

Economist (1999) "Sweatshop Wars", February 25.

Economist (2000a) "Tea Party: States Rights. Massachusetts v Myanmar", March 25.

Economist (2000b) "The World's View of Multinationals", January 27.

Edelman, M. (1977) *The Symbolic Uses of Politics*, Urbana: University of Illinois Press.

Edelman, M. (1977) *Political Language: Words that Succeed and Policies that Fail.* New York: Academic Press.

Edstrom, A. and Galbraith, J. R. (1977) "Transfers of Managers as a Coordination and Control Strategy in Multinational Organizations", *Administrative Science Quarterly*, **22**, 248–263.

El Pais (1998) "Philips Withdraws from Burma", October 4.

Elliott, K. A., Schott, J. J. and Hufbauer, G. C. (2001) *Economic Sanctions Reconsidered*, third edition. Washington, DC: Institute for International Economics.

Emery, F. E. and Trist, E. (1965) "The Causal Texture of Organizational Environments", *Human Relations*, **18**, 21–31.

Encarnation, D. J. and Wells, L. T. (1986) "Competitive Strategies in Global Industries: A View from Host Governments". In M. E. Porter (Ed.), *Competition in Global Industries*, 267–290. Boston: Harvard Business School Press.

Etzioni, A. (1961) *A Comparative Analysis of Complex Organizations*. New York: Free Press.

Etzioni, A. (1988) *The Moral Dimension. Toward a New Economics*. New York: Free Press.

Evans, P. B. (1979) *Dependent Development: The Alliance of Multinational, State and Local Capital in Brazil*. Princeton, NJ: Princeton University Press.

Evans, P. B. (1981) "Recent Research on Multinational Corporations", *Annual Review of Sociology*, **7**, 199–223.

Evans, P. B., Rueschemeyer, D. and Skocpol, T. (1986) *Bringing the State Back In*. New York: Cambridge University Press.

Evans, P. B. and Timberlake, M. (1980) "Dependence, Inequality and the Growth of the Tertiary: A Comparative Analysis of Less Developed Countries", *American Sociological Review*, **45**, 531–552.

Farrell, D. and Petersen, J. C. (1982) "Patterns of Political Behavior in Organizations", *Academy of Management Review*, **7**, 3, 403–412.

Fayerweather, J. (1969) *International Business Management: A Conceptual Framework*. New York: McGraw-Hill.

Fayerweather, J. (1982) *International Business Strategy and Administration*. Cambridge, MA: Ballinger Publishing.

Feldman, M. S. and March, J. G. (1981) "Information in Organizations as Signal and Symbol", *Administrative Science Quarterly*, **26**, 171–186.

Ferguson, C. E. (1980) "The Relationship of Business Size to Stability: An Empirical Approach", *Journal of Industrial Economics*, **9**, 43–62.

Finkelstein, S. and Hambrick, D. C. (1988) "Chief Executive Compensation: A Synthesis and Reconciliation", *Strategic Management Journal*, **9**, 543–558.

Finkelstein, S. and Hambrick, D. C. (1989) "Chief Executive Compensation: A Study of the Intersection of Markets and Political Processes", *Strategic Management Journal*, **10**, 121–134.

Finley, B. (2000) "Giving Buyers the Facts Plan would Certify Working Conditions", *Denver Post*, November 26.

Frank, R. H. and Freeman, R. T. (1978) The *Distributional Consequences of Direct Foreign Investment*. New York: Academic Press.

Franko, L. G. (1974) "The Move toward a Multidivisional Structure in European Organizations", *Administrative Science Quarterly*, **19**, 493–506.

Franko, L. G. (1976) *The European Multinationals: A Renewed Challenge to American and British Big Business*. Stamford, CT: Graylock.

Freeman, R. E. (1984) *Strategic Management: A Stakeholder Approach*. Marshfield, MA: Pitman Publishing.

Friedlander, F. and Pickle, H. (1968) "Components of Effectiveness in Small Organizations", *Administrative Science Quarterly*, **13**, 2, 289–304.

Fry, L. W., Keim, G. D. and Meiners, R. E. (1982) "Corporate Contributions: Altruistic or For-profit"?, *Academy of Management Journal*, **25**, 95–108.

Fujii, Y. (2000) "ILO Takes First Step in Implementing Myanmar Sanctions", *Kyodo News*, December 8.

Galaskiewicz, J. (1985) "Interorganizational Relations", *Annual Review of Sociology*, **11**, 281–304.

Galbraith, J. K. (1967) *The New Industrial State*. Boston: Houghton Mifflin.

Galbraith, J. K. (1973) *Economics and the Public Purpose*. Boston: Houghton Mifflin.

Gamson, W. and Scotch, N. (1964) "Scapegoating in Baseball", *American Journal of Sociology*, **70**, 69–75.

Gandz, J. and Murray, V. V. (1980) "The Experience of Workplace Politics", *Academy of Management Journal*, **23**, 237–251.

GAO/NSIAD-88-165 (1988) *South Africa. Trends in Trade, Lending and Investment*. United States General Accounting Office, Report to Congressional Requesters.

Gerlach, L. P. and Palmer, G. B. (1981) "Adaptation through Evolving Interdependence". In P. C. Nystrom and W. H. Starbuck (Eds.), *Handbook of Organizational Design*, **1**, 323–381. New York: Oxford University Press.

Ghauri, P. N. (1992) "New Structures in MNCs Based in Small Countries: A Network Approach", *European Management Journal*, **10**, 3, 357–364.

Ghertman, M. (1988) "Foreign Subsidiary and Parents' Roles during Strategic Investment and Divestment Decisions", *Journal of International Business Studies*, **19**, 1, 47–67.

Ghoshal, S. (1987) "Global Strategy: An Organizing Framework", *Strategic Management Journal*, **8**, 425–440.

Giddy, I. H. (1978) "The Demise of the Product Cycle Model in International Business Theory", *Columbia Journal of World Business*, Spring, 90–97.

Gilmour, S. C. (1973) *The Divestment Decision Process*. Doctoral dissertation, Harvard Business School, Cambridge, MA.

Gilpin, R. (1975) "Three Models of the Future", *International Organization*, **29**,1, 37–60.

Gilpin, R. (1987) *The Political Economy of International Relations*. Princeton, NJ: Princeton University Press.

Gladwin, T. N. (1982) "Conflict Management in International Business". In I. Walter and T. Murray (Eds.) *Handbook of International Business*, **41**, 1–30. New York: John Wiley.

Gladwin, T. N. and Walter, I. (1980) *Multinationals under Fire*. New York: John Wiley.

Gladwin, T. N. and Walter, I. (1983) "How Multinationals can Manage Social Conflict". In W. H. Goldberg (Ed.), *Governments and Multinationals*. Cambridge, MA: Oelgeschlager, Gunn and Hain.

Glasberg, D. S. and Schwartz, M. (1983) "Ownership and Control of Corporations", *Annual Review of Sociology*, **9**, 311–332.

Gordon, R. A. (1945) *Business Leadership in the Large Corporation*. Washington, DC: Brookings Institute.

Gorecki, P. K. (1976) "The Determinants of Entry by Domestic and Foreign Enterprises in Canadian Manufacturing Industries: Some Comments and Empirical Evidence", *Review of Economics and Statistics*, **58**, 485–488.

Graham, E. M. (1978) "Transatlantic Investment by Multinational Firms: A Rivalistic Phenomenon"? *Journal of Post-Keynesian Economics*, **1**, Fall, 82–89.

Granovetter, M. (1985) "Economic Action and Social Structure: The Problem of Embeddedness", *American Journal of Sociology*, **91**, 3, 481–510.

Greenhalgh, L. and Rosenblatt, Z. (1984) "Job Insecurity: Toward Conceptual Clarity", *Academy of Management Review*, **9**, 3, 438–448.

Grinyer, P. H. and Norburn, D. (1975) "Planning for Existing Markets: Perceptions of Executives and Financial Performance", *Journal of the Royal Statistical Society*, Series A, **138**, 70–97.

Grinyer, P. H. and Spender, J. (1979) *Turnaround*. London: Associated Business Press.

Grosse, R. E. (1982) "Regional Offices in Multinational Firms". In A. M. Rugman (Ed.), *New Theories of the Multinational Enterprise*, 107–132. New York: St. Martin's Press.

Guth, W. D. (1976) "Toward a Social System Theory of Corporate Strategy", *Journal of Business*, **49**, 3, 374–388.

Guth, W. D. and Macmillan, I. (1986) "Strategy Implementation versus Middle Management Self-interest", *Strategic Management Journal*, **7**, 4, 313–327.

Guth, W. D. and Taguri, R. (1965) "Personal Values and Corporate Strategy", *Harvard Business Review*, **43**, 5, 123–132.

Haley, G. T. and Haley, U. C. V. (1998) "Boxing with Shadows: Competing Effectively with the Overseas Chinese and Overseas Indian Business Networks in the Asian Arena", *Journal of Organizational Change Management*, **11**, 4, 301–320.

Haley, G. T., Tan, C. T. and Haley, U. C. V. (1998) *New Asian Emperors: The Overseas Chinese, their Strategies and Competitive Advantages*. Oxford and Boston: Butterworth-Heinemann.

Haley, U. C. V. (1990a) "Corporate Contributions as Managerial Masques: Reframing Corporate Contributions as Strategies to Influence Society", *Journal of Management Studies*, **28**, 5, 485–509.

Haley, U. C. V. (1990b) *From Catalysts to Chameleons: Multinational Firms as Participants in Political Environments*. Doctoral dissertation, Stern School of Business, New York University, New York, NY.

Haley, U. C. V. (1997) "The MBTI Personality Inventory and Decision-Making Styles: Identifying and Managing Cognitive Trails in Strategic Decision Making". In C. Fitzgerald and L. K. Kirby (Eds.), *Developing Leaders. Research and Applications in Psychological Type and Leadership Development*, 187–223. Palo Alto, CA: Consulting Psychologists Press.

Haley, U. C. V. (1998) "Virtual Singapores: Shaping International Competitive Environments through Business-Government Partnerships", *Journal of Organizational Change Management*, **11**, 4, 338–356.

Haley, U. C. V. (2000a) *Strategic Management in the Asia Pacific: Harnessing Regional and Organizational Change for Competitive Advantage*. Oxford and Boston: Butterworth-Heinemann.

Haley, U. C. V. (2000b) "Corporate Governance and Restructuring in Asia: An Overview", *Seoul Journal of Economics*, **13**, 3, 225–251.

Haley, U. C. V. (2000c) "The Hair of the Dog that Bit You: Successful Market Strategies in Post-crisis South-East Asia", *Marketing Intelligence and Planning*, **18**, 5, 236–246.

Haley, U. C. V. and Haley, G. T. (1997) "When the Tourists Flew In: Strategic Implications of Foreign Direct Investment in Vietnam's Tourism Industry", *Management Decision*, **35**, 8, 595–604.

Haley, U. C. V. and Low, L. (1998) "Crafted Culture: Governmental Sculpting of Modern Singapore and Effects on Business Environments", *Journal of Organizational Change Management*, **11**, 6, 530–553.

Haley, U. C. V., Low, L. and Toh, M. H. (1996) "Singapore Incorporated: Reinterpreting Singapore's Business Environments through a Corporate Metaphor", *Management Decision*, **34**, 9, 17–28.

Haley, U. C. V. and Richter, F.-J. (2001) *Asian Post-Crisis Management: Corporate and Governmental Strategies for Sustainable Competitive Advantage*. London and New York: Macmillan/Palgrave.

Haley, U. C. V. and Stumpf, S. A. (1989) "Cognitive Trails in Strategic Decision-making: Linking Theories of Personalities and Cognitions", *Journal of Management Studies*, **26**, 5, 479–497.

Hamel, G. and Prahalad, C. K. (1983) "Managing Strategic Responsibility in the MNC", *Strategic Management Journal*, **4**, 341–351.

Hannan, M. T. and Freeman, J. H. (1977) "The Population Ecology of Organizations", *American Journal of Sociology*, **32**, 929–964.

Harrigan, K. R. (1980) "The Effect of Exit Barriers upon Strategic Flexibility", *Strategic Management Journal*, **1**, 165–176.

Harrigan, K. R. (1981) "Deterrents to Divestiture", *Academy of Management Journal*, **24**, 2, 306–323.

Harrigan, K. R. (1985) "Exit Barriers and Vertical Integration", *Academy of Management Journal*, **28**, 3, 686–697.

Hatten, K. T., Schendel, D. E. and Cooper, A. C. (1978) "A Strategic Model for the U.S. Brewing Industry: 1952–1971", *Academy of Management Journal*, **21**, 592–610.

Hauck, D. (1987) *What Happens When U.S. Companies Sell their South African Operations*. Washington, DC: Investor Responsibility Research Center.

Hawkins, R. G. and Walter, I. (1979) "International Investment and the Multinational Corporation". In R. Amacher (Ed.), *Challenges to a Liberal International Economic Order*. Washington, DC: American Enterprise Institute.

Hawkins, R. G. and Walter, 1. (1981) "Planning Multinational Operations". In P. C. Nystrom and W. H. Starbuck (Eds.), *Handbook of Organizational Design*, **1**, 253–267. New York: Oxford University Press.

Heclo, H. (1974) *Modern Social Policies in Britain and Sweden*. New Haven, CT: Yale University Press.

Hedberg, B. L. T. (1974) "Reframing as a Way to Cope with Organizational Stagnation", Working Paper, International Institute of Management, Berlin.

Hedberg, B. L. T., Nystrom, P. C. and Starbuck, W. H. (1976) "Camping on Seesaws: Prescriptions for a Self-designing Organization", *Administrative Science Quarterly*, **21**, 41–65.

Hedlund, G. (1980) "The Role of Foreign Subsidiaries in Strategic Decision-Making in Swedish Multinational Corporations", *Strategic Management Journal*, **1**, 23–36.

Hedlund, G. (1981) "Autonomy of Subsidiaries and Formalization of Headquarters-Subsidiary Relationships in Swedish MNCs". In L. Otterbeck (Ed.), *The Management of Headquarters-Subsidiary Relationships in Multinational Corporations*, 25–78. Hampshire, England: Gower.

Hennart, J. F. (1982) *A Theory of Multinational Enterprise*. Ann Arbor: University of Michigan Press.

Herman, E. S. (1981) *Corporate Control. Corporate Power*. New York: Cambridge University Press.

Hermann, C. F. (1963) "Some Consequences of Crisis which Limit the Viability of Organizations", *Administrative Science Quarterly*, **16**, 533–547.

Hetter, K. (2000) "5th Avenue March Protests Labor Abuse", *Newsday*, December 7.

Hirsch, P. M. (1972) "Processing Fads and Fashions: An Organization-set Analysis of Cultural Industry Systems", *American Journal of Sociology*, **77**, 4, 639–659.

Hirschman, A. O. (1969) "How to Divest in Latin America and Why", Essays in International Finance No. 76, International Finance Section, Princeton University.

Hirschman, A. O. (1970) *Exit, Voice and Loyalty. Responses to Decline in Firms, Organizations and States*. Cambridge, MA: Harvard University Press.

Hirschman, A. O. (1984a) "Exit, Voice and Loyalty: Further Reflections and a Survey of Recent Contributions". In A. O. Hirschman (Ed.), *Essays in Trespassing. Economics to Politics and Beyond*, 213–235. New York: Cambridge University Press.

Hirschman, A. O. (1984b) "Exit, Voice and the State". In A. O. Hirschman (Ed.), *Essays in Trespassing. Economics to Politics and Beyond*, 246–265. New York: Cambridge University Press.

Hout, T., Porter, M. E. and Rudden, E. (1982) "How Global Companies Win Out", *Harvard Business Review*, September–October, 98–108.

Hrebiniak, L. G. and Joyce, W. F. (1985) "Organizational Adaptation: Strategic Choice and Environmental Determinism", *Administrative Science Quarterly*, **30**, 336–349.

Huntington, S. (1973) "Transnational Organizations in World Politics", *World Politics*, 25.

Hymer, S. H. (1960/1976) *The International Operations of National Firms: A Study of Direct Foreign Investment*. Cambridge, MA: MIT Press.

Hymer, S. H. (1970) "The Efficiency (Contradictions) of Multinational Corporations", *American Economic Review*, May, 441–448.

Hymer, S. H. (1971) "The Multinational Corporation and the Law of Uneven Development". In J. W. Bhagwati, *Economics and the World Order*, 113–140. New York: Macmillan Publishing.

Hymer, S. H. and Rowthorne, R. (1970) "Multinational Corporations and International Oligopoly: The Non-American Challenge". In C. P. Kindleberger (Ed.), *The International Corporation*, 57–91. Cambridge, MA: MIT Press.

Jacobs, D. (1974) "Dependency and Vulnerability: An Exchange Approach to the Control of Organizations", *Administrative Science Quarterly*, **19**, 45–49.

Jacquemin, A. P. and de Lichtbuer, M. C. (1973) "Size, Structure, Stability and Performance of the Largest British and EEC Firms", *European Economic Review*, **4**, 393–408.

Jacquillat, B. and Solnik, B. (1978) "Multinationals are Poor Tools for Diversification", *The Journal of Portfolio Management*, Winter, 8–12.

Janis, I. L. (1972) *Victims of Groupthink*. Boston: Houghton-Mifflin.

Jedel, M. J. and Kujawa, D. (1976) "Management and Employment Practices of Foreign Direct Investors in the United States". In, US Department of Commerce, *Foreign Direct Investment in the United States: Report of the Secretary of Commerce to the Congress in Compliance with the Foreign Investment Study Act of 1974*, Appendix 1. Washington, DC: US Government Printing Office.

Jensen, M. C. and Meckling, W. H. (1976) "Theory of the Firm: Managerial Behavior, Agency Costs and Ownership Structure", *Journal of Financial Economics*, **3**, 305–360.

Johnson, H. G. (1965) "An Economic Theory of Protectionism, Tariff Bargaining and the Formation of Custom Unions", *Journal of Political Economy*, **73**, 3.

Johnson, H. G. (1967) *Economic Nationalism in New and Old States.* Chicago: University of Chicago Press.

Johnson, H. G. (1970) "The Efficiency and Welfare Implications of the International Corporation". In C. P. Kindleberger (Ed.), *The International Corporation.* Cambridge, MA: MIT Press.

Jones, K. A. and Walter, I. (1982) "Politics, Economics and the International Steel Industry", *Institute of Electrical Engineers. IEE Proceedings*, June 129, A, 4.

Judge, G. G., Griffiths, W. E., Hill, R. C., Lutkepohl, H. and Lee, T. C. (1985) *The Theory and Practice of Econometrics.* New York: John Wiley.

Kaempfer, W. H., Lehman, J. A. and Lowenberg, A. D. (1987) "Divestment, Investment Sanctions and Disinvestment: An Evaluation of Anti-Apartheid Policy Instruments", *International Organization*, **41**, 3, 457–473.

Kamens, D. (1977) "Legitimating Myths and Educational Organizations: The Relationship between Organizational Ideology and Formal Structure", *Annual Review of Sociology*, **42**, 208–219.

Karakaya, F. and Stahl, M. J. (1991) *Entry Barriers and Market Entry Decisions.* Westport, CT: Quorum.

Katz, D. and Kahn, R. (1966) *The Social Psychology of Organizations.* New York: John Wiley.

Katzenstein, P. J. (1978) *Between Power and Plenty: Foreign Economic Policies of Advanced Industrial States.* Madison, WI: University of Wisconsin Press.

Katzenstein, P. J. (1985) *Small States in World Markets.* Ithaca, NY: Cornell University Press.

Kaufman, H. (1960) *The Forest Ranger: A Study in Administrative Behavior.* Baltimore, MD: Johns Hopkins University Press.

Kaufman, H. (1976) *Are Government Organizations Immortal?* Washington, DC: Brookings Institute.

Keisler, S. and Sproull, L. (1982) "Managerial Response to Changing Environments: Perspectives on Problem-Sensing from Social Cognition", *Administrative Science Quarterly*, **27**, 548–570.

Kerr, J. L. (1985) "Diversification Strategies and Managerial Rewards: An Empirical Study", *Academy of Management Journal*, **1**, 155–179.

Kessler, F. (1985) "Goodyear Toughs It Out", *Fortune*, September 30, 24–26.

Khandwalla, P. N. (1974) "Mass Output Orientation and Organizational Structure", *Administrative Science Quarterly*, **19**, 74–97.

Khandwalla, P. N. (1981) "Properties of Competing Organizations". In P. C. Nystrom and W. H. Starbuck (Eds.) *Handbook of Organizational Design*, **1**, 409–432. New York: Oxford University Press.

Kibbe, J. and Hauck, D. (1988) *Leaving South Africa: The Impact of U.S. Corporate Disinvestment*. Washington, DC: Investor Responsibility Research Center.

Kim, W. C. (1988) "The Effects of Competition and Corporate Political Responsiveness on Multinational Bargaining Power", *Strategic Management Journal*, **9**, 289–295.

Kimberly, J. R. (1980) "The Life Cycle Analogy and the Study of Organizations: Introduction". In J. R. Kimberly, R. H. Miles and Associates (Eds.) *The Organizational Life Cycle*, 1–17. San Francisco: Jossey-Bass.

Kindleberger, C. P. (1965) *Economic Development*. New York: McGraw-Hill.

Kindleberger, C. P. (1969) *American Business Abroad: Six Lectures on Direct Investment*. New Haven, CT: Yale University Press.

Knickerbocker, F. T. (1973) *Oligopolistic Reaction and Multinational Enterprise*. Boston: Graduate School of Business Administration, Harvard University.

Kogut, B. (1986) "Foreign Direct Investment as a Sequential Process". In C. P. Kindleberger and D. P. Audretsch (Eds.), *The Multinational Corporation in the 1980s*, 38–56. Cambridge, MA: MIT Press.

Kolarska, L. and Aldrich, H. (1980) "Exit, Voice and Silence: Consumers' and Managers' Responses to Organizational Decline", *Organization Studies*, 41–58.

Kotter, J. and Sathe, V. (1978) "Problems of Human Resource Management in Rapidly Growing Companies", *California Management Review*, **21**, 29–36.

Krasner, S. D. (1978) *Defending the National Interest. Raw Materials Investments and U.S. Foreign Policy*. Princeton, NJ: Princeton University Press.

Kriger, M. P. (1988) "The Increasing Role of Subsidiary Boards in MNCs: An Empirical Study", *Strategic Management Journal*, **9**, 347–360.

Krippendorff, K. (1980) *Content Analysis: An Introduction to its Methodology.* Beverly Hills, CA: Sage Publications.

Lanzilotti, R. F. (1958) "Pricing Objectives in Large Companies", *American Economic Review*, **48**, 921–940.

Larimer, T. and McCarthy, T. (1998) "Sneaker Gulag: Are Asian Workers Really Exploited?", *Time International*, May 11.

Lasswell, H. D., Leites, N. and Associates (1949) *Language of Politics.* South Norwalk, CT: George W. Stewart.

Leape, J., Baskin, B. and Underhill, S. (1985) *Business in the Shadow of Apartheid. U.S. Firms in South Africa.* Lexington, MA: Lexington Books.

Leblebici, H. and Salancik, G. R. (1982) "Stability in Interorganizational Exchanges: Rulemaking Processes of the Chicago Board of Trade", *Administrative Science Quarterly*, **27**, 227–242.

Lentz, A. and Tschirgi, H. (1963) "The Ethical Content of Annual Reports", *Journal of Business*, **36**, 387–393.

Lenway, S. A. (1988) "Between War and Commerce: Economic Sanctions as a Tool of Statecraft", *International Organization*, **42**, 2, 397–426.

Lepper, M. R. and Greene, D (1978) *The Hidden Costs of Reward: New Perspectives on the Psychology of Human Motivation.* Hillsdale, NJ: Lawrence Erlbaum.

Lessard, D. R. (1979) "Transfer Process, Taxes and Financial Markets: Implications of International Financial Transfers within the Multinational Firm". In R. G. Hawkins (Ed.), *Economic Issues of Multinational Firms.* Greenwich, CT: Jai Press.

Levine, C. H. (1978) "Organizational Decline and Cutback Management", *Public Administration Review*, **38**, 316–325.

Levine, C. H. (1979) "More on Cutback Management: Hard Questions for Hard Times", *Public Administration Review*, **39**, 179–183.

Levine, S. and White, P. E. (1961) "Exchange as a Conceptual Framework for the Study of Interorganizational Relationships", *Administrative Science Quarterly*, **5**, 583–601.

Lewis-Blake, M. S. (1980) *Applied Regression: An Introduction.* Sage University Papers, Quantitative Applications in the Social Sciences. Beverly Hills, CA: Sage Publications.

Lindblom, C. E. (1959) "The Science of 'Muddling Through'", *Public Administration Review*, **19**, 79–88.

Lipset, S. M. (1950) *Agrarian Socialism.* Berkeley, CA: University of California Press.

Litwak, E. and Hylton, L. F. (1966) "Interorganizational Analysis: A Hypothesis on Coordinating Agencies", *Administrative Science Quarterly*, **11**, 31–58.

Lodahl, T. M. and Mitchell, S. M. (1980) "Drift in the Development of Innovative Organizations". In J. R. Kimberly, R. H. Miles and Associates (Eds.), *The Organizational Life Cycle.* San Francisco: Jossey-Bass.

Lorsch, J. W. and Allen, S. A. (1973) *Managing Diversity and Interdependence.* Cambridge, MA: Division of Research, Harvard Business School.

Love, J. (1985) *The U.S. Anti-Apartheid Movement.* New York: Praeger Publishers.

Mace, M. L. (1971) *Directors: Myth and Reality.* Cambridge, MA: Division of Research, Harvard Business School.

Machlup, F. (1967) "Theories of the Firm: Marginalist, Behavioral, Managerial", *American Economic Review*, **57**, 1–33.

Maddala, G. S. (1977) *Econometrics.* New York: McGraw-Hill.

Magee, S. P. (1976) "Technology and the Appropriability Theory of the Multinational Corporation". In J .Bhagwati (Ed.), *The New International Economic Order.* Cambridge, MA: MIT Press.

Magee, S. P. (1977) "Multinational Corporations, the Industry Technology Cycle and Development", *Journal of World Trade Law*, July/August, 297–321.

Mahini, A. and Wells, L. T. (1986) "Government Relations in the Global Firm". In M. E. Porter (Ed.), *Competition in Global Industries*, 291–312. Boston, MA: Harvard Business School Press.

March, J. G. (1962) "The Business Firm as a Political Coalition", *Journal of Politics*, **24**, 662–678.

March, J. G. (1986) "The Power of Power". In D. Easton (Ed.), *Varieties of Political Theory.* Englewood Cliffs, NJ: Prentice-Hall.

March, J. G. (1981a) "Footnotes to Organizational Change", *Administrative Science Quarterly*, **26**, 563–577.

March, J. G. (1981b) "Decisions in Organizations and Theories of Choice". In A. Van de Ven and W. Joyce (Eds.), *Perspectives on Organizational Design and Performance*. New York: John Wiley.

March, J. G. (1982) "Theories of Choice and Making Decisions", *Transaction/ SOCIETY*, **20**, 29–39.

March, J. G. (1984) "Notes on Ambiguity and Executive Compensation", *Scandinavian Journal of Management Studies*, August, 63–64.

March, J. G. and Olsen, J. P. (1976) *Ambiguity and Choice in Organizations*. Bergen, Norway: Universitetsforlaget.

March, J. G. and Olsen, J. P. (1983) "The New Institutionalism: Organizational Factors in Political Life", *American Political Science Review*, **78**, 734–749.

March, J. G. and Olsen, J. P. (1989) *Rediscovering Institutions*. New York: Macmillan.

March, J. G. and Simon, H. A. (1958) *Organizations*. New York: John Wiley.

Markus, G. B. (1986) "The Impact of Personal and National Economic Conditions on the Presidential Vote: A Pooled Cross-sectional Analysis". Paper presented at the Third Annual Methodology Conference, Harvard University, Cambridge, MA.

Marris, R. (1967) *The Economic Theory of "Managerial" Capitalism*. London: Macmillan.

Marris, R. L. and Wood, A. (1971) *The Corporate Economy*. London: Macmillan.

Martin, J. (1980) "Stories and Scripts in Organizational Settings", Working Paper No. 543, Stanford Business School.

McCaffrey, D. P. (1982) "Corporate Resources and Regulatory Pressures: Toward Explaining a Discrepancy", *Administrative Science Quarterly*, **27**, 398–419.

McCarthy, S. (2000) "Ten Years of Chaos in Burma: Foreign Investment and Economic Liberalization under the SLORC-SPDC, 1988 to 1998", *Pacific Affairs*, Summer.

McEachern, W. A. (1975) *Managerial Control and Performance*. Lexington, MA: D.C. Heath.

Merton, R. K. (1968) *Social Theory and Social Structure*. New York: Free Press.

Mesarovic, M. D., Macko, D. and Takahara, Y. (1970) *Theory of Hierarchical Multilevel Systems*. New York: Academic Press.

Metcalfe, J. L. (1974) "Systems Models, Economic Models and the Causal Texture of Organizational Environments: An Approach to Macro-organization Theory", *Human Relations*, **27**, 639–663.

Meyer, J. W. and Rowan, B. (1978) "Institutionalized Organizations: Formal Structure as Myth and Ceremony", *American Journal of Sociology*, **83**, 340–363.

Michels, R. (1962) *Political Parties*. New York: Collier.

Miles, R. E. and Cameron, K. S. (1982) *Coffin Nails and Corporate Strategies*. Englewood Cliffs, NJ: Prentice-Hall.

Miles, R. E. and Snow, C. C. (1978) *Organizational Strategy, Structure and Process*. New York: McGraw-Hill.

Miller, A. (1998) *Strategic Management*, third edition. Boston, MA: McGraw-Hill.

Miller, D. and Friesen, P. H. (1980) "Momentum and Revolution in Organizational Adaptation", *Academy of Management Journal*, **22**, 591–614.

Miller, D. and Friesen, P. H. (1984) *Organizations: A Quantum View*. Englewood Cliffs, NJ: Prentice Hall.

Miller, G. A. (1958) "The Magical Number Seven, Plus or Minus Two: Some Limits on our Capacity for Processing Information", *Psychological Review*, **63**, 81–97.

Mintzberg, H. (1979) *The Structuring of Organizations*. Englewood Cliffs, NJ: Prentice-Hall.

Mintzberg, H. (1984) "Power and Organization Life Cycles", *Academy of Management Review*, **9**, 2, 207–224.

Mintzberg, H., Raisinghani, D. and Theoret, A. (1976) "The Structure of 'Unstructured' Decision Processes", *Administrative Science Quarterly*, **21**, 246–275.

Mintzberg, H. and Waters, J. A. (1982) "Tracking Structure in an Entrepreneurial Firm", *Academy of Management Journal*, **25**, 465–499.

Mitnick, B. M. (1987) "The Theory of Agency and Organizational Analysis", Working Paper No. 639, Graduate School of Business, University of Pittsburgh.

Monsen, R. J. and Downs, A. (1965) "A Theory of Large Managerial Firms", *Journal of Political Economy*, **73**, 221–236.

Montgomery, C. A. (1982) "The Measurement of Firm Diversification: Some New Empirical Evidence", *Academy of Management Journal*, **25**, 2, 299–307.

Moran, T. H. (1978) "Multinational Corporations and Dependency: A Dialogue for Dependentistas and Non-dependentistas", *International Organization*, **32**, 1, 79–100.

Morgan, G. (1986) *Images of Organization*. Beverly Hills, CA: Sage Publications.

Morison, E. (1966) *Men, Machines and Modern Times*. Cambridge, MA: MIT Press.

Mowday, R. T. (1978) "The Exercise of Upward Influence in Organizations", *Administrative Science Quarterly*, **23**, 137–156.

Moyer, R. (1970) "Reciprocity: Retrospect and Prospect", *Journal of Marketing*, October, 47–54.

Nelson R. R. and Winter, S. G. (1982) *An Evolutionary Theory of Economic Change*. Cambridge, MA: Harvard University Press.

Newman, A. and Bowers, C. (1984) *Foreign Investment in South Africa and Namibia. A Directory of US, Canadian and British Corporations Operating in South Africa and Namibia*. Washington, DC: Investor Responsibility Research Center.

Newman, W. H. and Logan, J. P. (1955) *Management of Expanding Enterprises*. New York: Columbia University Press.

Newsweek (1989) May 8, 42.

Nike Watch Campaign (2000) "Updates",

http://www.caa.org.au/campaigns/nike/news.html

Noble, C. (2000) "USA: Massachusetts Seeks Again to Bar Myanmar Business", *Reuters English News Service*, December 8.

Norburn, D. and Birley, S. (1988) "The Top Management Team and Corporate Performance", *Strategic Management Journal*, **9**, 225–237.

Nordlinger, E. (1981) *On the Autonomy of the Democratic State*. Cambridge, MA: Harvard University Press.

Normann, R. (1971) "Organizational Innovativeness: Product Variation and Reorientation", *Administrative Science Quarterly*, **16**, 203–215.

North R B., Holsti, O., Zaninovich, M. G. and Zinnes, D. A. (1963) *Content Analysis: A Handbook with Applications for the Study of International Crisis*. Evanston, IL: Northwestern University Press.

Nye, J. S. (1986) "The Multinational Corporation in the 1980s". In C. P. Kindleberger and D. P. Audretsch (Eds.), *The Multinational Corporation in the 1980s*, 1–17. Cambridge, MA: MIT Press.

Olsen, J. P. (1981) "Integrated Organizational Participation in Government". In P. C. Nystrom and W. H. Starbuck (Eds.), *Handbook of Organizational Design*, **2**, 492–516. New York: Oxford University Press.

Olson, M. (1982) *The Rise and Decline of Nations*. New Haven, CT: Yale University Press.

O'Reilly, C. (1978) "The Intentional Distortion of Information in Organization Communication", *Human Relations*, **31**, 173–193.

O'Rourke, D. (1997) *Smoke for a Hired Gun: A Critique of Nike's Labor and Environmental Auditing in Vietnam as Performed by Ernst and Young*. San Francisco: Transnational Resource Action Center.

Ostrom, C. W. (1978) *Time Series Analysis*. Sage University Paper No. 9. Newbury Park, CA: Sage Publications.

Pahl, R. E. and Winkler, J. T. (1974) "The Economic Elite: Theory and Practise". In, P. Stanworth and A. Giddens (Eds.), *Elites and Power in British Society*, 102–122. Cambridge, England: Cambridge University Press.

Palamountain, J. C. (1955) *The Politics of Distribution*. Cambridge, MA: Harvard University Press.

Parry, T. G. (1980) *The Multinational Enterprise. International Investment and Host-Country Impacts*. Greenwich, CT: JAI Press.

Paul, K. (1987) "The Inadequacy of Sullivan Reporting". In S. P. Sethi (Ed.), *The South African Quagmire. In Search of a Peaceful Path to Democratic Pluralism*, 403–412. Cambridge, MA: Ballinger.

Paul, K. and Duffy, S. (1988) "Corporate Responses to the Call for South African Withdrawal", *Corporate Social Performance and Policy*, **10**, 211–240.

Pelz, D. and Andrews, F. (1966) *Scientists in Organizations*. New York: John Wiley.

Penrose, E. T. (1952) "Biological Analogies in the Theory of the Firm", *American Economic Review*, **4**, 804–819.

Penrose, E. T. (1959) "Profit Sharing between Producing Countries and Oil Companies in the Middle East", *Economic Journal*, June.

Pennings, J. M. (1980) *Interlocking Directorates*. San Francisco: Jossey-Bass.

Pennings, J. M. (1981) "Strategically Interdependent Organizations". In P. C. Nystrom and W. H. Starbuck (Eds.), *Handbook of Organizational Design*, **1**, 433–455. New York: Oxford University Press.

Perrow, C. (1961) "The Analysis of Goals in Complex Organizations", *American Journal of Sociology*, **62**, 854–866.

Peterson, E. A. (1977) "Interest Group Incorporation in Sweden: A Summary of Arguments and Findings", Working Paper, Yale University.

Pettigrew, A. M. (1973) *The Politics of Organizational Decision Making*. London: Tavistock.

Pettigrew, A. M. (1979) "On Studying Organizational Culture", *Administrative Science Quarterly*, **24**, 570–581.

Pfeffer, J. (1972a) "Size and Composition of Corporate Boards of Directors: The Organization and its Environment", *Administrative Science Quarterly*, **17**, 218–228.

Pfeffer, J. (1972b) "Merger as a Response to Organizational Interdependence", *Administrative Science Quarterly*, **17**, 382–394.

Pfeffer, J. (1973) "Size, Composition and Function of Hospital Boards of Directors: A Study of Organization-Environment Linkage", *Administrative Science Quarterly*, **18**, 349–364.

Pfeffer, J. (1981) "Management as Symbolic Action: The Creation and Maintenance of Organizational Paradigms". In B. Staw (Ed.), *Research in Organizational Behavior*, **3**, 1–52. Greenwich, CT: JAI Press.

Pfeffer, J. (1987) "A Resource Dependence Perspective on Intercorporate Relations". In M. S. Mizruchi and M. Schwartz (Eds.), *Intercorporate Relations: The Structural Analysis of Business*, 25–55. New York: Cambridge University Press.

Pfeffer, J. (1997) *New Directions for Organization Theory*. Oxford and New York: Oxford University Press.

Pfeffer, J. and Salancik, G. R. (1978) *The External Control of Organizations: A Resource Dependence Perspective*. New York: Harper and Row.

Pitts, R. A. (1974) "Incentive Compensation and Organization Design", *Personnel Journal*, **53**, 338–348.

Pondy, L. R. (1969) "Effects of Size, Complexity and Ownership on Administrative Intensity", *Administrative Science Quarterly*, **14**, 1, 47–61.

Porter, M. E. (1976) "Please Note Location of Nearest Exit: Exit Barriers and Planning", *California Management Review*, **19**, 21–33.

Porter, M. E. (1980) *Competitive Strategy: Techniques for Analyzing Industries and Competitors*. New York: Free Press.

Porter, M. E. (1986) *Competition in Global Industries*. Boston, MA: Harvard Business School Press.

Porter, M. E. (1998a) *The Competitive Advantage of Nations: With a New Introduction*. New York: Free Press.

Porter, M. E. (1998b) *Competitive Advantage: Creating and Sustaining Superior Performance*. New York: Free Press.

Poynter, T. A. (1982) "Government Intervention in Less Developed Countries: The Experience of Multinational Companies", *Journal of International Business Studies*, Spring/Summer, 9–25.

Prahalad, C. K. and Doz, Y. L. (1981) "An Approach to Strategic Control in MNCs", *Sloan Management Review*, Summer, 5–13.

Prasso, S. (2000) "Can a State Have its Own Foreign Policy?", *Business Week*, March 20.

Provan, K. G., Beyer, J. M. and Kryutbosch, C. (1980) "Environmental Linkages and Power in Resource-Dependence Relations between Organizations", *Administrative Science Quarterly*, **25**, 200–225.

Pugel, T. A. and Walter, I. (1985) "US Corporate Interests and the Political Economy of Trade Policy", *Review of Economics and Statistics*, August, **3**, 465–473.

Rhenman, E. (1973) *Organization Theory for Long-range Planning*. New York: John Wiley.

Richardson, R. J. (1987) "Directorship Interlocks and Corporate Profitability", *Administrative Science Quarterly*, **32**, 367–386.

Roberts, D. R. (1956) "A General Theory of Executive Compensation Based on Statistically Tested Propositions", *Quarterly Journal of Economics*, **20**, 270–294.

Roberts, D. R. (1959) *Executive Compensation*. Glencoe, IL: Free Press.

Robinson, R. (1976) "The World Economy and the Distribution of Income Within States: A Cross-National Study", *American Sociological Review*, **41**, 638–659.

Rosen, S. J. and Kurth, J. R.(1974) *Testing Theories of Economic Imperialism*. Lexington, MA: Lexington Books.

Ross, L., Lepper, M. R. and Hubbard, M. (1975) "Perseverance in Self-Perception and Social Perception: Biased Attributional Processes in the Debriefing Paradigm", *Journal of Personality and Social Psychology*, **32**, 880–892.

Rothman, D. J. (1972) "Of Prisons, Asylums and other Decaying Institutions", *The Public Interest*, **26**, 3–17.

Rothman, R. (1981) "Political Symbolism". In S. L. Long (Ed.), *Handbook of Political Behavior*, **2**, 285–340. New York: Plenum.

Rowthorne, R. and Hymer, S. H. (1970) *International Big Business*. Cambridge, England: Cambridge University Press.

Ruggie, J. G. (1983) *The Antinomies of Interdependence: National Welfare and the International Division of Labor*. New York: Columbia University Press.

Rugman, A. M. (1982) "Internalization and Non-Equity Forms of International Involvement". In A. M. Rugman (Ed.), *New Theories of the Multinational Enterprise*, 9–23. New York: St. Martin's Press.

Rumelt, R. P. (1974) *Strategy, Structure and Economic Performance*. Cambridge, MA: Harvard University Press.

Salancik, G. R. (1977) "Commitment and the Control of Organizational Behavior and Belief". In B. M. Staw and G. R. Salancik (Eds.), *New Directions in Organizational Behavior*. Chicago: St. Clair Press.

Salancik, G. R. and Conway, M. (1975) "Attitude Inferences from Salient and Relevant Cognitive Content About Behavior", *Journal of Personality and Social Psychology*, **32**, 829–840.

Salancik, G. R. and Pfeffer, J. (1974) "The Bases and Use of Power in Organizational Decision Making: The Case of a University", *Administrative Science Quarterly*, **19**, 453–473.

Salancik, G. R., Staw, B. M. and Pondy, L. R. (1980) "Administrative Turnover as a Response to Unmanaged Organizational Interdependence", *Academy of Management Journal*, **23**, 3, 422–437.

Salter, M. S. (1973) "Tailor Incentive Compensation to Strategy", *Harvard Business Review*, **51**, 3, 94–102.

Sampson, A. (1973) *The Sovereign State of ITT*. New York: Stein and Day.

Sarason, S. (1972) *The Creation of Settings and the Future Societies*. San Francisco: Jossey-Bass.

Sayrs, L. W. (1989) *Pooled Time Series Analysis*. Sage University Paper No. 70, Quantitative Applications in the Social Sciences. Newbury Park, CA: Sage Publications.

Scherer, F. M. (1970) *Industrial Market Structure and Economic Performance.* Chicago: Rand McNally.

Scherer, F. M., Beckenstein, A., Kaufer, E., Murphy, R. D. and Bougeon-Maassen, F. (1975) *The Economics of Multi-Plant Operation.* Cambridge, MA: Harvard University Press.

Schollhammer, H. (1971) "Long-range Planning in the Multinational Firms", *Columbia Journal of World Business*, **6**, 5, 79–86.

Schmookler, J. (1966) *Invention and Economic Growth.* Cambridge, MA: Harvard University Press.

Seidman, A. (1986) *The Roots of Crisis in Southern Africa.* Trenton, NJ: Africa World Press.

Selznick, P. (1949) *T.V.A and the Grass Roots.* Berkeley, CA: University of California Press.

Selznick, P. (1957) *Leaders in Administration.* Evanston, IL: Northwestern University Press.

Sethi, S. P. (1987) *The South African Quagmire. In Search of a Peaceful Path to Democratic Pluralism.* Cambridge, MA: Ballinger.

Shambaugh, P. (1978) "The Development of the Small Group", *Human Relations*, **31**, 283–295.

Shapiro, D. M. (1988) "Entry, Exit and the Theory of the Multinational Corporation". In C. P. Kindleberger and D. P. Audretsch (Eds.), *The Multinational Corporation in the 1980s*, 103–122. Cambridge, MA: MIT Press.

Shen, T. Y. (1981) "Technology and Organizational Economics". In P. C. Nystrom and W. H. Starbuck (Eds.), *Handbook of Organizational Design*, **1**, 268–289. New York: Oxford University Press.

Shubik, M. (1961) "Approaches to the Study of Decision-Making Relevant to the Firm", *Journal of Business*, **34**, 101–118.

Sigelman, L. (1977) "Reporting the News: An Organizational Analysis", *American Journal of Sociology*, **79**, 132–151.

Simon, H. A. (1945) *Administrative Behavior: A Study of Decision Making Processes in Administrative Organizations.* New York: Macmillan.

Simon, H. A. (1955) "A Behavioral Model of Rational Choice", *Quarterly Journal of Economics*, **69**, 99–118.

Simon, H. A. (1957) *Models of Man*. New York: John Wiley.

Simon, H. A. (1964) "On the Concept of Organizational Goal", *Administrative Science Quarterly*, **9**, 1–22.

Simon, H. A. (1986) "Rationality in Psychology and Economics", *Journal of Business*, **59**, 4, 209–224.

Singh, A. (1971) *Take-overs*. Cambridge, England: Cambridge University Press.

Skelly, D. F. and Hobbs, J. R. (1988) "Statistics of Income Studies of International Income and Taxes", *SOI Bulletin*, **8**, 2, 25–40.

Skocpol, T. (1979) *States and Social Revolutions: A Comparative Analysis of France, Russia and China*. New York: Cambridge University Press.

Smith, A. (1776) *An Inquiry into the Nature and Causes of the Wealth of Nations*.

Smith, G. (1982) "The Bell/Western Union Patent Agreement of 1879", Working Paper, Winthrop Research Group, Cambridge, MA.

Stahl, M. J. and Grisby, D. W. (1997) *Total Quality and Global Competition*. Oxford: Blackwell.

Starbuck, W. H. (1965) "Organizational Growth and Development". In J. G. March (Ed.), *Handbook of Organizations*, 451–553. Chicago: Rand McNally.

Starbuck, W. H. (1978) "Organizations and their Environments". In M. D. Dunnette (Ed.), *Handbook of Industrial and Organizational Psychology*, 1069–1123. Chicago: Rand McNally.

Starbuck, W. H. (1985) "Acting First and Thinking Later: Theory versus Reality in Strategic Change". In J. M. Pennings (Ed.), *Organizational Strategy and Change*, 336–372. San Francisco: Jossey Bass.

Starbuck, W. H. and Nystrom, P. C. (1981) "Designing and Understanding Organizations". In P. C. Nystrom and W. H. Starbuck (Eds.), *Handbook of Organizational Design*, **1**, ix–xxii. New York: Oxford University Press.

Staw, B. M. and Ross, J. J. (1978) "Commitment to a Policy Decision: A Multi-Theoretical Perspective", *Administrative Science Quarterly*, **23**, 40–64.

Staw, B. M., Sandelands, L. E. and Dutton, J. E. (1981) "Threat-Rigidity Effects in Organizational Behavior: A Multi-level Analysis", *Administrative Science Quarterly*, **26**, 501–524.

Stephan, A. C. (1978) *The State and Society: Peru in Comparative Perspective*. Princeton, NJ: Princeton University Press.

Stinchcombe, A. L. (1965) "Social Structure and Organizations". In J. G. March (Ed.), *Handbook of Organizations*, 142–193. Chicago: Rand McNally.

Stinchcombe, A. L., McDill, M. S. and Walker, D. R. (1968) "Demography of Organizations", *American Journal of Sociology*, **74**, 221–229.

Stobaugh, R. B. (1968) *The Product Life Cycle. U.S. Exports. and International Investment*. Doctoral dissertation, Harvard Business School, Cambridge, MA.

Stopford, J. M. (1984) *World Directory of Multinational Enterprises*. Detroit, MI: Book Tower.

Stopford, J. M. and Wells, L. T. (1968) *Managing the Multinational Enterprise*. New York: Basic Books.

Tatum, L. (1987) *South Africa. Challenge and Hope*. New York: Hill and Wang.

Teece, D. J.(1976) *Vertical Integration and Vertical Divestiture in the U.S. Oil Industry*. Palo Alto, CA: Institute for Energy Studies, Stanford University.

Tolbert, P. and Zucker, L. G. (1983) "Institutional Sources of Change in the Formal Structure of Organizations: The Diffusion of Civil Service Reform, 1880–1935", *Administrative Science Quarterly*, **28**, 22–39.

Tornedon, R. J. and Boddewyn, J. J. (1974) "Foreign Divestments: Too Many Mistakes", *Columbia Journal of World Business*, **9**, 3, 87–94.

Tushman, M. L. and Romanelli, E. (1985) "Organizational Evolution: A Metamorphosis Model of Convergence and Reorientation", *Research in Organizational Behavior*, **7**, 171–222.

Tversky, A. and Kahneman, D. (1982) "Judgment under Uncertainty: Heuristics and Biases". In D. Kahneman, P. Slovic and A. Tversky (Eds.), *Judgment under Uncertainty: Heuristics and Biases*, 3–20. New York: Cambridge University Press.

Ungson, G. and Steers, R. M. (1984) "Motivation and Politics in Executive Compensation", *Academy of Management Review*, **9**, 313–323.

Useem, M. (1984) *The Inner Circle*. New York: Oxford University Press.

Van Maanen, J. (1975) "Police Socialization: A Longitudinal Examination of Job Attitudes in an Urban Police Department", *Administrative Science Quarterly*, **20**, 207–228.

Vernon, R. (1986) "International Investment and International Trade in the Product Cycle", *Quarterly Journal of Economics*, May, 190–207.

Vernon, R. (1967) "Long-run Trends in Concession Contracts", *Proceedings of the American Society of International Law*, April.

Vernon, R (1971) *Sovereignty at Bay*. New York: Basic Books.

Vernon, R. (1979) "The Product Cycle Hypothesis in a New International Environment", *Oxford Bulletin of Economics and Statistics*, **41**, 255–267.

Wain, B. (2000) "Don't Isolate Myanmar", *Asian Wall Street Journal*, December 1.

Wallace, A. F. C. (1956) "Revitalization Movements", *American Anthropologist*, **58**, April.

Walter, I. (1982) "Country-Risk Assessment". In I. Walter and T. Murray (Eds.), *The Handbook of International Business*, **21**, 1–20. New York: John Wiley.

Wamsley, G. and Zald, M. N. (1973) *The Political Economy of Public Organizations*. Lexington, MA: D.C. Heath.

Weedon, D. R. (1987) "The Evolution of Sullivan Principle Compliance". In S. P. Sethi (Ed.), *The South African Quagmire. In Search of a Peaceful Path to Democratic Pluralism*, 393–402. Cambridge, MA: Ballinger.

Weick, K. E. (1979) *The Social Psychology of Organizing*. Reading, MA: Addison-Wesley Publishing.

Wells, L. T. (1972) *The Product Life Cycle and International Trade*. Cambridge, MA: Graduate School of Business Administration, Harvard University.

West, C. T. and Schwenk, C. R. (1996) "Top Management Team Strategic Consensus, Demographic Homogeneity and Firm Performance: A Report of Resounding Nonfindings", *Strategic Management Journal*, **17**, 7, 571–576.

Whetten, D. A. (1980) "Sources, Responses and Effects of Organizational Decline". In J. R. Kimberly, R. H. Miles and Associates (Eds.), *The Organizational Life Cycle*. San Francisco: Jossey-Bass.

Whetten, D. A. (1981) "Organizational Responses to Scarcity. Exploring the Obstacles to Innovative Approaches to Retrenchment in Organizations", *Education Administrative Quarterly*, **17**, 80–97.

Whetten, D. A. (1987) "Organizational Growth and Decline Processes", *Annual Review of Sociology*, **13**, 335–358.

White, H. C. (1970) *Chains of Opportunity*. Cambridge, MA: Harvard University Press.

Wildavsky, A. (1964) *Politics of the Budgetary Process*. Boston: Little, Brown.

Wilensky, H. L. (1967) *Organizational Intelligence*. New York: Basic Books.

Williamson, O. E. (1963) "A Model of Rational Managerial Behavior". In R. M. Cyert and J. G. March, *A Behavioral Theory of the Firm*, Englewood Cliffs, NJ: Prentice-Hall.

Williamson, O. E. (1975) *Markets and Hierarchies: Analysis and Antitrust Implications*. New York: Free Press.

Wolfe, A. W. (1967) "The African Mineral Industry: Evolution of a Supranational Level of Integration", *Social Problems*, Fall, **11**, 2, 153–164.

Wolfe, A. W. (1977) "The Supranational Organization of Production: An Evolutionary Perspective", *Current Anthropology*, **18**, 615–635.

Wolman, H. (1972) "Organization Theory and Community Action Agencies", *Public Administration Review*, **32**, 33–42.

Yarmolinsky, A. (1975) "Institutional Paralysis", *Daedalus*, **104**,1, 61–67.

Yuchtman, E. and Seashore, S. E. (1967) "A System Resource Approach to Organizational Effectiveness", *Administrative Science Quarterly*, **32**, 891–903.

Zald, M. N. (1965) "Who Shall Rule? A Political Analysis of Succession in a Large Welfare Organization", *Pacific Sociological Review*, **8**, 52–60.

Zaleznik, A. and Kets de Vries, M. F. R. (1975) *Power and the Corporate Mind*. Boston, MA: Houghton-Mifflin.

Index

suppression of, 118–120, 195–198, 209
symbolic actions, 118–119, 195–196

Work practices, 88
World, 36–39
World Council of Churches, 128
World Directory of Multinational
   Enterprises, 154

Young, Andrew, 220

Zenex Oil Ltd, 62